Economic Stabilization For Developing Countries

Economic Stabilization For Developing Countries

Anthony Clunies Ross
Professor of Economics
University of Strathclyde

Edward Elgar

Published by
Edward Elgar Publishing Limited
Gower House
Croft Road
Aldershot
Hants GU11 3HR
England

Edward Elgar Publishing Company
Old Post Road
Brookfield
Vermont 05036
USA

British Library Cataloguing in Publication Data

Clunies Ross, Anthony *1932–*
Economic stabilization for developing countries.
1. Developing countries. Economic conditions
I. Title
330.91724

Printed in Great Britain by
Billing & Sons Ltd, Worcester

ISBN 1 85278 314 1
1 85278 452 0 (paperback)

Contents

Foreword vii

PART 1: PURPOSES AND CONCEPTS

1 Meaning and purpose of economic stabilization 3

2 National income, product, and expenditure 15

3 Money and the balance of payments 24

4 Exchange rates and international money 34

PART 2: STANDARD MODELS FOR STABILIZATION

5 Keynesian and Monetarist approaches 53

6 Managing the external balance 76

PART 3: MODELS FOR DEVELOPING COUNTRIES

7 Relevant differences among types of economy 95

8 Structuralism: model or attitude of mind? 108

PART 4: INTERNATIONAL APPROACHES TO STABILIZATION

9 Commodity-price stabilization 125

10 Earnings compensation and insurance 143

11 Debt and borrowing 156

PART 5: DOMESTIC INSTRUMENTS OF STABILIZATION

12 Stabilization targets and instruments 169

13 Fiscal rules 182

14 Choosing exchange-rate regimes and policies 197

15 Wage policies 222

16 Interest-rate policies 235

17 Adjusting from gross imbalance 244

PART 6: CASE-STUDIES AND CONCLUSIONS

18 Some recent experiments and experiences 255

19 Concluding lessons 277

Further reading 281

Bibliography 286

Index 295

Foreword

This book is designed as a text for people who need to understand the policy questions raised by economic stabilization in developing countries.

Stabilization is considered not just as a matter of balancing aggregate supply and demand at a constant price level, but more fundamentally as maintaining the conditions in which fluctuations in real national expenditure (and hence in living standards and levels of investment) can be minimized.

Stabilization in Third World countries has assumed enormous importance in the 1970s and 1980s in face of the disturbances of external origin that they have had to face, largely as a result of the oil-price shocks and the subsequent failures in the management of the world economy. This book leads up to the two main questions, of what the world can do (Part 4), and of what the governments of the countries concerned can do for themselves (mainly Part 5), to protect them against similar experiences in future. It takes the view that action from both sides is necessary. Four case studies, touching altogether on eight countries, are given in Chapter 18.

There is of course a great variety among the economies of so-called developing countries. For purposes of macroeconomic management, some are best considered by the same concepts as the industrialized. Yet there is an important category of countries, including most of those heavily dependent on primary-commodity exports, in which the habits of thought developed over management of the United States or Japan can be positively misleading. As a corrective, Part 5 of this book treats a stylized version of the primary-commodity-dependent country as the standard case, with the others as deviations from it.

The book is based on a course of classes which I have given each year since 1987-88, under the auspices of the Centre for Development Studies and the Department of Political Economy at the University of Glasgow. The course was for students, mainly from developing countries, and with varying degrees of exposure to economics, who were taking the first year of one or other of several two-year postgraduate programmes. Most were from finance, statistical or planning departments of government, or from central banks. Parts of the book's content have also been served over several years to postgraduate students of similar backgrounds, and to (mainly Scottish and Norwegian) fourth-year undergraduates, at the University of Strathclyde.

Those who read the book are not assumed to start with an advanced knowledge of economics, but will need the usual introduction to macroeconomics provided by any one of the many standard first-year economics textbooks, such as Wonnacott and Wonnacott (1990) or Begg, Dornbusch and Fischer (1988). Those who have no knowledge at all of the methods of analysis in microeconomics are also advised to work through the elementary microeconomic chapters of any one such text, at least to the point of understanding the simple model of price-formation in a competitive market ('supply and demand'). Market analysis cannot really be avoided, and in one or two places the argument also assumes a rough understanding of the analysis of the behaviour of buyers and sellers under monopoly or monopsony.

The book begins with some very elementary exposition of the concepts and definitions involved in macroeconomic policy, on the assumption that many who have taken elementary courses in economics are often quite vague about these things. The first four chapters should be easy enough for anyone new to the subject. It is when Chapter 5 begins that the reader without any background will probably need to go to a standard textbook.

One element lacking in this book that the officer performing a policy or information function in a finance or planning department or central bank needs is some preparation in statistics: not only the elements of stochastic analysis with an entrée to econometrics, but the understanding and simple manipulation of price and quantity indices, time-series, growth rates, social accounts (dealt with briefly here) and demographic aggregates. There are many elementary books on statistical analysis and econometrics, but to find most of the other elements under one cover is rarer. A text that meets this need is Karmel and Polasek (1978). The government economist also needs an understanding of allocation theory and project appraisal, but these can to some extent be separated from the macreconomic issues considered here.

Thanks

The elements that I hope may be distinctive and valuable in this work I owe largely to others, in particular to Ross Garnaut, the influence of whose published and unpublished ideas on Chapter 13 especially (and of his activities on what is recorded in the last part of Chapter 18) is pervasive, though he, like all others mentioned here, can take no responsibility for what use I have made of their contributions. Jim Love, as often before, put me much in his debt by reading through the whole draft at a late stage, giving valuable comments and judicious encouragement. Mozammel Huq, Peter McGregor, Roger Sandilands, and Bill Stewart, have read bits of the text or its precursors, and their ideas and knowledge have more or less explicitly filtered in. Sandra Branney gave me much time and expert guidance in helping to get the printing right, and on this score I have benefited also from the collective wisdom and help of Moira Devaney, Morag Pryce, Irene Love and Kathleen Tyrrell. Mozammel Huq lent me several pieces of not-readily-accessible material on Ghana for Chapter 18, as well as giving me a copy of his own excellent book on the subject; Roger Sandilands provided material on Colombia from his book on indexation and his biography of Lauchlin Currie, then in preparation; and John Langmore, beside much else in encouragement and challenge, sent me a copy of the ACFOA study on developing-country debt. David Vines, among many kindnesses, has provided me with much stimulus in matters macroeconomic, and, if no effects of that stimulus had seeped through here, that would certainly be my fault. I am also in the debt, for background information and results of investigations, to certain students whom I have supervised, notably Rosinah Tatedi, Amos Mmolawa, Lee Geok Lian, Graeme Langlands, Anita Gibb, and Chan Wai Ling. It will be clear that I have drawn heavily on certain special issues of *World Development*, and on one of the *Oxford Review of Economic Policy*, whose value I gratefully acknowledge. My thanks also to Frank Stephen who acted as midwife for a review issue of the *Journal of Economic Studies*, **15** (2), 1988, which I prepared covering recent articles on stabilization targets and instruments in developing countries. That exercise has provided much of the raw material for the last few chapters herein.

Anthony Clunies Ross

March 1991

Part 1
Purposes and Concepts

1 Meaning and purpose of economic stabilization

The objective: stabilization

'Stabilization' became an unpopular notion in many 'less developed' countries (hereafter often 'LDCs') in the 1980s because of the unpleasant measures associated with the term. Nevertheless stability is what both households and governments dearly long to maintain. When stability is lacking, households feel the want of it acutely, and in extreme cases governments may fall under elections or coups.

Stability in what? We can best sum this up by naming two main variables: **real national expenditure** (E) and the **general price level** (P). A third variable that has in some sense to be stabilized is the **external balance** (B) or balance of payments. Fluctuations in national expenditure are likely to entail even greater proportional fluctuations in consumption, that is, in living standards, on the part of a number of the households that make up the nation. Changes, particularly unforeseen changes, in the price level are also likely to cause changes in the living standards of many households.

Of course it can be argued that fluctuations imply movements *up* as well as *down*, and that the changes brought about by unexpected movements in the rate of price-inflation in itself are changes from which some people gain while others lose. So what is the fuss about? A formal answer to this question will be given below. For the moment it is enough to appeal to common experience: the ups never seem to compensate for the downs, even if arithmetically they are of the same size; the losers always seem to lose more than the gainers gain.

(a) Real national expenditure

Notice that the variable to be stabilized is described as *national expenditure* (E) rather than *national income* (Y). In practice this distinction may often make very little difference, and some writers will talk of stabilizing income rather than expenditure. The point of referring here to expenditure rather than income as the variable to be stabilized is that expenditure represents the value of the goods and services that are used in the period concerned, either for consumption or for investment. A nation's income may fall, for example because of a fall in the world price of its exports, but if it can manage its economy so that the actual real value of the spending of its residents and government does not fall, then those residents may find their standard of living unaffected, and the investment programmes directed at providing for the future may also go ahead without interruption.

Why exactly do people not like fluctuations in their living standards? Why do the ups not compensate for the downs? Why is a spending power of £1000 (in constant prices) that is received *regularly* year after year better than an *irregular* annual spending power that *averages* £1000 a year? Analysis can give two fundamental reasons in answer to this question, one that might be regarded as a logical necessity, the other as a feature of human behaviour. These two happen for the present purpose to work in the same direction.

The first is the **diminishing marginal utility of income or wealth.** This is simply a reflection of the fact that, if a person has only one pound, she buys what she regards as the most essential things first; a second pound would be used for goods that are less essential, and a third for others that are less important again. So an *extra* pound, or the proceeds of an extra hour's subsistence work, will be more important, more valuable, to the poorer person than to the richer, more important to most of us than to say the Sultan of Brunei. Stated sufficiently carefully and applied to a single person rather than between people, this principle must of necessity be true. If supposed to operate approximately also *between* people, it provides incidentally an argument that may be used for the equalization of income and wealth. If the utility or value of income is measured on the vertical axis of a diagram and wealth or income on the horizontal axis, then the line showing the relationship between them would be rising but with a decreasing slope (Figure 1.1). The decreasing slope represents the 'diminishing marginal utility' of income.

Diminishing marginal utility means that a movement of 100 shillings *down* represents a bigger loss of value to anyone than a movement of 100 shillings *up* represents a gain. Thus it is better to stay at a steady level of income than on a fluctuating one that has the same average.

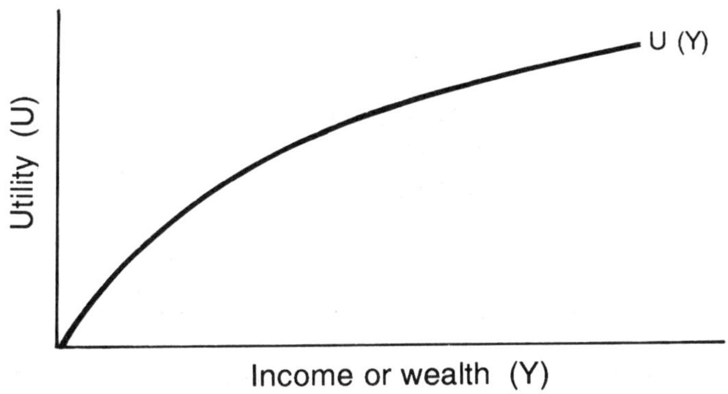

Figure 1.1 Diminishing marginal utility of income

The second reason is one that incidentally can be used *against* the equalization of wealth. This is that **we find it particularly distressing to have our expectations disappointed.** It seems true to say that it matters much more to us if we lose 100 shillings that we expected to enjoy than if we gain 100 shillings that we never thought to have. This appears to be a fact of human nature which may well be true also for other animals. We do not like being forced to adjust to going without something to which we have grown accustomed. A state of life that might be perfectly acceptable to me if I were used to it becomes distasteful if I am reduced to it from something grander. Adjustment to enlarged opportunities can be pleasant because any change in that direction can be freely chosen or rejected. The need to adjust to reduced circumstances is always unwelcome because the change that it involves is enforced. This effect can be expressed on the utility-wealth or utility-income function by showing the line kinked at the particular person's accustomed level of wealth or income (Figure 1.2). As her accustomed level changes, the position of the kink will move up or down.

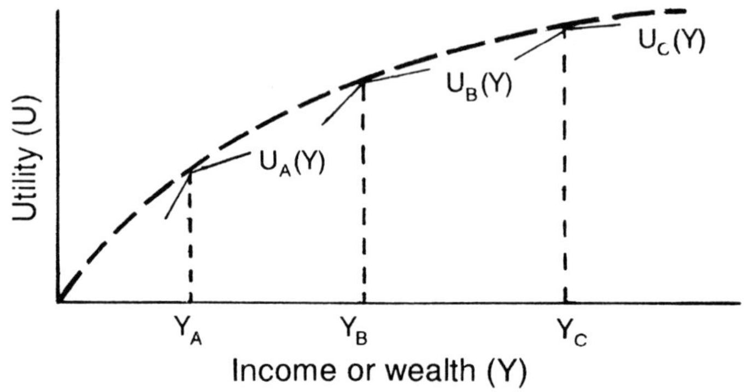

Y_A is the accustomed or expected income of person A, and $U_A(Y)$ is her utility-income function.

Figure 1.2 Effect on utility of disappointed expectations

The effect of diminishing marginal utility in favouring stability is enhanced by the effect of disappointed expectations, represented by the the kinked utility-income function.

Diminishing marginal utility (possibly the disappointed-expectations effect as well) is generally taken to be the reason for the phenomenon of *risk-aversion.* People are said to be 'risk-averse' if they prefer a *certain* return of say 1000 pesos to an 'expected' but uncertain return of 1000 pesos, for example a 50 per cent prospect of 2000 pesos and a 50 per cent prospect of nothing. If the person is subject to diminishing marginal utility of returns, then the expected (that is, mean) utility of the return in the latter case will be lower than in the former, that is lower than the utility of the *certain* 1000 pesos. Such a person will behave in a risk-averse way if she understands the probabilities involved: she will prefer a stable income of 1000 pesos a year to an unstable one which *averages* 1000 pesos a year (Figure 1.3).

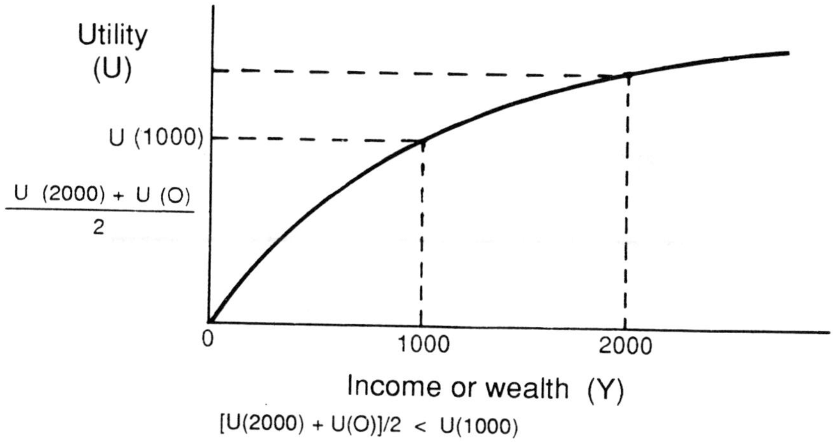

Figure 1.3 Risk-aversion

This seems to be a common-sense explanation of why individuals and households prefer stability in their incomes and expenditures to instability. Instability of *national* income and expenditure does of course tend to mean instability *for the households who compose the nation.* Furthermore **falls in income will not be evenly spread.** It is quite likely that some people will experience quite drastic reductions even if the national reduction is only say 5 per cent. If a 5 per cent reduction in real national income could be distributed to everyone in roughly the same proportion, it might well seem tolerable and not even a source of serious political discontent. But probably no nation, certainly none in the Third World, is so neatly organized that it can achieve anything like this degree of equality of sacrifice. The changes associated with a 5 per cent reduction in national income may actually mean gains for some and 50 per cent or 80 per cent reductions for others. How disturbing these changes are politically will depend on the power and influence of those who incur serious losses.

(b) Prices

All the reasons for wanting stable national expenditure, once voiced, are obvious enough. It is not quite so obvious why *instability in the price level* is so irritating, and why, especially when it goes far beyond what is expected, it can be politically destabilizing. There are probably four main reasons, at least two of them very closely connected with the reasons for the dislike of instability of income and living standards. Remember that what we are trying to explain is why people do not like inflation even if *real* national income per head is constant or rising. (If rises in the price level are not matched by rises in *nominal* national income, then of course *real* national income will be falling; there is no puzzle over why *that* should be objectionable.)

(i) The first reason is that inflation makes it **difficult for households and enterprises to budget**. If the rate of inflation were constant over long periods, people might adapt their budgeting practices, but the case seems to be that, the *faster* the rate of inflation is, the *more variable* it is likely to be, at least if variability is measured by the year-to-year change in the rate as expressed in percentage points of inflation. 'Indexing' contracts for inflation is not a complete solution. Varying rates of inflation introduce an additional degree of uncertainty to life when most of us value security.

(ii) The second reason is that, whenever the rate of inflation is higher than expected, people think that the income or wealth that they have is greater than it turns out in real-purchasing-power terms to be. There is thus a high incidence of **disappointed expectations**.

(iii) The third reason is that changing rates of inflation are almost inevitably associated with a **changing distribution** of real income. People in countries such as Brazil, with long experience of high and variable inflation, use formal or informal indexation to moderate the changes in distribution, but this again is a part-answer, and informal devices take time to become established. The losers are likely to feel their losses more than the gainers feel their gains. Moreover the redistribution does not follow any principle of social justice; it is quite likely that the poorer elements tend to be the losers.

(iv) The fourth reason is that, once inflation has started, it often tends to accelerate unless unpopular measures are taken to halt it. This **accelerating tendency** of inflation is recognized by both policy-makers and the general public. There is the feeling that we don't know where it will end. There have been cases of what is described as hyperinflation: Germany in the early 1920s, China just after the Second World War, Indonesia in 1965-66, Chile in 1973-74, Argentina in 1976 and 1983 and 1989, Bolivia and Israel in 1984-85. Past a certain point people get rid of domestic money or of any fixed-interest asset expressed in domestic currency as fast as possible. The functions of domestic money as a store of value and unit of account disappear, and it becomes of only limited usefulness as a medium of exchange. Economic life in a specialized economy without a convenient form of money becomes difficult. Hyperinflation is truly something to fear.

(c) External balance

Apart from real national expenditure and the price level, there is a third variable to which stabilization policy is directed. This is the *external balance* or *balance of payments* (B). This is an account of the flows of *money* into and out of the hands of the residents of the nation. Important subdivisions of this account are the *balance of trade in goods and services*, which represents the difference between what the country produces and what it uses, and the slightly different *balance of payments on current account*, which is the difference between what the country earns from exports and property income and receives as gifts from abroad and what it pays for imports and as property income and gives abroad.

Why is the external balance important?

To buy from abroad, residents of a country use either some foreign currency or their own, and those of most Third World countries have to use the currencies of the main trading powers. So there is a potential liquidity problem: a country has to make sure that enough foreign currencies continue to be available to its residents for the foreign purchases that they need to make. Its **international reserves** are its residents' holdings of foreign currencies and claims on foreign currencies. These have to be maintained at a suitable level. Purchases of goods or assets overseas run these reserves down; sales of goods or assets overseas replenish them. The balance between these two movements is therefore important, and that roughly is what the external balance is. So a government may properly have objectives over the external balance.

However, external-balance objectives are of a different order from national-expenditure or price-level objectives. Instability in national expenditure or in the price level is fairly directly painful. A fall in external reserves is not. The fall in reserves is a matter of concern only because action may have to be taken subsequently to reverse it, *and such action may entail reducing income and expenditure or raising the price level.* Since reserves do fall from time to time, we might hope that matters can be arranged so that these falls do not affect the aggregates that are of direct importance for welfare.

In some circumstances, moreover, the external balance can be left to look after itself without incurring the hazard of an absolute shortage of international liquidity. So maintenance of a particular state of the external balance does not *always* need to be an *explicit* objective.

How stable is stable?

How stable do we want these aggregates (E, P and B) to be? And in what precise sense stable?

(a) Prices

For the price level, the answer is easiest. All other things being equal, we should want the general price level to be constant: we should want an inflation rate of zero. But it is conceivable that not all other things are equal: that in certain circumstances a completely stable price level may require sacrifices in some other objective. Indeed it is believed by some that a really stable price level, or even a stable positive rate of inflation, sometimes requires some sacrifice of income and employment below the full-capacity level of the economy. If that were the case, some compromise would need to be reached between the stability of the price level and running the maximum level of income and employment.

(b) Real national expenditure

What are appropriate targets for stabilization of real expenditure? On the whole residents will be happy enough about rises in income and expenditure but will not like falls. A government will therefore properly be disposed *to prevent falls* in national expenditure as far as possible. It might go farther than that and try *to avoid any marked reduction in the rate of growth* of national expenditure. We should want a *stable growth-path* of income and expenditure. Insofar as it is possible to pursue stability in the income or expenditure *of particular classes of people*, such as coffee-growers or building workers, this would also be desirable.

A related objective is full employment or internal balance. Beside stabilizing expenditure at some level or other, we shall want as far as possible to maintain **internal balance.** Internal balance is commonly taken to mean equality of supply and demand in the labour market. This is the idea behind 'full employment' as it has been understood in affluent countries. The term 'full employment' is often avoided in discussion of objectives in developing countries as having misleading connotations. It belongs to a world in which able-bodied adults without pressing housework duties will normally seek wage employment because they usually have no other adequate prospective source of income. This is not the case in most Third World countries; and in fact most affluent countries have themselves reached this position only recently, mainly over the last century, and in some there has recently even been a slight movement away from wage employment toward self-employment and household enterprise.

In most LDCs, unskilled wage employment competes for workers, at least to some extent, with household enterprises in agriculture and in the rest of what is called the 'informal sector'. If workers could move freely and costlessly between household agriculture and wage employment, we should expect a higher wage to make more people willing to accept wage employment. It is not always as simple as that because a worker's land may be a long way from the towns or other sites where paid jobs are widely available, and movement between the two may be costly. These obstacles may interfere with the response of wage-labour supply to its price. This might lead to temporary excesses in either supply of, or demand for, wage-labour.

There may, however, be a more important reason for urban unemployment. In some coutries minimum wages are set by law or convention and observed more or less in government employment and by firms in the 'modern', 'organized' sector. If the wages set are above those that would be necessary to equate supply and demand for wage-labour, we should expect excess supply, in other words involuntary unemployment: unemployment of people who would be willing to work at existing wages.

Harris and Todaro (1968, 1970), writing about East Africa, postulated that there might be an equilibrium (that is, a sustainable position) of involuntary unemployment under these conditions. Even though the unemployed might not be landless and could move back into household agriculture, they might fail to do this because their **expected wage** in the modern sector (that is, the wage that they would earn if employed multiplied by the probability of employment) was not less than the income that they could expect to earn (or the addition that they could expect to make to family income) in household agriculture. Where presenting for wage work involved rural-urban movement, workers could be expected to move to towns until there was no 'expected gain' from doing so, that is until the rate of urban unemployment had risen so high that, multiplied by the urban wage rate on offer, it would give an 'expected wage' no higher than their rural alternative income. Unemployed workers in towns will presumably be supported by gainfully employed relatives and friends. This model implies that, if there is involuntary unemployment in towns among workers who are mainly not landless, its rate and absolute size can not be reduced by increasing the number of urban jobs alone, since this will attract proportionately more workers; what will be necessary in order to reduce unemployment is either to reduce urban real wages or to increase the non-wage income of the rural workers who might otherwise be looking for urban jobs.

Neither of these responses may be easy to achieve. Nevertheless, where there is much urban unemployment of people who have access to gainful activities in the rural household sector, such movement of real urban wages or real rural marginal income may be taken as a general objective to be pursued as far as possible. This is because the unemployed workers are a wasted resource; *prima facie* real national income would be higher if they were gainfully occupied.

An important qualification must be made to the conclusions drawn from the Harris-Todaro model. The growth of urban employment may be so fast and extensive, as over the past quarter-century in Taiwan and South Korea, that it renders rural labour 'scarce', pushing up its marginal returns and rewards, and so increasing the 'expected wage' that rural workers will require before they become interested in urban jobs. In other words, the wage level that will produce 'internal balance' rises closer to the actual urban wage, and the unemployment rate falls. This seems to have happened in those LDCs that have industrialized very rapidly through labour-intensive activities, usually as a result of export-expansion.

However, wage rates, wherever they are institutionally fixed rather than being determined in a free market, inevitably come into consideration in stabilization policy. We should like real national expenditure not only to be stable but to be as high as resources allow it consistently to be. This means having *the trend level of real national income* as high as the supply of labour and other productive factors permit. Reducing involuntary unemployment by aligning unskilled wages more closely with marginal rural income will tend to increase the real income of the society. It should not be assumed, without consideration of all those involved, that such a change would be detrimental to social justice.

Internal balance may be regarded as an aspect of allocation and distribution, rather than stabilization, policy, but it will be considered here as part of the objective for national expenditure.

(c) External balance

There is the even more elusive question of the appropriate targets in the 'stabilization' of the external balance. 'Stabilization' is put in quotation marks because it is probably not the external balance itself that we should try to stabilize. Rather, the manipulation of the external balance should be used to help stabilize expenditure and the price level. To achieve stability in these last two it may be necessary to accept instability in the international reserves and in the part of the external balance which represents the change in those reserves. Management of the economy will need to be such that fluctuations in the external balance and the reserves can be accommodated without requiring measures that would disturb the course of real income and expenditure or shift the price level.

Objectives in the external balance probably have in practice to concern the *cumulative value or average value over several years* of certain subdivisions within it, such as the movement in reserves or else what is called the 'basic' external balance. One formulation of the objective might be that the actual value of reserves should not fall below a certain level. However the target is set, the purpose of the exercise is to ensure uninterrupted access of residents to foreign purchasing power, and to do this without the need for internal adjustment that seriously interferes with the real-expenditure and price-level objectives.

Is understanding stabilization issues any use?

All this may sound a long way from the world of the 1970s and 1980s in the course of which developing countries suffered quite drastic disturbances from overseas.

From such disturbances countries such as Zambia and Malawi and Sri Lanka and many others have seemed at the time to have no satisfactory means of defending themselves. International agencies have often seemed to be unsympathetic to their plight, and joint defensive action by groups of developing countries has been rare. The changes could often not have been foreseen; at least few people claim to have predicted the violent movements of the world economy since 1973. Should we give up and accept that nothing can be done?

The justification for trying to understand stabilization issues is the hope that some combination of national and international measures may be found which at least avoids a recurrence of the extreme instability of the past two decades. Even if that were not possible, it would be good for a core of people to have enough understanding of the issues to prevent governments from taking 'corrective' measures that actually make the position worse. One way or another, governments and international agencies will be choosing between alternatives. There are decisions that they simply have to make. They must budget. They must have an exchange-rate policy, even if that policy is to leave it all to market forces. What they decide to do may make things better or worse. If they or their advisers understand the issues and have a rudimentary knowledge of relevant experience, they seem more likely to make things better and less likely to make them worse.

2 National income, product, and expenditure

This chapter is not a complete introduction to national-accounting concepts. It is concerned only with summarizing the meanings and relationships of those concepts as they need to be understood in framing stabilization policy.

'National income' is designed to be a measure of the 'potential material welfare' in a nation. What it means in terms of potential welfare can only be grasped if it is given 'per head' of the population. It also ignores the distribution of income, an important element in welfare, for which other forms of measurement are needed. Even certain elements in 'potential material welfare' are also ignored.

The concept of national income (most commonly expressed in its 'gross' form, gross national product) is widely used in comparisons over time (growth rates) and in international comparisons. We leave out here any account of how it is computed and the difficulties of counting it adequately, especially of properly expressing the output and income of the 'subsistence sector' (the part of output not bought or sold) and the cost of environmental damage and depletion of natural resources. We make only slight reference to problems of adjusting for changes in price level. We also make no reference to the difficulties (some would say the impossibility) of making meaningful international comparisons.

Income, product and expenditure

Just as we find it useful to think of the income and expenditure of households and of the output of enterprises, there are good reasons to apply the concepts of income, product and expenditure to groups of people. The aggregates (income, product and expenditure) are most often discussed and calculated for 'countries', that is for groups of people each comprising all those under one sovereign power, but they might just as well be used for regions within a nation or for the whole world.

National income, product and expenditure are of course flow concepts, which have to be expressed as so much per unit time (usually, but not necessarily, a year).

National (or regional) income is defined so that it corresponds as closely as possible to the income of a household as commonly understood.

National income (Y), product (D) and expenditure (E) are defined in such a way that they are equal *in a closed economy* (that is, in one that has no transactions with the world outside itself).

IN A CLOSED ECONOMY, $Y = D = E$ (by definition)

Income of an earner can be defined as the amount that he, she, or it, receives in return for productive services. Thus, on this definition, gifts and social-security benefits received would *not* be included as part of the income of the recipient.

National **income** is the sum of all the incomes in this sense received by all the 'earners' in the nation. Earners include companies and the government as well as individuals or households, but, to avoid double-counting, company or co-operative income (profit) that becomes part of household income (in the form of dividends) is included as part of company income *or* of household income *but not both*. Government income for this purpose does not include tax receipts but does include any surplus or profit that the government makes on its business activity. Income can be in the form of wages, interest, dividends, undistributed corporate profits, government profits, or rent.

Since all income is received on account of productive services supplied, then (provided the economy is 'closed') **product**, if it is valued by the value of productive services that go to make it up, must be equal to income.

In order to value product in this way, however, we can not simply include all the gross output of every productive unit. This is because the value of a car includes the value of the steel and tyres and the rest that are components in its production. To include the whole gross value of output of the steel and tyre plants, as well as that of the car-assembly plant (not to mention the car sale-room), would be double-counting, indeed multiple-counting.

So the part of output of each productive unit that is included is the gross output *minus* any components that are bought in. This is called the **value-added** (VA).

VA = gross output - material inputs

VA of all units added together thus comprises the value of the productive services that are contributed.

National **expenditure** is similarly defined so as to equal **income** in a closed economy. This is achieved by including what are called 'final' expenditures only, not 'intermediate' expenditures.

The final expenditures of a period are those on consumption or on investment (i.e. for future production), but investment has to include any accumulation over the period (intended or unintended) of stocks (inventories) of goods. Thus spending by a car-assembly plant to buy steel is not included in final expenditure, just as, in the computation of product, the value of the steel is deducted from the value of the product of the car plant. Any *increase of steel holding*, however, by either the car plant or the steel plant, is included as expenditure (on investment) for the period over which it occurs; and correspondingly any running down of steel stocks is regarded as a negative item in expenditure.

IN AN OPEN ECONOMY,

income, product and expenditure are not necessarily equal.

D	=	E	+	X	-	M
(product)		(expenditure)		(exports)		(imports)

and Y	=	D	-	Ya
(income)		(product)		(net factor income sent abroad)

where:
X represents exports of goods and services.
M represents imports of goods and services.
Ya, 'net factor income sent abroad', represents property

income (profit, interest, rent and royalties) paid overseas *minus* property income received from overseas.

All actual national economies are 'open'.

The first of these two identities follows naturally from a commonsense interpretation of the terms. We produce exports but do not buy them; so they come into product but not expenditure. We buy imports but do not produce them; so they come into expenditure but not into product.

Similarly the second identity is easily understood if you think of product as what is produced within a country's borders and income as what is earned by its residents. Of sugar produced in the country, the part of value that goes to the foreign investor who owns shares in the sugar-processing factory comes into the country's product but not into its income.

Personal disposable income is individuals' income (including that of unincorporated businesses but *not* including the part of company profit that is *not* paid to individuals) *minus* direct taxes paid by individuals *plus* social-security and other benefits received by them. These tax and benefit payments are known as **transfers.**

The term **national disposable income** is also used. By analogy with personal disposable income, this consists of national income *plus* net transfers received from abroad (R). **Transfers from abroad** are those receipts that come as free gifts: aid received as grants or gifts from governments or private bodies overseas, remittances of workers who are living abroad, and cash and other possessions brought in by immigrants; corresponding movements out are deducted to give the net figure.

One further complication: these aggregates may be expressed **gross** or **net.** Gross income, product or expenditure is the aggregate inclusive of (that is without deduction of) **depreciation** of capital goods ('consumption of fixed capital', in the terms used in Figure 2.1 below). Net is the corresponding measure with depreciation deducted. Value-added can similarly be estimated gross or net of depreciation. The sum of gross values-added is gross domestic product.

Because the gross measures are more easily and reliably measured, they are the ones usually cited.

Strictly 'national income' is defined as a 'net' measure, but the corresponding measure most commonly cited is what is really gross national income but is (confusingly) called **gross national product** (GNP).

Gross 'product' in the sense used above is called **gross domestic product** (GDP).
Gross 'expenditure' is similarly often called **gross domestic expenditure** (GDE).

Basic concept	Gross measure	Net measure
Income	gross national product	national income, net national product
Product	gross domestic product	net domestic product
Expenditure	gross (domestic) expenditure	net (domestic) expenditure

Table 2.1 Names of the national aggregates

There is another complication. The aggregates can be expressed either **at purchasers' prices** or **at producers' prices.** 'At purchasers' prices' or 'at market prices' means with **net indirect taxes** included in the prices. 'At producers' prices' or 'at factor cost' means with net indirect taxes excluded from the prices, so that the prices correspond to those received by the suppliers or producers. 'Net indirect taxes' means indirect taxes *minus* indirect subsidies, that is subsidies applied to the sale of goods.
Figure 2.1 (p. 23) shows the inter-relations of the national-accounting aggregates. The terms used are (with slight adaptations) those laid down in the UN System of National Accounts of 1968.

Consumption, saving and investment

Income is either consumed or saved:

$$Y = C_n + S_n$$

where C_n and S_n are (domestic) consumption and saving (private and government).

Expenditure goes on either consumption or investment:

$$E = C_n + I_n$$

where C_n and I_n are (domestic) consumption and investment (private and government).

Commonly this is expressed as

$$E = C + I + G$$

where C is private consumption
I is private investment
G is government spending (both consumption and investment).

Similarly it is common to write

$$Y = C + S + T$$

where C is private consumption
S is private saving
T is net transfers to government (including any profit earned on government business activities).

But, if international transfers are present, the amount that can be devoted to consumption, savings, and transfers to government, is augmented or reduced by the net transfers in or out, and we take the right side above as equal now to national disposable income (Y + R):

$$Y + R = C + S + T$$

where R is net inward international transfers

Comparisons over time

Comparisons of a country's national aggregates over time for the purpose of estimating their rate of growth or decline require adjustments for changes in the price level.

A time-series of a particular variable in which the prices used for each year's aggregate are simply those of the year in question is described as one 'in money terms' or 'in nominal terms' or 'in current prices'. But for the comparison to tell us anything useful we need to cite all the figures in a single set of prices, normally the actual prices of a particular year such as 1980. Series converted in this way are said to be 'in real terms' or 'in constant 1980 prices'.

To change a time-series in current prices to one in constant 1980 prices we need to divide the figure for each year by the value for that year of an index of the price level, when the index is arbitrarily given a value of one for 1980. (All values of the index are usually presented multiplied by 100 for neatness' sake.) That index will again have to be based on a particular 'basket' of goods; it will be a relative measure of the price of that basket. The basket will need to have goods within it represented in the proportions in which they are bought in real life. But in real life the proportions in which various goods are bought change from year to year. So there is no one right basket to use. The results are likely to be different according to which basket is used. This is referred to as an 'index-number problem'.

However, changes in consumption patterns are unlikely to be great in any one country from one year to the next. Thus comparisons of national income in one country *over a reasonably short period* are not likely to be greatly affected by this index-number problem. The longer the period, the less satisfactory comparisons made with the use of price indexes will be.

If we are trying to find an estimate of the price level in 1990 against that of 1980 as base and are using the 1980 (base-year) pattern of purchases or sales to construct the 'basket', the result is called a Laspeyres index; if we use the 1990 (given-year) pattern, it is called a Paasche index. In practice an index is usually worked out for a run of years or months on a fixed basket, which is not necessarily that of the base year. Then another index series with a more up-to-date basket is worked out for a later run of years or months overlapping with the period of the previous one. If comparisons are needed between the years covered in the two different series, they are 'linked' into a 'chain-index': for example the later series is carried back in time beyond the period that it strictly covers by taking the index numbers in the older series for the years not covered in the new series and multiplying them by the ratio that the new-series index bears to the old for a year in which they overlap. However this may sound, it is really very simple, and faced with the problem you will see that it is the only way.

The same principles apply to the construction and use of price indexes, whether they indicate, say, consumer prices for low-income urban families or a nation's export prices or the prices of the items in GDP.

To talk of a *basket* of goods simplifies the issue slightly. The prices that are used to make the index can seldom be those of the complete range of goods bought by consumers or sold as exports. *Representatives* of classes and sub-classes of the total range of goods are used. These are described as a 'regimen'. The price of each item used is given an index (or 'relative') number in relation to that of the base year, and then a weighted average of these relatives is worked out, the weighting factor being in each case a fraction indicating the importance (in total consumer spending or export receipts or whatever it is) *not of the actual item itself but of the class which it represents.* The weighting factors must of course add to one. The classes or sub-classes or sub-sub-classes represented must correspondingly cover the whole range. (See, for examples of this, and much else of value to those who use numbers to convey economic information, Karmel and Polasek, 1978.)

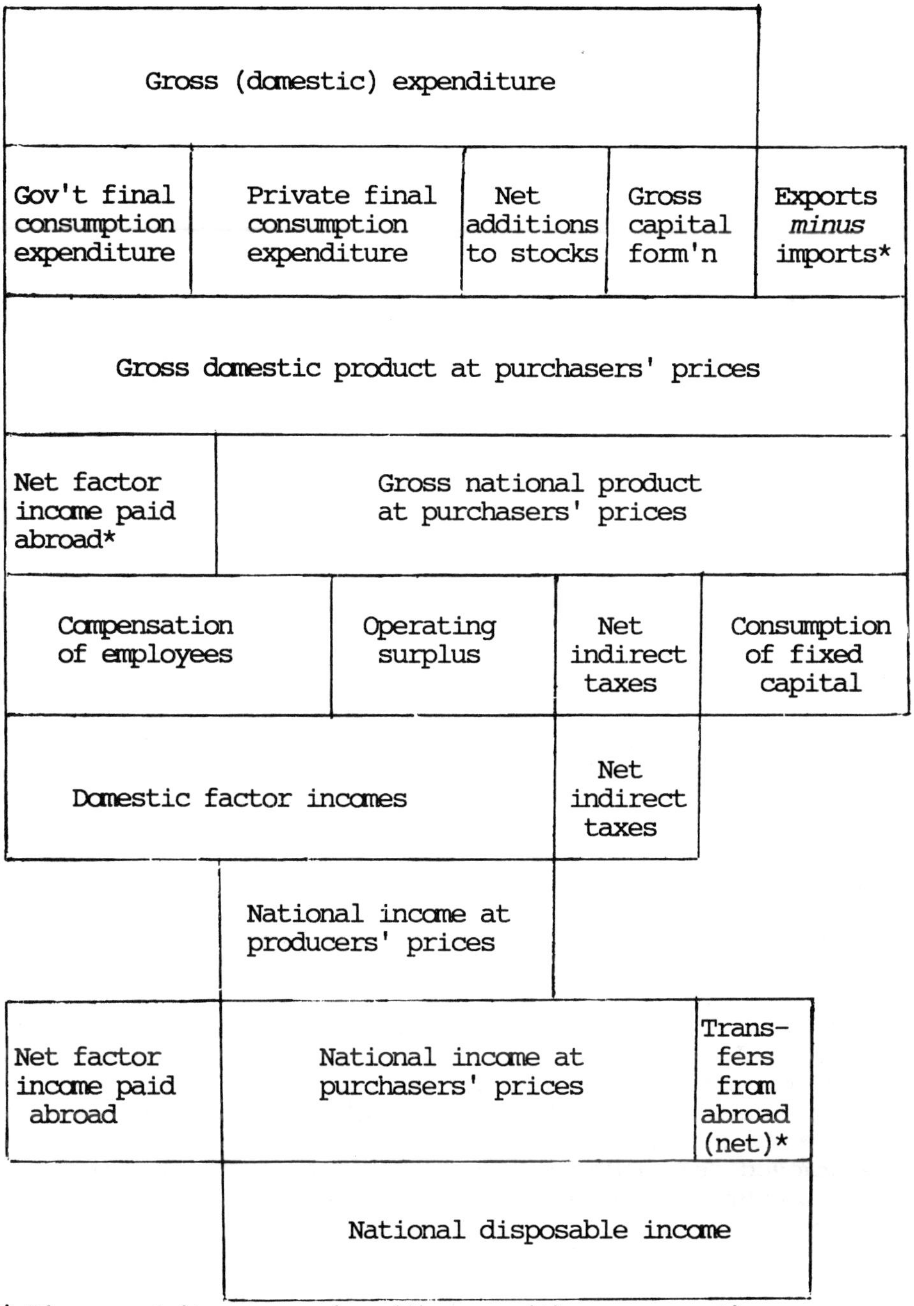

* These net items may be either positive or negative.
Figure 2.1 Interrelationships of national aggregates

3 Money and the balance of payments

Money, as the term is used in economics, is a particular kind of asset. It can be defined as **a highly liquid asset,** or as **an asset which is used as a medium of exchange.** Some would define it as an asset which is used as a medium of exchange, a unit of account and a store of value.

Assets

Assets need to be distinguished from **goods** (commodities, 'goods and services') though the same objects may serve as both. Whereas a good is something which is bought or made so that it can be used, an asset is a means of holding **wealth.** It is a claim on commodities. A **liability** is a 'negative asset', so that the wealth of a person is his assets *minus* his liabilities. A painting or a gold bracelet may serve as both a good and an asset. If it is bought to be enjoyed as a thing of beauty or display, it is a good. If it is bought as a means of holding wealth, it is an asset. It may of course be bought for both purposes at once.

Liquidity: the characteristic of money

At different places and times, various commodities have served as money. What is meant by this is principally that each has served as a **medium of exchange**: instead of exchanging goods for each other directly, someone selling cassava and wanting to buy a chicken sells the cassava not directly for the chicken but for some other item that she is not interested in using, such as silver or shells or cigarettes, and then uses this other item to buy the chicken. Typically the things used in this intermediary role have been durable and fairly easily portable; to say that they are portable implies that they have a relatively high value for their weight and volume. Forms of money such as notes, that have no 'intrinsic' value but are used as money only because some institution agrees to treat them as such, are a fairly recent invention. These are called 'token-money' or 'fiat-money'.

In order to be useful as money, a good or token needs to have a relatively *stable* value in terms of other things. Coffee or sugar would not be a useful form of money today because the value of each of them, in terms of other things in general, is extremely variable. When gold or silver or bronze or shells or pigs have had a fairly stable value in people's estimation, one or other of these items has been found convenient as a medium of exchange. In the Western world, the first approach to **coins** came about 2500 years ago when Greek city authorities in Asia Minor started putting marks on lumps of metal to certify that they were of a certain weight and purity.

This stability of value is one of the two characteristics that are covered by the term **liquidity**. To be 'liquid' an asset has to be (i) readily exchangeable for goods and other assets at (ii) relatively stable rates. Of course the rates of exchange cannot be stable against every other commodity individually. If the value of coffee varies greatly, no asset, however 'liquid', is likely to have a stable rate of exchange with coffee. But to be counted as liquid an asset will need to have a fairly stable, and therefore predictable, rate of exchange against other items in general.

If a particular asset is liquid enough to be used as a **medium of exchange**, it is also likely to be useful as a **unit of account** and as a **store of value**. The system of coins and notes that we commonly use as money do serve to provide units for accounting: we keep business accounts and express national budgets and all manner of other values in kwachas or shillings or rupees. We also use these forms of money in normal times as a store of value, though if there is a very high rate of inflation in the currency concerned its use as a store of value becomes much reduced.

Liquidity is not an all-or-nothing quality. There are degrees of liquidity. In the modern world coins and currency notes are generally regarded as the most liquid assets; they are money in the highest degree. But cheque-account (or 'sight') deposits at banks are very little less liquid than currency notes, and on the whole practice is tending in many countries to remove any difference in liquidity between them.

In order to draw the line somewhere, it was common in texts of twenty years and more ago to regard money as including coins and notes and cheque-account or sight deposits at banks. But in liquidity there is often very little difference between cheque deposits and the next most liquid forms of asset, which are 'savings' deposits and 'time' deposits. If time deposits mean what they say, you have to leave them in the bank for a certain time before withdrawing them, but in practice this is not always enforced. Whether we include these other forms of bank deposit as money is fairly arbitrary. And then there are very similar kinds of deposit in other institutions, such as savings-and-loan societies or credit unions. Holdings of short-term government bonds provide a fairly liquid asset too; if they are redeemable, say, ninety days after issue at a set price, their value will generally be fairly predictable. There is no natural and obvious place in which to draw the line so as to say that all the assets on one side of it are money and all on the other side are not.

Clearly less liquid than these assets that have been mentioned are longer-term government bonds, at least in their most common form, where their value on the market may move quite markedly up or down. Company shares ('stocks' in American parlance) are if anything less liquid again; there is a ready market for some of them and not for others, and unlike most bonds (loan certificates) they do not have a fixed redemption value and hence may become completely worthless. Less liquid again perhaps than many shares are land and buildings. Goods that readily wear out, such as motor vehicles, or are perishable, such as fresh vegetables, are less liquid again, if they are to be considered potentially as assets.

Definitions of the money supply

How do we define the money supply of a nation at a particular time? There are now various different definitions simultaneously in use and distinguished by symbols such as M0, M1, M2 or M3.

Note that most of them are concerned in principle with adding up the money in the hands of what is called 'the public'. The public for this purpose includes every resident (individual or institution) *other than the government and the banks*. So my deposits with my bank (which are *what the bank owes me*) are included, but except where otherwise specified one bank's deposits with another bank or with the central bank, or the government's deposits with any bank, are not included.

Probably this convention arose because of the view that the spending of the government was controllable by the policy-makers and that they could and should also control directly the behaviour of the banks; so what was of interest was the money in the hands that could *not* directly be controlled, those of 'the public' (that is, the non-bank private sector).

M1, sometimes called 'the narrow definition of the money supply', covers notes, coins and 'sight' (or cheque or current-account) bank deposits in the hands of the public.

M2 and **M3** include, with variants, other bank deposits of the public, and **M4** covers in addition deposits in other institutions. The precise definitions appear to vary from one country to another, which is probably unavoidable since their financial institutions differ in form. Sometimes deposits of government and its agencies are included with those of the public. Sometimes the holdings in the definition are confined to those denominated in the national currency.

M0, or 'base money', is different in concept. It covers all the notes and coins that are on issue, but no deposits except the banks' own deposits with the central bank. It is now often favoured as the most useful way of thinking about money for policy purposes by those who believe that the government cannot reliably control bank lending and therefore cannot control the public's bank deposits and who think that it is most appropriate to use an aggregate that is controllable.

Various people have considered one or other definition of the money supply the most relevant. As financial institutions change, the relevance of any particular definition may wax or wane. Those who regard the money supply as an important indicator or instrument increasingly tend to use several definitions of it together. An effect, known in Britain as **Goodhart's Law**, has been observed. This is that, as the authorities try to restrict the holding of certain forms of liquid asset, holders tend to shift to other forms. So trying to control the money supply by one definition will not necessarily have the desired effect of controlling the public's 'liquidity', which can be thought of either as its total holdings of liquid assets or as the readiness with which it can exchange its assets for other assets or for goods and services.

The demand for money and the income-velocity of money

The income-velocity of money is defined by an identity known as the **Quantity Equation:**

$$PY = MV$$

where P is a price-level index
Y is real national income
M is the money supply
V is the income-velocity of money

In other words,

$$V = PY/M,$$

i.e., the ratio of nominal national income to the amount of money held.

These are both purely definitional statements, defining V, and in themselves they tell us nothing about the world. They imply that V is an (inverse) indicator of the demand for money in relation to income. The less the proportion of their income that people want to hold as money, the 'faster' money moves from hand to hand in allowing income to be generated; in other words, the less money is needed for a particular level of income.

If the only reason for holding money were for convenience in making 'transactions', that is spending on either final or intermediate goods and services, you would expect V to be fairly stable. It may change slowly over the long term as arrangements for making payments change, but very little from month to month. That the income-velocity of money is exponents know that actual series of V fluctuate considerably from month to month, but they regard these as random variations about flat and stable trend lines. Keynes took into account the fact that people also hold money for speculative reasons, that is because they think other assets are likely to fall in price, and he supposed that the amount held for this reason would vary considerably, so that there was no reason to expect V to be stable.

Classical and Monetarist theorists also assume that there is a natural tendency for real income to return to its full-capacity level, and the full-capacity level of income will change only slowly. Accordingly their models suppose that in the short or 'medium' term both V and Y will be stable. This means that P will move proportionately with M.

The means by which this would happen is roughly as follows. People start by holding the amount of money they choose to hold given the level of their incomes. The authorities allow the money supply to be increased. Now people find that they are holding more money than they think they need. They will pay out the excess either to buy extra goods and services or to buy other assets. This will not reduce the amount of money in the system, but the extra spending on goods and services (on the assumption mentioned that output is at full capacity) must raise their prices. The extra spending on assets other than money will raise the prices of those assets, reducing the interest or yield on them and thus reducing the cost of funds for investment; the increase in investment plans will also involve extra spending on goods and services and raise their prices. The raising of prices will raise the level of income in nominal terms (PY). This will go on until PY has risen enough to equal V *times* M. Then the public will be satisfied to hold the higher quantity of money.

Taken literally the Classicals' and Monetarists' suppositions would mean that doubling the money supply would double the price level. They adopt something like this as a working assumption and a guide to policy, and try to find such a relationship behind the complex phenomena that are actually observed. The Keynesians, not supposing any particular stability in either V or Y, have doubted that this assumption is useful.

The view that there is some strong proportional relationship between the quantity of money and the price level is called the **Quantity Theory**, which must be distinguished from the purely definitional Quantity Equation.

The balance of payments

A country's balance of (international) payments is an account which sums up the **movements of money** over a period between residents of the country and residents of the rest of the world.

The reason for compiling the balance of payments is that the residents of the country need to maintain their access to liquid assets that can be used to make purchases from the rest of the world. To make sure that they will continue to have this access, *either* the country's own currency must be kept acceptable in the rest of the world *or* the country must keep a stock of other liquid assets that are acceptable.

Most LDCs' currencies are not much used in international trade, and therefore for them the problem presents itself as one of making sure that they have adequate stocks of currencies that *are* so used or of other assets (such as IMF Special Drawing Rights, certain other IMF credits, and gold) that can be readily converted into such currencies.

The balance-of-payments account itself deals only with **flows**, not with stocks, though much of the interest of the account is in the effect that these flows have on the **stock of international reserves**, which is what the country's supply of internationally-usable liquid assets is called.

If all autonomous items are included, we can say that the movements of money to residents of the country from the world outside *minus* the movements of money from them to the world outside will *equal* the rise in the country's international reserves over the period concerned.

However the interest in the account goes beyond that. It divides up the various kinds of transaction that cause money to move in or out. The transactions are conventionally divided between a *current account* and a *capital account*. These are further subdivided in the following way.

Current account:

Exports and imports of 'merchandise'

Exports and imports of 'services' (transport, shipping, insurance, tourist services, know-how sold for royalties)

Property income receipts and payments (profit remittances, dividends, interest, rent)

Transfers (international governmental and private grants, emigrants' and immigrants' remittances and what money they take or bring with them).

Capital account:

Long-term capital movements (international purchases and sales of capital assets such as land, buildings, capital equipment, shares, bonds)

Short-term autonomous capital movements (exchanges of liquid assets across currencies).

Under each of these items there are 'credit' transactions that move money in and 'debit' transactions that move it out. The excess of the credit flows over the debit flows we can take as the **net official monetary movements inward** or **net increase in reserves.** This is the balancing item. To add it (algebraically) to the debit items will make the total in the debit column equal the total in the credit column.

Names are given to the excess of credit over debit items in various subdivisions of this account. The excess of credit over debit:

For the first subdivision, is the **balance of merchandise trade;**

For the first two subdivisions, is the **balance of trade in goods and services** [= X - M], now often simply called the balance of trade;

For the first four subdivisions, is the **balance on current account** [= X - M - Ya + R];

For the first five subdivisions, is the **basic balance;**

For all six, is the **net balance** or **net monetary movement.**

Here the term 'external balance' will be used generally for these balances. Where the expression is not otherwise specified, it can be taken to mean either the *basic balance* or the *net balance*.

If the balance on capital account is taken to include the net increase in reserves as an item on the debit side, then the balance on capital account has an equal magnitude, and is treated as having the opposite sign, to the balance on current account.

The existence of a 'problem' or 'crisis' over the external balance means generally that there are grounds for fearing that the country's international reserves will run out if existing tendencies continue. Some adjustment is held to be necessary. What forms that adjustment might take will be discussed later.

The **current account** measures the country's net increase in claims on the rest of the world. (In a loose sense it is said that the current account represents the amount of net 'lending' from the country to the rest of the world over the period covered.) A surplus of $100 million on the current account for the period indicates that the foreign assets of the country's residents (including internationally-usable cash) have risen by $100 million more than their foreign liabilities. They have sold (and received in property income) internationally $100 million more than they have bought (and paid in property income) internationally. So their holdings of cash, bonds, shares, land and the like, that represent claims upon the residents of other countries, must have risen by $100 million more (or fallen by $100 million less) than the corresponding claims that the residents of other countries have upon them. The **capital account** records these changes in claims, and, according to the definitional rule given two paragraphs back, it must have an overall value of -$100 million. This implies that, by the accounting convention, an increase in the country's international reserves, just like an increase in its holdings of foreign shares, is a negative item in the capital account.

One small qualification to what has been said is that, since the balance-of-payments items are given in current prices, changes in the real value of its foreign financial assets and liabilities that occur purely because of changes in price level will not in practice be included in the balance-of-payments account. The net change in the country's foreign-asset position may therefore be slightly different from the amount indicated by the current-account balance. The greater the rate of inflation in the currency in which the foreign financial assets and liabilities are denominated, and the greater the difference between the aggregates of assets and liabilities, the bigger this discrepancy will be.

Current-account surplus and domestic surplus

From the definitions of terms given in Chapter 2, with the symbols used there,

$$
\begin{aligned}
Y &= E + X - M - Ya \\
&= (C + I + G) + X - M - Ya \\
\text{and} \quad Y + R &= C + S + T \\
\text{Thus} \quad C + S + T - R &= C + I + G + X - M - Ya \\
\text{So} \quad S + T - R &= I + G + X - M - Ya \\
\text{and} \quad X - M - Ya + R &= (S - I) + (T - G)
\end{aligned}
$$

And the right side of this equation may be written, in the terms used in Chapter 2, as:

$$S_n - I_n$$

that is, 'total national saving minus total national investment'.

What this means is that the external current-account surplus, (X - M - Ya + R), is by definition equal to the excess of domestic saving over domestic investment, which we might call the 'domestic surplus'. This is made up of the private domestic surplus (S - I) and the government domestic surplus (T - G).

Countries with current-account deficits, such as the US through the 1980s, Canada and Australia most of the time, the UK in the late 1980s, and most developing countries in the 1970s and before, have an excess of domestic investment over domestic saving: some of their domestic investment must be financed by overseas capital. Countries with current-account surpluses, such as Japan, Taiwan and West Germany in the 1970s and 1980s, have an excess of domestic saving over domestic investment: their surplus savings can be used to finance investment elsewhere.

4 Exchange rates and international money

International reserves

A country's international reserves are holdings by the country's banking system (mostly its central bank as a rule) of assets that the residents of the country can use as liquid (money-type) claims on the rest of the world and that therefore represent its holdings of **money available for international transactions.** The items held as reserves in recent years have been:

(a) gold;
(b) currencies of other countries (normally only those of major trading countries whose currencies are 'convertible');
(c) certain claims on the IMF (International Monetary Fund) including Special Drawing Rights (SDRs) and the first quarter or 'tranche' of the country's IMF quota.

This implies incidentally that two major trading countries can increase each other's reserves by doing a swap of currencies, such as pounds for lire.

Exchange rates

The exchange rate of the cedi is used here to mean the number of units of another currency for which it is bought and sold. In this sense, **depreciation or devaluation** of the currency means lowering the exchange rate and **appreciation** means raising it. (Confusingly, however, many writers use 'raising' and 'lowering' in the opposite sense; they think of the cedi's exchange rate as the number of cedis per other currency unit. They therefore describe depreciation as a *rise* in the exchange rate.) The figure cited is often a mean between buying and selling prices.

There is an exchange rate of the cedi against the naira, against the mark, and so on. For historical reasons a currency is often quoted against the US dollar, but there is really more sense in quoting its 'exchange-rate index' or 'effective exchange rate' (EER), which compares it with a 'basket' of other currencies in relation to its value in, say, 1975 or 1980. (The index is expressed so that it is higher if the currency's exchange rate is higher in the sense used here.) Quoting a currency's value against the Special Drawing Right (SDR), as is now quite often done, is really quoting it against a particular basket.

There have been changing fashions on whether to have **fixed** or **flexible** exchange rates. An alternative classification is **pegged** or **floating**, which normally means something slightly different.

For a period before 1914 the major trading nations used what was called the 'gold standard' to fix their exchange rates. (Those developing countries that were then colonies mostly used either the currency of the imperial power or one pegged to it.) For a government to be on the gold standard meant that it had agreed to buy and sell its currency for gold at a fixed rate or between very narrow limits. This fixed the exchange rates between currencies and made them more like one currency for purposes of international trade: a price in one currency could be converted at a known fixed rate into a price in another.

The gold standard was also supposed to prevent a country from going too far into 'deficit' or 'surplus' on its balance of payments, because of a supposed effect called the 'specie-flow mechanism' described by David Hume in 1752 and in some fashion by others before him (Allen, 1987). Gold (or currencies substituting for it) naturally tended to flow into surplus countries and out of deficit ones. Since the money supply in each country was supposed to be related to its gold holdings, a fall in gold holdings (arising as a result of a balance-of-payments deficit) would lead to a fall in money supply and consequently, it was believed, to a fall in the price level. The fall in prices within the country would tend to reduce import payments and probably to increase export receipts, so that the balance-of-payments deficit would tend to be corrected. The opposite adjustment would happen in the case of a country in balance-of-payments surplus. It is a matter of dispute how far these adjustments actually happened. They suppose a high degree of flexibility in prices.

During the 1914-18 War most countries abandoned the gold standard. It was restored fitfully after that war, and most countries which had returned to it (as Britain had done in 1925) abandoned it in the early 1930s.

The 1930s was a time of changing exchange rates among the major trading nations, since most governments thought it unsatisfactory in the prevailing depression to be bound by fixed rates. (The US from early 1933 was an exception.) The experiences of this period gave flexible rates a bad name. It was held that governments used their exchange rates to 'export' unemployment.

There was thus a hope during the Second World War for a return to stable rates once the fighting was over. However, not everyone was enchanted with the gold standard. Keynes blamed much of Britain's unemployment of the late 1920s on the attempt to restore and maintain it at the wrong rate. The Keynesians took the view that, if the specie-flow mechanism or 'gold-standard adjustment mechanism' worked at all to give each country a sustainable balance of payments, it did so mainly because *real income* (and not, or not only, prices) would fall in a deficit country in response to the withdrawal of gold.

So floating rates and permanently fixed rates were both suspect. What was wanted seemed to be a system that would 'peg' exchange rates for fairly long periods but not fix them for ever, allowing them to be adjusted if a country were in persistent surplus or deficit. To allow countries to sustain the deficits that would be unavoidable if exchange rates were to be constant for long periods, while at the same time avoiding the departures from full employment which Keynes believed the specie-flow mechanism was likely to entail (if it worked at all), there must be a system of international loans or overdrafts of currencies to accommodate temporary deficits. Then countries might manage their own domestic money supplies according to the needs of employment and output and not tie them to gold flows.

Accordingly Keynes, working in the UK Treasury in 1943, devised a proposal for an international central bank (the 'International Clearing Union') that would in effect give extensive 'overdrafts' to deficit countries and pile up positive balances for countries in surplus. The institution would require exchange-rate changes (up or down) if the surplus or deficit persisted for too long, but normally stable exchange rates could prevail without compelling the countries affected to vary their money supplies in ways that might have ill effects on their own employment and income. The UK government presented this scheme to its allies at a conference in 1944.

US officials thought this scheme too radical for their Senate to approve. They supposed that it would mean that the US would be in surplus and most of the rest in deficit, and that America would thus in effect be extending enormous loans to the rest of the world if the International Clearing Union were set up. Instead they proposed the outline of what was to become the International Monetary Fund (IMF). This followed somewhat similar principles but in a much more cautious way: borrowing rights from the IMF were to be discretionary and much more limited than the UK had proposed. The IMF system (known as the 'Bretton Woods' system after the place where the Allied financial conference was held in 1944) was still, however, directed at keeping exchange rates generally stable but allowing them to be changed in case of what was called 'fundamental disequilibrium'.

This system prevailed until 1971. The US dollar was the peg on which the rest in fact depended. The dollar was kept at a fixed rate to gold (for official transactions) from 1933 to 1971. The other members accepted rates expressed in dollars for their own currencies, with a narrow band of permissible variation around these rates.

What made the US end the system in 1971 was that the dollar, so long as it remained the peg, could not be devalued against the rest. Yet the US balance-of-payments deficits on account of current and long-term-capital transactions had been high and persistent. So in August 1971 President Nixon abandoned the fixed dollar price of gold, and in response the other major currencies were allowed to 'float' with more or less freedom.

Attempts, from December 1971 on, at a general restoration of pegged rates were short-lived.

However, the then EEC countries (except Britain, which remained outside until 1990) joined from early 1979 in the Exchange Rate Mechanism (ERM) of the European Monetary

System (EMS) which again pegs rates of members' currencies to each other within fairly narrow limits. (This followed on a rather similar system with fewer members, known familiarly as the 'Snake in the Tunnel'.) However, these rates are less permanent than under the Bretton Woods system, and formally there is no one peg currency against which all the others are fixed, as was the case with the dollar until 1971. There had been at least twelve realignments of ERM currencies' rates by early 1989, that is in the first ten years. The EMS thus forms one group with its own system of rates among its members.

A number of Third World countries also have exchange rates pegged, though not necessarily permanently, either to one of the major currencies or to a 'basket' of currencies, increasingly the latter.

The dollar, yen and pound, however, remained through the 1980s 'independently floating', their rates to an important extent determined by 'the market', but with a greater or less degree of deliberate influence exerted by their authorities. In early 1990 four other industrialized and fourteen developing countries were also listed by the IMF as independent floaters. The values of the dollar, yen, and pound, since 1979, have fluctuated greatly against each other and against the EMS-ERM currencies as a bloc. An example is the 33 per cent rise of the pound against the dollar from late 1977 to late 1980. The yen and mark both appreciated against the dollar by about 100 per cent over thirty months or so from early 1985.

During the Bretton Woods period (to 1971) the external balance was potentially a matter of concern to most countries; it has remained so to the majority of LDCs (until the mid-1980s, almost all), which for whatever reason have not trusted market-floating and have pegged their rates, or else have followed what is called by the IMF 'managed floating', where the rate appears to be kept in control but is not announced. Governments on pegged rates have often resisted the idea of devaluing their currencies. For those industrialized countries, and possibly also those developing countries, such as in the late 1980s Nigeria and Ghana, that have now 'market-floated' their currencies, the fear of being left without foreign exchange is probably no longer much of a worry in itself since it is assumed that exchange-rate movements will remove any marked deficit before reserves are exhausted. It is the *domestic effects* of the exchange-rate changes that assumed importance in the 1980s for market-floaters such as the UK and US. These effects include the high interest rates sometimes judged necessary to 'support' an exchange rate that, to judge by the external current account, seems too high, but is being kept there for some other purpose such as stabilizing domestic prices; and also the loss of competitiveness in internationally tradable goods if the exchange rate appreciates faster than the ratio of foreign-currency trading prices to domestic prices rises. These effects are the more disturbing if the exchange rate, instead of moving slowly and consistently in one direction according to long-run changes in the real capacities and productive structures of the particular economy and of the outside world, shifts erratically in accordance with short-term shortages and surpluses or changes in the expectations of those speculating in currencies.

Effects of exchange-rate changes

Downward movement ('devaluation' or 'depreciation') of a country's exchange rate will normally have three types of short-term effect.

(a) Devaluation is usually expected to increase a surplus or reduce a deficit on the external balance of trade in goods and services, though this result depends on certain elasticity conditions and on certain conditions of constancy in nominal expenditure and in the domestic component of prices.

If nominal expenditure and the domestic component of prices are both unaffected by the devaluation (compensating action being taken if necessary to ensure this), one effect will be to reduce the *foreign currency spent on imports* by making them more expensive in home currency. This is partly a real-income effect, in that the real value of any given cash income is reduced because import prices are increased, and partly a substitution effect, in that imports cost more in relation to substitute goods.

On the same two conditions, the devaluation will tend to increase the *quantity of exports sold* by reducing their prices in foreign currency or by making them more profitable to home producers, and it *may* as a result increase (but may diminish) *foreign currency earned for exports.*

The 'may' in the last sentence (the effect depends on the price-elasticity of demand for the country's exports) indicates that, even under constant nominal expenditure and a constant domestic component of prices, devaluation will not *necessarily* reduce any deficit on the balance of trade. On those conditions, however, it is *generally expected* to do so, though the desired effects on the export side may be slow to appear.

Moreover it is very likely that, unless compensatory action is taken, the changes that go with the devaluation *will* increase nominal expenditure (they will after all increase home-currency earnings for exports) or increase the domestic component of prices, and that these influences will reduce or cancel the elements (the changes in spending-power and in relative prices) that would tend to reduce the external trade deficit. (These qualifications will be explored in Chapter 6.)

(b) Devaluation is generally expected if anything to add to aggregate demand and so (if there is unused capacity) increase output and employment. The part of this effect originating on the import side depends on a diversion of demand through a change in relative prices between imported goods on the one hand and home-produced goods and producer-services on the other; the part originating on the export side depends on an increase in the real purchasing-power of export income over home-produced goods and producer services; thus the effect can be expected to apply unless and until the domestic component of prices has risen in full proportion to the devaluation. Moreover if, as in countries with low internal economic integration, the demand for imports is very inelastic to their price, or if imports are heavily constrained by administrative controls designed to equate them with a fairly fixed inflow of foreign-exchange earnings, the depressing 'tax-like' effect of higher import prices, the real-income effect, may outweigh any stimulating substitution effect on output from the import side.

(c) Devaluation will raise the price level, principally through raising the price of imports (important in most countries, since 20 per cent or more, often much more, of all expenditure is generally on imports). There may be exceptions to this rule, as discussed below, when there has been a high degree of administrative control of access to foreign exchange for importing, especially if devaluation allows these controls to be relaxed.

It follows from what has been said that just how effective any exchange-rate change can be in raising output and employment depends on whether other prices not *directly* affected by the change alter in sympathy with import prices. Very important among these 'other prices' are wages.

Suppose the exchange value of the kwacha were reduced from an index of 60 to an index of 50. Import prices could be expected to rise by a fifth, 20 per cent. If imports constitute ultimately 30 per cent of expenditure, we might expect the general level of prices to rise by about 6 per cent (0.2 *times* 0.3). A producer competing with imports and using an average selection of imported inputs in his production would thus find his own costs rising by 6 per cent while the costs of the imports with which he is competing rise by 20 per cent. He thus gains a (20 - 6 =) 14 percentage-point advantage to help him undersell the imports. (And a similar advantage accrues to exports.)

But if wages were to rise in response by 6 per cent because the price level has risen by 6 per cent, then (on the assumption that wage costs ultimately make up the 70 per cent of total costs that is not accounted for by imports) there would be a further increase in prices of (0.06 *times* 0.7 =) 0.042, about 4 per cent. Prices would now have risen altogether by 10 per cent and the margin of advantage to producers competing with foreign goods would have fallen to about 10 percentage points. Wages might then try to make up for the extra 4 per cent added to prices, and so on.

It is clear that, if other prices and wages are moving to restore their relativities with import prices after a devaluation, the initial advantage, to home producers, of higher foreign prices will gradually be whittled away. So, unless there is some restraint on wages (which will be a main element in the domestic component of costs), the boost to output and employment (and to the trade balance) resulting from a devaluation may be temporary.

It is also important to remember that, if the *nominal* value of government expenditure is unchanged in response to a devaluation, its *real* value will fall. Keeping nominal expenditure unchanged requires sacrifices, which it will be tempting to avoid.

Upward movement ('appreciation') of the exchange rate will tend to have all the opposite effects to devaluation, tending (on similar assumptions) to push the balance of trade towards deficit and reducing the level of output and employment and the price level. The more domestic prices and wages *fall* in response, the less will be the depressing effect on income and employment.

But it seems to be generally much easier to make prices rise through depreciation than to cause them to fall through appreciation. There is a kind of ratchet effect.

Exchange-rate changes therefore may tend to be disappointing in their effects: devaluation often seems to give more rise in prices and less rise in output than might have been expected if money-wages and nontradables' prices had not responded upwards; and appreciation seems to give less fall in prices and more fall in output than might have been expected if import-price reductions had been fully passed on into all domestic prices.

Trade restrictions

Import duties, import quotas, or foreign-exchange restrictions, may be used to restrict import spending. Where they act to restrict the import of goods that have domestically produced substitutes (an important proviso), they also in the short term tend to raise output and employment, the price level, and the external trade surplus, provided the exchange rate is fixed or else does not move upward in response. Some of the qualifications made above about the effects of exchange-rate changes, however, are also relevant here, for similar reasons.

The main objection to these measures is that (by contrast with the corresponding devaluation) they switch trade flows in an inefficient way. If the import-duty (tariff) rates among products differ, the system is favouring some as against others, thus encouraging some domestic industries at the expense of others, usually for no good reason connected with their real costs and benefits. Similarly the imposing of import controls at all (rather than devaluing) is favouring industries that compete with imports as against actual and potential export industries, often again for no good reason. Quantitative investigations made of the likely allocative effects of the systems of import duties and controls in a number of developing countries have shown that these are often quite horrendously wasteful. (See for example Little *et al.*, 1970, ch. 5, esp. table on p. 174.)

Exchange-rate changes under trade or exchange restrictions

Where there are administrative restrictions on all transactions on the import side, altering the exchange rate may have no effect on import quantities or on import payments in foreign currency. These will depend on what value of transactions is permitted under the restrictions. It is also possible that a devaluation will not raise the domestic price level under these conditions. Where the import of tradables is restricted, their domestic price may well reflect their scarcity value rather than simply reflecting their price to the importer. Thus lowering the exchange rate without reducing the availability of the foreign exchange for buying imports may not have the effect of raising their domestic prices. They may remain no more and no less scarce than before. If lowering the exchange rate simultaneously increases the flow of foreign exchange available and so reduces its scarcity, the domestic price level may even fall (or the rate of inflation be reduced) as a result.

Reducing the exchange rate in a process of liberalization

Where the exchange rate has been greatly overvalued (and foreign exchange correspondingly under-priced internally), liberalization may be advised as a means to a price system which gives a more efficient allocation of resources. At times there may be enormous distortion and waste to be overcome by such a change. Correction inevitably involves changing the exchange rate so that it reflects more closely the real cost and value of foreign exchange in relation to other inputs. However, it has to be remembered that the reason for this change in exchange rate is primarily that of improving *allocation*. It can not necessarily be expected to improve the external balance at the same time, certainly not quickly; and the devaluation should not be regarded as failing simply because there was no simultaneous increase in the external balance.

Influencing short-term capital flows

In the foreign-exchange markets, there are trade (and other current) flows and also capital flows. At present the volume of international capital flows is many times as high in value as the volume of international trade flows. Much of the capital flowing is short-term capital, that is, holdings of money and near-money moving between currencies.

Short-term capital is encouraged to move by changes (and expected changes) in differentials of nominal interest rates between countries. With the differences in nominal interest rates, holders of these assets will also take account of how they expect exchange rates to move in the near future. These two considerations will between them determine the difference in expected returns between holding the assets in one currency and holding them in another. So a change in a country's interest rates may be a quick-acting weapon for encouraging short-term capital to move in or out.

If the 'expected' devaluation of the franc against the yen over the next three months is 1.5 per cent, which corresponds to an annual rate of a little over 6 per cent, then it would seem that short-term interest rates on franc securities will need to have an annual interest rate about 6 percentage points higher than those on corresponding yen securities to make the two kinds of securities equally attractive. This hypothesis is known as that of **covered interest parity**. The reference to 'covering' concerns forward cover. If the market expects the franc to devalue by 1.5 per cent against the yen over three months, the cost of buying yen forward three months for francs, that is the extra cost of a guarantee of being able to buy yen at a preset price near the current price for francs in three months' time, will be about 1.5 per cent: the three-month forward price of yen in terms of francs will be about 101.5 per cent of the current ('spot') price. The cost of forward cover, in other words, will be a measure of the expected exchange-rate change. There is covered interest parity if the interest earned from holdings in the two currencies is equal once the cost of forward cover against exchange risks has been taken into account.

When exchange rates are allowed to float independently of official currency-market intervention, they respond to demand and supply for the currency concerned. Short-term capital flows may naturally make a difference to the demand for various currencies. If, as a result of a rise in French short-term interest rates, operators want to sell other currencies and buy francs to a greater extent than before, this will tend to make the exchange rate of the franc rise.

How to move the exchange rate

When the exchange rate is **pegged**, the central bank or other authority undertakes that it will trade other currencies with its own at the pegged rate. The peg may be to a precise rate or else to a range of rates within which the country's authorities will be prepared to buy or sell. To shift the peg, it simply alters the rate at which it will trade, say from $2.80 per £1 yesterday to $2.40 today. When the exchange rate is **floating**, the authorities may influence it by buying or selling currencies themselves; or they may influence it by general policies of a fiscal or monetary kind that affect the demand for, or the supply of, their currency. Floating does not imply that the authorities show no care or concern for the exchange rate. Since 'floating' may be consistent with varying degrees of deliberate intervention, and 'pegging' may allow variation within a range of rates, there is no very obvious line between the two. Here we may take a currency as pegged if the rate at which, or the range within which, its national authorities are resolved to hold it for the time being, or the rule by which that rate or range will be set, is public knowledge.

Fiscal expansion will tend to increase imports. If the money supply is fixed, however, it will also raise the interest rate. Raising imports will of course cause money to flow out. But raising the interest rate will cause money to flow in. So it is not clear what effect fiscal expansion or contraction with a fixed money supply will have on the exchange rate.

Fiscal expansion accompanied by sufficient monetary expansion to prevent interest rates from rising, however, will definitely cause money to flow out, and will hence tend to reduce (devalue) the exchange rate. In small Third World countries with undeveloped capital markets, fiscal expansion *will* normally be accompanied by monetary expansion.

Monetary expansion on its own will lower interest rates, and by expanding nominal income it will also raise imports at any given exchange rate. On both scores it will cause money to flow out and hence tend to devalue the exchange rate.

Wage restraint, by keeping down domestic costs, will probably tend to cause money to flow in on account of trade for the same reason (changes in relative prices) that devaluation will tend to do so. This would tend to raise a floating exchange rate.

What is called **sterilized intervention** by governments in foreign-exchange markets to alter or to support an exchange rate is intervention which does not rely on changing the home country's interest rates. Sterilized intervention to raise the price of one's own currency involves buying up securities in that currency for foreign exchange and selling foreign-currency securities to do so, and *not* simultaneously selling home-currency securities on the domestic market to raise home interest rates; the authorities would sell home-currency securities on the domestic market only insofar as that might be necessary to prevent interest rates on home securities from actually falling.

If the only considerations that led a holder to prefer one currency to another were the relative expected yields on holding them (which would imply that considerations of risk played no part in leading a holder to favour one currency in which he would shortly have to make payments for example, or to favour a spread of currencies), that is, if currencies were *perfect substitutes* for one another, sterilized intervention could have no effect on the exchange rate. In that case, as fast as the French authorities switched from yen to francs without changing the franc securities' interest rates, other holders would switch from francs to yen, so that there would be no change in the franc-yen price. Probably currencies are generally not perfect substitutes, so that sterilized intervention may still have some role to play. National controls over the international flow of capital can help to increase the effectiveness of intervention that does not affect domestic interest rates (sterilized intervention), in that it creates partly separate domestic and international markets for the country's currency.

Exchange-rate determination in a free market

What would determine exchange rates if there were no administrative controls, or other trade intervention such as duties, on trade and exchange?

It is natural to think that there would be some approximation to **purchasing-power parity**, that is, that if a Kenyan shilling bought ten times as great a real value of goods in Kenya as an Indonesian rupiah does in Indonesia the exchange rate of the shilling would be 10 rupiah. This has been argued to follow from the 'law of one price', the rule that, in a free market, the same good cannot, except to an extent explained by transport costs, have two different prices at the same time. If you can buy twice as much sugar for a shilling in Kenya as for a shilling in Tanzania but one Kenyan shilling exchanges for one Tanzanian shilling, then sugar will do its best to find its way from Kenya to Tanzania, and people will try to sell Tanzanian shillings for Kenyan shillings, until either the price ratio for sugar or the exchange rate changes.

Every traveller, however, knows that actual exchange rates seem very far from following purchasing-power parity. Quite apart from all trade and exchange interventions, there are several reasons why this should be so.

First, there are of course **transport costs**. Goods have differing costs of movement, and some are produced only in particular areas.

Second, **only certain kinds of good are traded internationally**; there are reasons why the prices of many nontraded goods in relation to those of traded goods should be systematically different from one country to another, principally because of *vastly different real-wage levels* and the fact that a number of nontraded goods, especially personal services, have a high low-skilled labour content. That such international differences in the purchasing power of wages over traded goods (and the *marginal* product of labour) can continue to exist is partly due to the 'natural' and imposed barriers to migration. Differences in the efficiency of non-traded elements in production, such as distribution systems, and also the relative scarcity of natural resources such as land, may also have a bearing on the country-to-country differences in the relative prices of nontraded and traded goods. Combinations of these factors (combined with different degrees of agricultural protection) help to explain why North American or British travellers find board and accommodation cheap in Bombay but dear in Tokyo. (It should be added that consumption patterns differ from one country to another, so that it is impossible to make unambiguous comparisons of living costs.)

Third, a unit of currency is a **financial asset**, and to understand its value we have to see it as traded in an asset market. Its value may be heavily affected by speculative factors, that is by what its value is believed likely to be in the near future. Also, when the external balance goes markedly into surplus or deficit, a market exchange rate will adjust up or down as the case may be and will go on adjusting until it has equated the demand with the supply of the currency. Such an adjustment will eventually affect trade flows, but that change in response to the exchange-rate adjustment may take time. The exchange rate may therefore well 'overshoot' in relation to the level of exchange rate that would mark the eventual equilibrium, because there will be no mechanism to make it take account of the trade changes that its movement will eventually bring about.

Fourth, there are **long-term capital movements**, which, if in total they are not balanced by trade flows in the opposite direction, will influence the relative scarcity of the currency independently of price parities. The fact that to invest in Botswana lawfully you need pula, and in Vietnam dong, creates a protected demand to some extent for these currencies.

The existence of trade and exchange interventions by governments, including restrictions, will provide additional reasons why exchange rates out of line with purchasing-power parities may be sustainable.

The real exchange rate

The real (effective) exchange rate (RER or REER) of a country is an index whose value takes account of movements in the ('nominal') exchange rate and also of relative movements of prices between the country and the rest of the world.

It can be regarded as an inverse measure of the country's **'competitiveness'** in the limited sense that it measures the effect on its competitiveness of price (including exchange-rate) changes. It does not take into account the contribution to competitiveness of relative changes in the efficiency of production. Thus, though Japan's real exchange rate by any ordinary measure rose greatly between 1985 and 1987, its industries showed very little fall in their capacity to compete in world trade. This was presumably because the industries that actually faced international competition found ways of improving their technical efficiency or choice of techniques or products or 'X-efficiency' or marketing or some other factor that did not directly depend on general relative-price changes.

As we express the RER here, the more the RER *rises*, the *less* competitive does it tend to make the country's products.

$$\text{RER} = \text{NER}\ \textit{times}\ \frac{\text{Domestic prices}}{\text{World prices}}$$

The higher the nominal exchange rate and the higher the domestic prices for any given set of world prices, the more difficult it is for the country to compete.

A variety of somewhat different indexes of the RER will be obtained by using different series for the indexes that go to make it up. There is no one right set of series. Which ones are suitable will depend on the purpose for which the RER is being calculated.

Usually it will be most relevant to treat the nominal ER ('nominal' as against 'real') here as what is called an 'effective' exchange rate (EER), that is, not one measured against a currency arbitrarily chosen but rather one measured against a basket of the currencies that are most relevant for the country's own trade. Countries' EER indexes are now commonly quoted against the basket of currencies represented by the SDR.

Similarly the 'world-price' index used should be chosen so that it reflects the movements in those external prices that are most likely to affect the country's trade; it may be a weighted average of some price indexes of the country's major trading partners, weighted according to their relative importance in its total trade or its imports or its exports. Since for a primary-exporting country the world prices affecting its price-competitiveness in the shortish term are the prices of those from whom it imports rather than the prices of those exporting the same goods or those buying its exports, a weighted average domestic-price index or export-price index *for its main import-supplier countries* may be judged the most relevant.

The domestic price index used also needs to be chosen according to the purpose of the enquiry. On the whole we should like to make it reflect as far as possible the 'domestic component' in prices. For this reason a domestic **wage or employment-cost index** may be most suitable in some cases.

In analysis a model is frequently used in which the products of a country are divided between 'tradable' and 'nontradable' goods, the prices of items within each group being supposed to move together in response to exchange-rate changes. Tradables are the kinds of goods that are internationally traded: imports and exports and those that compete with imports and exports. This is of course an abstraction to simplify a much more complex reality, but it is a useful one.

The division between tradable and nontradable goods fits most precisely in what is called a small-open-economy model (explained in Chapter 7). In this framework the REER can be thought of as measuring the ratio between the prices of nontradable and tradable goods.

A marked rise in the REER is likely to indicate changes which have a depressing effect on real income and employment. Argentina, Chile, Uruguay and the UK all suffered (as a partly unintended result of policy) large rises in their REERs around 1980. The effects on real output and employment were pretty disastrous.

Many LDCs keep their ERs and RERs consistently higher than they would be in a free market. This requires close restrictions on the use of foreign exchange and greatly reduces incentives for export growth. Since limits on the growth of export earnings form a principal constraint on economic growth, such policies need to be questioned.

Part 2
Standard Models for Stabilization

5 Keynesian and Monetarist approaches

Here we have to repeat what was said in the foreword. Readers who have not undergone some elementary course in macroeconomics will probably need to work through the relevant parts of a basic economics textbook before they can derive reasonable benefit from this chapter or from much of what follows. They will also need to have some idea of the rudiments of microeconomics, at least to the point of following simple models of market adjustment. Relevant readings are given in the section on further reading at the end of the book. This chapter will try to give a refresher on the elements of Keynesian and Monetarist models, but the account may be too brief for someone with no previous acquaintance with them.

The Keynesian revolution

J.M.Keynes's book *The General Theory of Employment, Interest and Money*, published in 1936, instituted a revolt against what he called 'Classical' economics. Classical economics, as Keynes interpreted it, held that under a free market there were natural mechanisms, working through price adjustment, that would tend to maintain a full employment of society's resources including labour. They would thus maintain national output and income at the highest level consistent with those resources and existing technical knowledge and capacity. Involuntary unemployment of labour would be only transient, and attempts by governments to intervene for the purpose of increasing the level of employment would be unnecessary and probably harmful.

This drew on various explicit or implicit assumptions. Among them were the beliefs (a) that both real wages and the price of any good or service would respond to excess supply by falling promptly; (b) that investors would take an accurate and consistent view of the prospects for investment; and (c) that money was held only for purposes of making purchases of goods and services.

Keynes's quest for an alternative model was motivated by a desire to understand and correct the high levels of apparently involuntary unemployment that had become chronic in Britain in the 1920s and the general catastrophic fall in world real income and employment that is dated from after the US stock-market collapse of October 1929. Classical macroeconomics seemed to be saying that all this could not happen. It was thus of little use in showing how these disasters could be averted.

Keynes argued that the three assumptions of the Classical model (mentioned in the last paragraph but one) were not realistic approximations to what actually happened in twentieth-century industrial economies. (a) Wages and prices were likely to be 'sticky' in a downward direction; (b) investors could not have accurate knowledge of the prospects for their investments and would be influenced in their decisions by unpredictable and irrational forces; and (c) money would be held not only for the purpose of making regular (and some unexpected) purchases of goods and services but also as an asset for speculation.

Rejecting the assumptions of the Classical model enabled Keynes to reject their conclusion: that the system would return fairly promptly to full employment after any disturbance: in other words, that there would be a stable equilibrium at full employment.

His model made use of the analytical concept of equilibrium, but he postulated that there might be an equilibrium level of income and of employment *other than at full employment*. From this starting-point, one might then ask how the system could be manipulated in order to produce an equilibrium *at full employment*.

Keynes's model (at least as formulated by his systematizers and simplifiers) worked by supposing that disturbances leading to departures from any given income equilibrium (situations in which demand and supply of output were unequal) would be followed by a restoration of equilibrium not through adjustment of prices but through adjustment of income levels. (An exposition of Keynes's own writings would show that he allowed more of a role to price changes than this implies, as will be mentioned below; but undoubtedly the important new element was the supposition that output and income adjusted.)

The model, in the form in which it entered the textbooks and probably influenced the understanding of millions of students over the third quarter of this century, supposed that, while output or income was below the full-employment level, the level of income (Y) would be determined by the level of 'aggregate demand': it was demand, not supply, that in those circumstances would set the pace. It was *only when full employment was reached* that supply conditions would set the limits and only then that any increase in demand would raise the price level alone rather than output.

At positions below full employment, the system would tend to move to an equilibrium by adjustment of Y ('aggregate supply') to the level of aggregate demand (AD). In the closed-economy model, AD, which would be the same as planned expenditure (E_P), would be made up of the private demand for consumption (C), the private demand for investment (I_P), and the government's demand for goods and services:

$$AD = E_P = C + I_P + G.$$

In the open-economy model, as Keynes's framework was developed by Harrod and others, aggregate demand would be equal to planned expenditure *plus* the foreign demand for our exports (X) *minus* our demand for imports (M):

$$AD = E_P + X - M = C + I_P + G + X - M.$$

To influence the level of output or income, then, a government would need to influence the level of one or other of the terms on the right side of this equation. C and M would both be closely related to income itself, though policy might alter both these relationships through subsidies, taxes, restrictions, or the exchange rate. X would be determined in part by conditions outside the country, though again subsidies, taxes, or the exchange rate, could affect the level. G would of course be determined by the government directly. I_P would be determined by investors' expectations of yields and by the interest rate. The interest rate would be determined in the market for money.

C and M would not be likely to be important autonomous sources of instability. (Their two-way relationship with Y is the reason for the 'multiplier' described by Keynes.) I_P, however, might fluctuate: investors' expectations, which form one part of its determinants, would be unstable; the interest rate, its other determinant, might also be unstable because the market for money, in which it is itself determined, is likely to be affected by instability in the speculative demand for money. Keynes said little if anything in this context about the instability of X, but export earnings are of course a source of great disturbance for many developing countries.

Because of the inevitable instability of I_P, Keynes believed that it might be necessary for government to use its own spending (G) in a compensatory manner to stabilize AD. To vary taxes with G would, partly at least, cancel this corrective effect. Therefore it might be necessary to run varying levels of government surpluses and deficits, with a tendency towards deficit when private investment demand was low and toward surplus when it was high. Such active use of the government budgetary balance came to be the main meaning of the term **fiscal policy**.

It would also in principle be possible for the government to influence the level of I_P itself through the interest rate (i) by varying the supply of money (Mn). However, for various reasons Keynes believed that such **monetary policy** would be rather ineffective or at least unreliable, especially in raising I_P when it was too low.

Equilibrium in the goods and money markets combined: the Keynesian closed-economy model

Treating government expenditure for simplicity as if it were part of private investment or consumption, and supposing a closed economy, we can represent the reaching of equilibrium in the goods and money markets combined under Keynesian mechanisms. The position of the equilibrium will be determined by five conditions:

(a) the money supply;
(b) the speculative-demand function for money (relating the demand for money to the interest rate);
(c) the investment-demand function (based on investors' expectations);

(d) the consumption or savings function (relating consumption to income);
(e) the transactions-demand function for money (relating the demand for money to the income level).

Of these, the Keynesians supposed, (a) can be largely set by the authorities; (d) and (e) are stable; but (b) and (c) are potentially unstable.

Rather than trying to represent these five conditions separately on a single diagram, which is awkward, we can summarize them in two functions, roughly as was done by two of Keynes's expositors, Hicks and Hansen.

One function or locus, expressing conditions (c) and (d), shows the combinations of i and Y which give equilibrium in the market for goods. The other, expressing conditions (a), (b) and (e), shows the combinations of i and Y which give equilibrium in the market for money.

These two functions are shown in Figure 5.1, which is known as the **IS–LM diagram**. The function showing goods-market equilibrium (the so-called IS or investment-savings function) slopes downward. The one showing money-market equilibrium (which is called the LM function) slopes upward. The point at which they intersect is the combination of i and Y which will give equilibrium in *both* markets. That intersection point is the one to which the system will tend at any given combination of the five conditions.

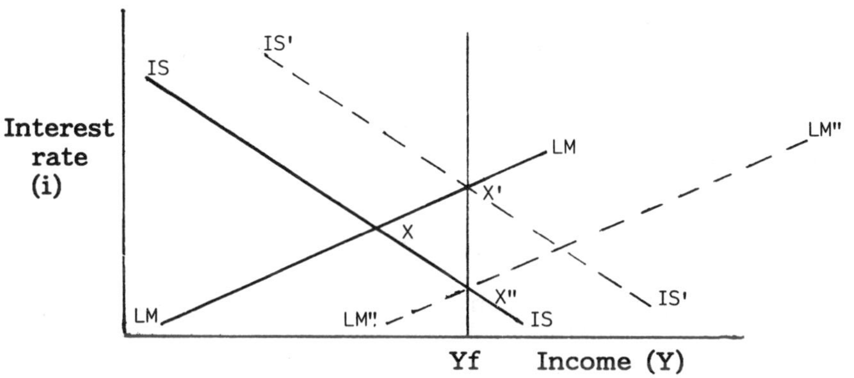

Figure 5.1 IS-LM joint equilibrium

If we think of government spending as part of total investment and consumption, changes in fiscal (budgetary) policy, as well as other changes in either the investment-demand function or the consumption function, can be shown by movements of the IS (goods-market equilibrium) function: expansion by the function's movement to the right, contraction to the left. Expansion will raise income as the new equilibrium is set, but it will also raise the interest rate through imposing bigger demands for transactions money on a constant money supply. This is shown at the new equilibrium point X'.

Changes in monetary policy or monetary conditions can be shown by movements of the LM (money-market equilibrium) function: expansion of the money supply (in relation to money demand) by its movement to the right, contraction to the left. Expansion may come about through an increase in the money supply or any change that makes people less desirous of holding money (a fall in the 'demand function for money'). Such expansion will raise income while at the same time lowering the interest rate as the new equilibrium is reached. This is shown at the equilibrium point X".

Equilibrium in the goods, money, and foreign-exchange, markets combined: the Keynesian open-economy model

The IS-LM diagram introduced above can be made relevant to an open economy by adding a further 'equilibrium' line to represent the combinations of i (interest rate) and Y (income) that will achieve 'equilibrium' in the foreign-exchange market. This line is BB (Figure 5.2).

We can give BB either of two slightly different meanings depending on what set of policy instruments we are exploring.

First, let us take the points on BB to represent not strictly equilibrium in the foreign-exchange market but rather *a satisfactory picture in the net balance of external payments under a particular pegged exchange rate.*

The upward slope of BB indicates the fact that, at any one pegged exchange rate, a rise in income will increase imports and that therefore interest rates will need to rise in order to attract the short-term capital flows that will leave the net external balance unaffected by the rise in income.

Suppose that there are now *two* objectives of policy: to achieve a certain value of Y (the 'full-employment' or 'internal-balance' level) and to maintain a certain level of the net external balance indicated by the BB line. So in the diagram the aim is to have all three lines (IS, LM and BB) intersecting on the vertical line at income Yf. Unless there is some happy coincidence, it is clear that *two* of the lines are likely to have to be moved for that to be possible, and (if the lines are continuous, differ from one to another in their slopes, and can be moved in parallel right or left, and at least one of them initially intersects Yf) it should be enough if we can move *any two* of them.

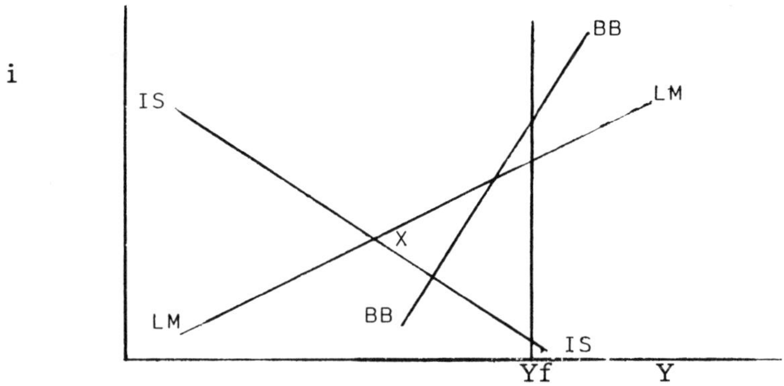

Figure 5.2 IS-LM equilibrium and BB: X at external surplus, internal 'deficit'

From the initial position shown in Figure 5.2, an intersection point ought to be achievable if we can move both the IS and the LM line each an appropriate distance to the right or left, as in Figure 5.3. Movement of the IS line to the right indicates fiscal expansion; movement of the LM line to the left indicates monetary contraction. The two will have to be capable of being moved independently if we are to be likely to achieve the result desired.

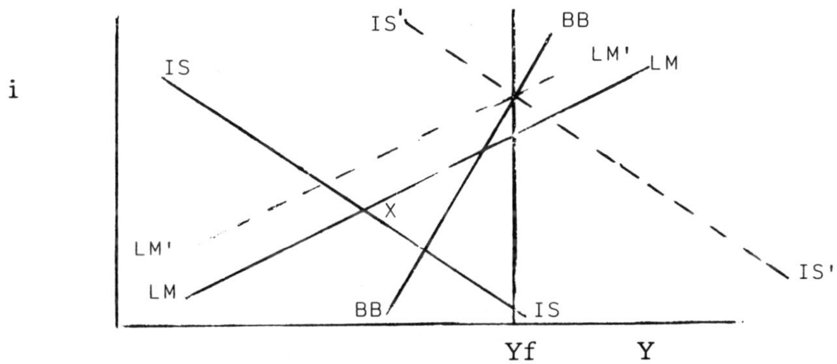

Figure 5.3 Fiscal and monetary measures to meet two targets

Alternatively we could achieve the result by moving the IS line to the right and the BB line downward, as in Figure 5.4. Movement of the BB line downward may be interpreted as the change produced by devaluation of the exchange rate, on the assumptions that (a) the devaluation itself is compensated as necessary so that nominal expenditure is unaffected and that (b) the elasticity conditions are fulfilled to make a devaluation tend toward surplus in the external current account. The downward movement of the BB line indicates that the required external-balance position comes to be achieved at a higher level of income or at a lower interest rate then before. (The devaluation may also act, independently of fiscal policy, to move the IS line to the right by switching demand to domestic products, and, independently of monetary changes, to move the LM line to the left by raising the price level and so reducing the real value of the money supply, but these effects are ignored in the diagram for the sake of simplicity.)

This is an illustration of the general rule that, to achieve two independent policy objectives, we are likely to need two independently manoeuvrable policy instruments. Here the objectives are a certain level of income and a certain external-balance position, and the instruments are fiscal and monetary policy, or fiscal and exchange-rate policy, or for that matter monetary and exchange-rate policy.

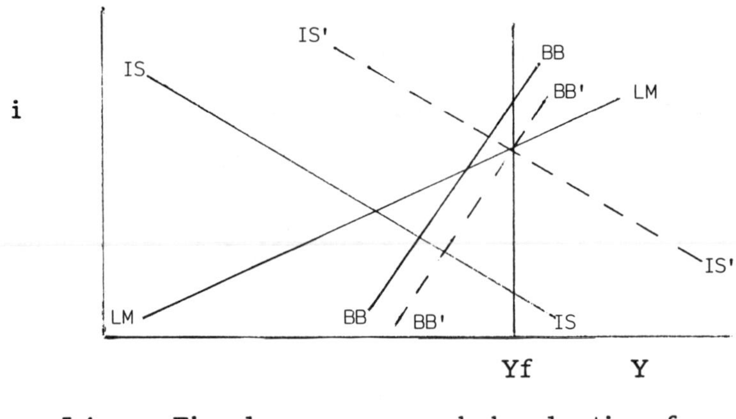

Figure 5.4 Fiscal measures and devaluation for two targets

The alternative way of seeing the BB line is relevant to a situation in which the exchange rate is not pegged but floating. Then it may be assumed that the exchange rate will move up or down in response to a surplus or shortage of foreign exchange in such a way as to maintain a desired external balance without the need of any policy-maker to look after it. But in that situation we may well want not only a certain level of income, Yf, but also a particular exchange rate, which may be desired in order either to stabilize domestic prices or to maintain the external competitiveness of the nation's tradable-goods industries.

So again there are two objectives. We can ignore external balance because it is being looked after by the floating exchange rate.

The BB line is now genuinely *an equilibrium locus* for the foreign-exchange market. It shows the combinations of i and Y that will give equilibrium in the foreign-exchange market *at some particular exchange rate* that happens to be desired.

Again we shall want all three equilibrium lines to intersect at income Yf, but this time the particular position of BB can not be changed; it represents one of the objectives that we are seeking. The exchange rate can no longer be used as an instrument because it is being left to find its own level in the market and in so doing to look after the external balance.

This time, then, we shall have to be able to move both IS and LM, in order to achieve an intersection (equilibrium in all three markets) at income Yf; in other words, we shall have to use both fiscal and monetary policy, and what happens appears just the same as in Figure 5.3.

For certain classes of LDC, monetary policy cannot very effectively be used independently of fiscal policy. With a floating exchange rate, they would then have only one instrument of the three so far mentioned that they could actually control. It would seem that they might achieve a certain desired level of income with this one (fiscal-monetary) instrument, *or* a certain desired exchange rate for price-stability purposes, but not both.

In fact most LDCs have pegged, or at least managed, exchange rates, so that the exchange rate *may* be used as an instrument, but then the external-balance objective has to be an additional target of policy. There are, however, two other potential instruments. One is **exchange controls**; they, to a point, enable a 'non-equilibrium' exchange rate to be maintained, but for reasons mentioned in Chapter 4 an 'overvalued' exchange rate maintained by exchange controls may not succeed in keeping down domestic prices as might be intended. The other instrument is **wage policy.**

Wage policy in the Keynesian framework

Keynes himself was sceptical over the usefulness of direct intervention by the authorities to set money-wages. However, he had no faith that wages would automatically adjust to the right 'market-clearing' level. He did in fact see a rise in prices (which he recognized as likely to follow from an expansion in aggregate demand even under conditions of less-than-full employment) as having a function in lowering *real* wages without the necessity of reducing money-wages. This way of lowering real wages, he thought, would be more easily accepted because it meant that all real wages fell in the same proportion, whereas he saw interference with money-wages as altering relativities, which would be resented. (This view depended probably on his assuming the very decentralized wage-fixing system of inter-War Britain with which he was familiar; the same would not seem so plausible in a centralized system such as post-War Sweden's.) The implication was that wage-setting was a political process. He believed that the success of stabilization policies of the kind he advanced depended on restraint on the part of trade-union negotiators.

By the 1950s and early 1960s several industrial countries that were being managed with broadly Keynesian policy assumptions made attempts at consistent national pay policies. Governments might be more or less heavily involved in these attempts. In Sweden and Japan the government participated directly in the arrangements only as an employer, and actual policy emerged from discussions between employers and employees: through centralized negotiations in Sweden, and through public debate, with both centralized and decentralized negotiations, in Japan.

There was a recognition that real wages might be set too high to make full employment possible. If the wage-workers were then prepared to accept some fall in real wages as demand in money terms expanded, full employment might be achieved. If, however, they responded by demanding a restoration of their previous real wages through money-wage rises, one of two results might ensue. The rise of demand in money terms might be halted, leaving the workers with their old level of real wages but failing to achieve full employment; or else there might be a further rise in demand in money terms followed by a further rise in prices and a further demand for a rise in money-wages. The latter outcome might succeed in raising employment if the rises in prices kept ahead of the rises in money-wages so that real wages were (on average over time) depressed. But of course the cost of this policy would be inflation. The faster the restoration of real wages after each price rise, the faster, other things being equal, would inflation have to proceed in order to keep real wages low enough for full employment to be maintained.

Wage policies were an attempt to make possible **full employment and stable prices simultaneously** by persuading workers to accept money-wage levels which, at stable prices, would give real-wage levels consistent with full employment. It is notable that Japan, Sweden, Austria, Norway and Switzerland kept high levels of employment right through the recessions of the 1970s and 1980s (only Austria faltering a little in the mid-1980s), and all except Switzerland observed some form of institutionalized national consensus over pay. This has to be remembered when we consider below the various strands of Monetarist, all of whom tend to become apoplectic over the notion of centralized arrangements for fixing wages, by government or otherwise.

Understanding of the mechanisms was complicated from 1958 by A. W. Phillips, who published his empirical findings on what has been called the **Phillips Curve**. These seemed to show a remarkably consistent relationship for several industrialized countries over quite long periods between rates of unemployment and rates of increase in money-wages. The lower unemployment was, the higher the rate at which money-wages (and therefore apparently prices) rose. This suggested that there was what is called a trade-off between high employment and stable prices: the more you wanted of one, the less you had to accept of the other. Phillips, when I heard him speak in 1959, raised the possibility that better wage-fixing arrangements might improve the trade-off, pushing the Phillips Curve for any country downward and to the left, in effect what national wage arrangements were trying to achieve. He did not apparently see his results as inconsistent with the approach that recognized political elements in wage-fixing.

What happened, however, from the late 1960s in a number of industrialized countries was that the Phillips Curve relationship moved or disappeared, but in the wrong direction. Higher rates of inflation *and* of unemployment became common. The much more depressing macroeconomic position of the 1970s gave fuel to the Monetarist reaction against Keynesian thinking.

It can be said that by implication a typical 'Keynesian' approach to wages accepts that there may be a range of real-wage levels (in individual occupations and also nationally on average) at which roughly the same number of people would be prepared to offer for work; the supply curve of labour, in other words, may be very steep. Wage negotiation is frequently carried out not in anything resembling a perfect market but by large bodies on both sides with a measure of monopoly-monopsony power. The politics of negotiation, in which governments and other national bodies can participate, may help to determine at what level wages are fixed.

Where there is a lower nominal wage (money-wage), a given national-income target may be achieved at a lower level of nominal expenditure. A lower nominal wage will also tend to mean a lower *real* exchange rate (higher international competitiveness) for any given *nominal* exchange rate. Thus, unless there is an excess demand for labour, a lower nominal wage will tend to mean higher real national income for a given price level and external position, both because it enables a given *real* level of domestic expenditure to be achieved with lower *nominal* domestic expenditure and because it allows higher international competitiveness to be achieved with a given *nominal* exchange rate.

Equilibrium in the goods, money, and foreign-exchange, markets, with wage policy as a potential instrument

Let us assume that wage policy does in certain circumstances work more or less as its advocates suppose and that it therefore forms a further potential instrument for helping to achieve stabilization objectives.

We can explore in Figure 5.5 its use with reference to the IS-LM-BB diagram presented above in Figure 5.2.

A question raised above was how a Third World country that did not have a significant domestic money and capital market, and could therefore not effectively run fiscal and monetary policies that were independent of each other, could achieve internal and external balance and stable domestic prices. This could be represented as *either* (a) pursuing *two* independent objectives (full-employment income, and an exchange-rate target designed to maintain a stable domestic price level), with only *one* independently movable instrument, *or* (b) pursuing *three* independent objectives, (full-employment income, an exchange-rate target for domestic-price stability, and external balance), with only *two* instruments (fiscal-monetary policy and the exchange rate).

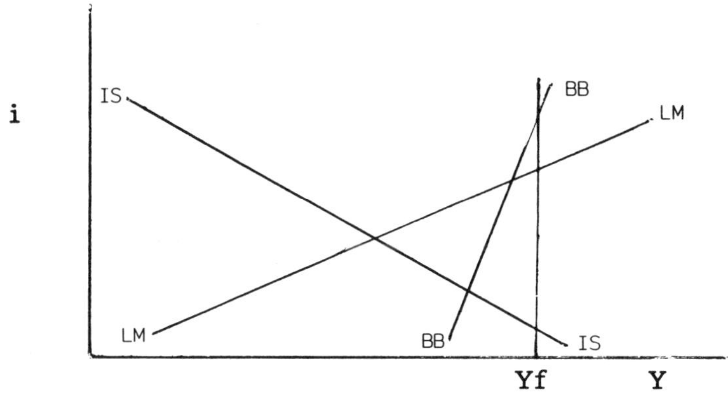

Figure 5.5 A position from which LM and IS must come to intersect on BB at income Yf

The answer was that these combinations of objectives could not be achieved unless at least one more instrument variable was used. The two extra candidates suggested for the role were exchange controls and wage policy.

How can we represent on the diagram the operation of wage policy in adding the capacity to achieve a further possible objective?

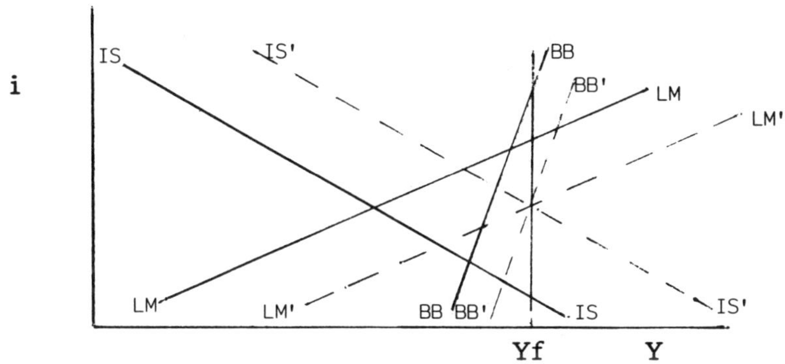

Figure 5.6 Fiscal-monetary measures as one instrument cannot attain two targets

Suppose then that we want to achieve (a) an income level, Yf, (b) external balance through a floating exchange rate, and at the same time (c) an exchange-rate level that will serve to stabilize domestic prices. In Figure 5.5, BB represents the combinations of Y and i which will be consistent with the particular equilibrium exchange rate that will stabilize domestic prices. The object of policy is to arrange it that LM and IS intersect on BB at the income level Yf. Then all three objectives will be achieved.

To attain these three objectives, what instruments do we have? The exchange rate is potentially one instrument, but that one is tied up as a floating rate in looking after external balance. If fiscal and monetary policy have to be treated as one, there is only one instrument for the two objectives that have to be actively pursued. Fiscal-monetary expansion alone may attain intersection of IS and LM at Yf, as in Figure 5.6, and the exchange rate, if it is floating, will fall to make that combination consistent with external balance, but this may easily mean, as in the case shown in Figure 5.6, that the exchange rate is below the one corresponding to BB, and the inflation objective will have to be sacrificed. How can wage control as a second instrument serve to make achievement of that extra objective possible?

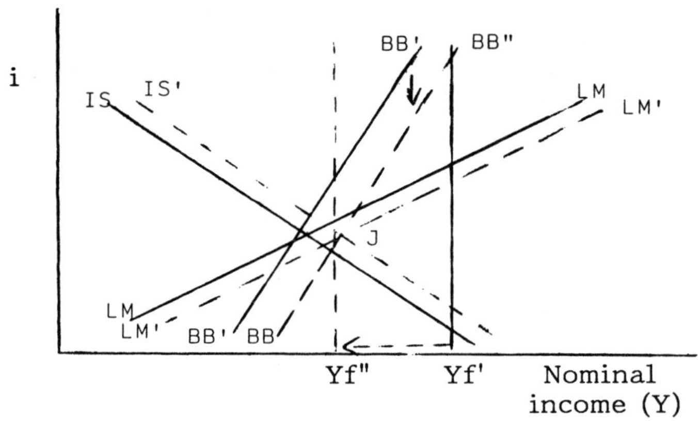

Figure 5.7 Suppressing money-wages reduces the target nominal income for internal balance and reduces the target nominal exchange rate for price stability; so wage policy and fiscal-monetary measures may achieve these two targets

For this purpose we have to distinguish between nominal and real magnitudes since changing the wage rate will make a given nominal expenditure mean more or less in real terms. If we take it then that the target income level is a target in real terms ('internal balance') but that the Y axis on the diagram, and the fiscal and monetary measures that move IS and LM, are expressed in nominal terms, then, the lower the domestic price level, the lower the *nominal* income that corresponds to full employment (internal balance), and hence the further the *target* level of nominal income moves to the left, say from Yf' to Yf" in Figure 5.7.

Similarly, if a given nominal exchange rate is associated with a lower real exchange rate than before, the *real* exchange rate necessary for achieving external balance at any particular interest rate will represent a higher *nominal* exchange rate than before and will therefore have a greater tendency to suppress domestic inflation; the exchange rate that is required to achieve domestic price stability will therefore be one that achieves external balance at a higher nominal income (Y) or a lower interest rate (i) than before. In other words, the money-wage reduction pushes the *target* BB line downward and to the right, say from BB' to BB" in Figure 5.7. (BB is steep to suggest a low sensitivity of external payments to interest rates.)

So, to summarize, reducing money-wages will make target BB lower (more to the right) than it otherwise would be; and it will move target Yf to the left (Figure 5.7). The required equilibrium is represented on the diagram by the intersection at one point of all four lines.

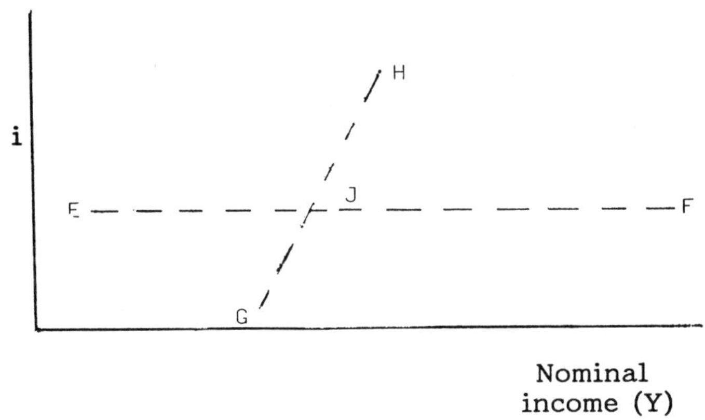

Figure 5.8 Anatomy of the changes in Figure 5.7

Suppose fiscal-monetary expansion or contraction will allow IS and LM to intersect at any chosen point along a roughly horizontal locus, EF, and the lowering or raising of the money-wage will allow the vertical line at Yf and target BB to intersect at any chosen point along an upward-sloping locus, GH. From the initial positions shown in the diagrams, it seems quite likely that there will be some point at which EF and GH will intersect. In the case illustrated, where EF and GH intersect at J in Figure 5.8, there will be some combination of fiscal-monetary expansion and money-wage reduction that will cause IS, LM, BB, and Yf, lines all to intersect at a point such as J.

Thus, in the case illustrated, though not necessarily in every case, it seems that, while external balance is achieved by a floating exchange rate (or for that matter by pegged-exchange-rate adjustment), the use of fiscal adjustment (without independent monetary adjustment) and wage control will suffice to achieve simultaneously a real-income and a price-level objective.

It need hardly be added that, even under the most favourable circumstances, the capacity of the authorities to influence money-wages may be severely limited in practice.

The Monetarist counterrevolution

The Keynesian attack on Classical macroeconomics rested on the view that:

(a) some prices, especially wages, do not readily adjust to shortages and surpluses;
(b) investment decisions are made in ignorance of the future and often with little relationship to the objective possibilities of the economy as set by its resources;
(c) the demand for money has an inconsistent relationship with income.

All this led to doubts over the self-correcting character of market economies.

Those commonly referred to as Monetarists since about 1970 in the North Atlantic nations question these judgements and, with whatever qualifications, reassert Classical views. The qualification that all of them make, however, to the form of the Classical doctrine that Keynes had in mind is that governments should control the supply of liquidity.

The protagonist of the Monetarist counterrevolution was Milton Friedman, and some writers confine the term Monetarist to the Friedman school.

The elements common to all forms of Monetarism are these:

(a) use of the concept of a 'natural rate of unemployment', a market-equilibrium employment level, set by a downward-sloping demand curve and an upward-sloping supply curve for labour, and setting a limit beyond which movements of nominal demand can only temporarily, if at all, raise the employment rate;
(b) belief that (except perhaps transitorily) there is a close and stable relationship between the demand for money (properly considered) and the level of income in money terms, so that systematic control of liquidity is central to control of the price level;
(c) belief that macroeconomic policy should consist of the pursuit of simple medium-term targets rather than of day-to-day 'fine-tuning' of a number of variables in response to the latest information.

At least three sub-groups of Monetarist can be described: **Friedmanites, New Classicals**, and **International Monetarists.** This is of course a simplification of a more complex variety of opinions.

The first two differ over the nature of the labour market and more broadly over how expectations are formed by economic agents. Friedman follows an 'adaptive-expectations' model and the New Classicals a 'rational-expectations' model. This means that Friedman accepts that market expectations may be systematically wrong, which enables him to provide an explanation for fluctuations in employment in spite of a belief that labour markets 'clear' readily. The explanation is that, when inflation rates are varying, wage-workers will interpret the real value of wage offers by recent past experience and will thus misjudge it, tending to settle for lower real wages than they intend when inflation is rising and for higher real wages than they intend when inflation is falling. Thus when inflation is rising employment rises above the natural rate, and when inflation is falling employment falls below the natural rate. Depressions are thus caused by unexpected falls in the rate of growth of the money supply, which produce unexpected falls in the price level or in the rate of inflation. Thus, when unemployment rose in the US to about a third of the workforce in the early 1930s, this was because the money supply had been allowed to fall drastically. If Keynesian policy for expanding employment had appeared to be successful, this could only be because it had unexpectedly raised the rate of inflation, and the policy could work only temporarily while the rise was unexpected. If rates of employment above the natural rate were to be maintained, they would require inflation continually faster than expected and therefore continually increasing, and this would be intolerable.

The New Classicals, on the other hand, regard it as implausible that any group of economic agents should *systematically* be wrong in their expectations of the future in the way that Friedman supposes. They believe therefore that employment will return readily to the natural rate regardless of rates of inflation. They thus come closer to Classical assumptions about employment. Their difficulty is then in explaining the variations in employment that actually occur.

Both Friedman and the New Classicals advocate the use of the money supply as the sole instrument for controlling the level of nominal demand, and they generally believe that it should be used according to a medium-term rule: a judgement should be made over the rate of growth of the money supply that is necessary to satisfy the demand for money as national income grows on its full-capacity path at stable prices. This rate should be maintained regardless of what appears to be happening in the short term to employment and prices.

The practical difficulties over this rule are two. One is that of deciding which definition of the money supply is the appropriate one for purposes of control. Money supply on the differing definitions rises at differing rates. What is wanted is the definition under which the demand for money is most closely related to the course of nominal income, but that seems to vary from country to country and from time to time. The second difficulty is that of actually controlling money supply according to whichever definition is adopted. This is especially acute in countries with developed banking systems. Unless the version used is M0 (base money), an element in money supply is bank (and possibly other) credit, and government controls over these elements are imperfect. The UK government, in trying heroically to follow a Friedman-type money-supply rule in the early 1980s, came up against both these difficulties and quietly replaced the rule (for several years) by something more like one proposed by International Monetarism as described below.

Friedman supporters and the New Classicals generally believe that wage rates, interest rates, prices and the exchange rate should all be left to the market without government intervention.

International Monetarists differ from both Friedman and the New Classicals by using an explicitly open-economy model. As it happens, by so doing they can claim to avoid the main practical difficulties of following a money-supply rule. Monetary policy, they propose, should not rely on controlling the money supply according to some particular definition. Instead it should be directed to maintaining a target level of the exchange rate. Money and credit should be expanded if the exchange rate appears to be rising too high and contracted if it appears to be falling too low. The exchange rate will be the indicator of whether monetary policy is too tight or too loose. The assumption behind this rule is that there will be a tendency for the *real* exchange rate (the relationship between tradables' and nontradables' prices) to return to an equilibrium level if disturbed. Thus if the exchange-rate target is a 3-per-cent-per-year appreciation against a basket of trading-partner currencies whose average domestic inflation rate is 3 per cent, maintaining the target will keep the country's own domestic price level roughly stable. It is a fact in countries whose currencies are widely held internationally that their exchange rates are fairly responsive to their short-term interest rates, so that it may often be possible to follow such a rule. Rather than using monetary policy to target the money supply and leaving interest rates and the exchange rate to look after themselves, this school would use monetary policy to move interest rates in order to target the exchange rate. However, like other Monetarists, they would leave wages and other prices to 'the market'.

Monetarists of all creeds regard unemployment as in some sense voluntary (unless a superior authority is fixing wages or controlling labour). Even Friedman's model supposes that workers are unemployed because they choose not to accept jobs on the terms that they think they are being offered. This is in conflict with the first premiss and reason-for-being of Keynes' theory. Differences between Keynesians and Monetarists over the workings of labour markets are probably the most fundamental. Keynesians as a consequence direct macroeconomic instruments to achieving specific employment and real-income targets. Monetarists do not.

Is there any resolution of the Keynesian-Monetarist controversy?

Keynesianism and Monetarism have increasingly been recognized as embodying different emphases rather than simply contradictions about the way the world works: they differ over *how* stable (or how quickly restored after a disturbance) are such entities as the income-velocity of money, or the investment-demand function, or the real offer-price of labour, or the real effective exchange rate. Monetarists see the economy as more fully under a benevolently self-adjusting mechanism than do Keynesians. It is also true to say that they tend to be people with somewhat different values or preferences. Monetarists often have a stronger dislike for government intervention and for inflation. Keynesians tend to have a stronger dislike for unemployment. There is no particular logical connection between these values and the corresponding views about how economies work, but values do often appear to influence economists' choices of models.

The Keynesian approach still probably dominates the presentation of macroeconomics in some of the popular introductory textbooks in North America and the Commonwealth, though it can no longer be represented as beyond controversy. There was a period, perhaps of several years before and after 1980, when Monetarist assumptions prevailed in academic research and writing. The apparent failure or weakness of various Monetarist experiments, and the general disasters of world macroeconomic management in the early 1980s, which were a heyday of Monetarism, have made it clear, however, that there is no easy victory for any pure version of Monetarist doctrine.

Monetarist insights that have commonly been fairly generally accepted include the following:

(a) Possibility of modelling expectations. One does not have to accept Friedman's particular view of the working of adaptive expectations in the labour market, or the New Classical belief in rational expectations, to regard expectations as extremely important in determining the rate of inflation and as having some consistent dependence on other events. Keynes too believed of course that investors' expectations affected the level of income and employment. Unlike the early Keynesians, Monetarists have assumed that there is some order in such expectations and have tried to model them. However 'political' wage bargaining becomes, it may well be influenced by whether the parties expect a boom or a slump, whether they expect prices to rise at 20 per cent or at 2 per cent, and these expectations may not be entirely unpredictable.

(b) Difficulty of effective fine-tuning. There is a problem about flying a plane on an undeviating course, responding to every small change in conditions, if you have no way of checking bearings and altitude or wind changes until half an hour after they have happened. It may not be quite as bad as that with macroeconomic management, but there is only a certain degree of precision with which macroeconomic targets are likely to be attained; trying to do better may be counter-productive.

(c) Value of clear longish-term policy rules. From the importance of expectations and the difficulty of fine-tuning we can see the attraction of fairly simple and explicit policy rules related to longer-term perspectives, such as Friedman's money-supply rule. Even if the elusiveness of the concept of the money supply and the difficulty of controlling it under most definitions make that particular rule unworkable, there are other possible candidates, such as an exchange-rate rule maintained directly by monetary measures or a fiscal or wage rule. Possible applications of such rules to developing countries will be discussed in Chapters 13 to 15.

(d) Concept of a natural or non-accelerating-inflation rate of unemployment (NRU or NAIRU). The idea that, with a given set of institutions in a market economy, employment can be consistently pressed only so far at any time, and that attempts to press it further by increasing demand will be inflationary and will achieve at best only transient further increases in employment, is now fairly well established in the minds of policy-makers. It is not necessarily inconsistent with Keynes's own views. No one would deny, however, that changes in institutions may change the NRU or NAIRU. The parties will differ on what kind of changes will be useful for this purpose. Keynesians, seeing the labour market as politicized, may look to rules of reasonable behaviour, pacts, social contracts, and tribunals. Monetarists may be interested only in what seems to make the market work 'better', that is, more like a text-book market model, or in changes of 'fundamental' conditions, such as of the marginal rewards to investment or of productivity on the demand side of the labour market, or of alternative means of support for workers' households on the supply side. The kinds of intervention referred to in the last sentence are all now commonly described as *'supply-side'* measures, because they are concerned with increasing the real aggregate *capacity* of the economy to supply goods and services. Informed policy-makers in

developing countries will probably consider both 'political' devices over wages and supply-side measures.

Keynesian *insights that persist include the following:*

(a) Elements of unpredictability in the behaviour of investors and asset-market operators. 'Rational expectations' may be a hypothesis worth exploring to see how much it can explain, but individual rationality in a world of uncertainty may dictate that the individual investor or asset-holder should act as he thinks others are acting, and this may generate sheep-like behaviour and render equilibria of real income and the income-velocity of money highly unstable. Destabilizing shocks may therefore come not only from events that have actually happened, such as earthquakes and floods and new inventions, but from the players' thoughts about what is going to happen, and from what they think others think is going to happen. Admittedly, in many LDCs, those that are heavily dependent on primary exports or on domestic food production, there are often large disturbances from the weather or pests or world markets or inward investment, and, especially where the domestic capital market is small or non-existent, these are often more important than disturbances arising from the thoughts of agents within the economy. Yet the problems so created are not necessarily entirely different.

(b) Long-term importance of the short term. Keynes's most famous dictum is that 'in the long run we are all dead'. The practical importance of this truism derives from the previous point. Departures from any real-output-expenditure equilibrium may be cumulative instead of self-correcting. In the world at large, not only individuals and companies but also governments may appear to act like sheep, all deflating or all reflating against each other rather than acting collectively to correct their joint position. Deliberate action may have to be taken by governments individually or collectively if any level of real output-expenditure, however appropriate to fundamental economic conditions, is to be preserved.

(c) Downward-inflexibility of money-wages. This is an aspect of the recognition that markets may not always 'clear' quickly through price changes. Monetary measures for price-disinflation that require for their effectiveness a piecemeal, market-driven fall in money-wages, or a sharp reduction in their rate of growth, are likely to be ineffective or sluggish in bringing growth of wages and other prices down and hence are likely to reduce real

output and employment. This immediate effect on output and employment, as we have seen, is not denied by the Friedman school of Monetarists.

(d) Political character of the labour market. This is related to the previous point and with it suggests that negotiations, pacts, reasoning, public information, and appeals to justice and public interest, may make real-wage adjustments possible and so have a part to play in macroeconomic management.

In conclusion

These insights from the two sides are not formally in conflict. Sensible policy should draw from both.

Deciding from empirical observations between different models of how the economy works is not simple. Econometric methods have often relied on taking one model at a time and estimating the parameters and their significance. This is not entirely satisfactory as a way of determining which of two rival models fits the facts better. Methods have been devised specifically to compare the explanatory power of the elements in alternative models that differ from one another, in order to show which of the conceivable mechanisms or relationships are the more important. These may help to resolve doctrinal differences about the way the world works. It is, however, quite likely that economies of different character may be predicted best by different models and that for any one economy the relevance of any model may change over time.

Those who attempt to simulate the behaviour of actual economies with a view to predicting their responses to various measures of policy are often eclectic among theoretical models, taking from different doctrines whatever they think is likely to be most realistic in the circumstances. A model is by its nature a simplified representation of the world, choosing to consider some among the many possible causative mechanisms and to ignore others.

Since human beings are creatures of feeling as well as intellect, it is also likely that people with differing values will continue to be drawn to differing explanations, whatever statistical studies appear to be telling them.

6 Managing the external balance

There are several distinct approaches to understanding and managing the external balance. We try to reconcile them.

The elasticity approach

The 'elasticity approach' deals only with the effect of *exchange-rate changes* on the *balance of trade in goods and services*. By implication it supposes that all other relevant factors are held constant. These would include fiscal and monetary variables and the wage rate (all in nominal terms) and the 'non-tradables' component of domestic prices. It is also implicitly assumed that there are no quantitative restrictions on trade. These are the assumptions of the model.

The effect of an exchange-rate devaluation on the external balance is taken to depend on the *switching of domestic expenditure* between foreign and home goods *and its contraction*, and on the *switching of domestic product* between home and foreign markets *and its expansion*. The extent of these various effects and their impact on money flows is indicated by the price-elasticities of supply and demand for imports and exports: others' supply and our demand for imports, and our supply and others' demand for exports.

The external balance is a net movement of money, and therefore it is the cash values attached to these changes that are relevant. If we are simply interested in whether a change of exchange rate moves the external balance positively or negatively, and there is a single exchange rate at any one time, then it does not matter whether these movements are measured in home or in foreign currency. Only the calculations are different. The movements are considered here *in foreign currency*.

On that basis it could be said that, in the conditions of the model, **devaluation** will always, if anything, *reduce payments for imports*; it may *raise or lower receipts for exports*. The more *price-elastic* is our *demand for imports*, the bigger will be the reduction in payments for imports. The more *price-elastic* is the *demand for our exports* (for a given elasticity of supply and pattern of price behaviour), the bigger will be the increase or the smaller the reduction in receipts for exports; in fact, it will be an increase (if anything) if the elasticity of demand for the exports has a magnitude greater than one, but a decrease (if anything) if the magnitude of that elasticity is less than one.

But elasticities of *supply* enter in too. The more *inelastic* the supply of *imports*, the more the world price will fall as a result of the fall in our demand for imports, and hence the more our payments for imports will be reduced. The more *elastic* the supply of our *exports* (in response to the higher domestic-currency prices for them that the devaluation will bring), the greater will be the effect (whether raising or lowering of receipts) that will be determined by the world's elasticity of demand for the exports.

The **Marshall-Lerner Condition** gives the necessary and sufficient condition, in terms of price-elasticities of the country's trade flows, for a depreciation of the exchange rate to 'improve' the balance of trade in goods and services, that is, to move it towards surplus, provided that the initial position is one of balance and in fact provided also that the macroeconomic variables mentioned at the beginning of the chapter are not affected. It is:

$$\frac{e_x\,(\eta_x - 1)}{e_x + \eta_x} + \frac{\eta_m\,(1 + e_m)}{e_m + \eta_m} > 0 \qquad (6.1)$$

where e_x, η_x, e_m, and η_m are the magnitudes of respectively the elasticities of supply of, and demand for, exports, and of supply of, and demand for, imports.

This is cited from Williamson (1983, p. 152). Williamson notes that the requirement that the initial position should be one of balance can be removed if the condition is reframed with the first term on the left side multiplied by a and the second term by (1 - a), where a is the initial proportion of exports in total trade.

The Condition is often expressed in a form which assumes that the two elasticities of supply are infinite. This would be so if the world prices of the country's imports were unaffected by the country's exchange-rate change and the world prices of the country's exports were reduced in exact proportion to the devaluation. The former would be approximately true for any country that was 'small' in relation to its import markets (which probably includes most countries). The latter suggests exports of differentiated products, such as manufactures or tourist services, but sold in conditions in which there is a high degree of competition domestically and the domestic market has an effect on the world price. Thus the country apparently has to be 'small' in its import markets but 'large' in its export markets. In these (perhaps rather peculiar) circumstances, the critical condition is that the sum of the magnitudes of the two elasticities of demand (for imports and exports) equals one. If the sum is greater than one, i.e., if

$$\eta_x + \eta_m > 1, \tag{6.2}$$

the effect will be to increase the balance, that is to increase the surplus or reduce the deficit.

It will be seen that the left side of (6.2) *minus* one represents the limit approached by the left side of (6.1) as e_x and e_m approach infinity.

Remember, however, that strictly (6.2) expresses the critical condition only in the following circumstances:

(a) The elasticities of supply of imports and exports are both infinite;
(b) The initial position is one of balance, that is, X = M.

However, departure from the former of these conditions, or departure from the latter in the direction likely to be of interest, namely that the initial position is one of deficit, will *lower* the critical value for the sum of the demand-elasticities. In other words, the simple statement of the Marshall-Lerner Condition given in (6.2) makes the conditions in which devaluation will 'improve' the balance of trade seem rather more restricted than they will in fact be in cases of interest.

Williamson points out (1983, p. 153 for derivation) that, while the statement of the Condition given above in (6.2) supposes that exporters reduce their world prices in the full proportion of the devaluation (which is implied by the infinite elasticity of export supply), if instead they reduce the prices by a proportion, z, less than one, which seems more likely to happen in fact with manufactured and tourist exports than what was supposed in the previous case (6.2), a different expression of the critical condition may be given, namely that

$$z(\eta_x - 1) + \eta_m > 0 \qquad (6.3)$$

This implies that, if $\eta_x > 1$, a bigger z means a bigger reduction in the deficit, while if $\eta_x < 1$, a bigger z means a smaller reduction or a larger increase in the deficit.

Where, however, export and import prices both remain *fixed* in foreign-currency terms, and consequently rise in proportion to the devaluation in home-currency terms (that is, where η_x and e_m are infinite), which is likely to be approximately true for 'small' exporters of primary products, the critical condition, derived from (6.1), is that

$$e_x + \eta_m > 0 \qquad (6.4)$$

There must be few people who could retail these conditions, with all their assumptions and qualifications, failing decent time for recollection. Those who try to memorize them often get them wrong. Perhaps the best advice is to remember the simple statements of the Condition in (6.3) and (6.4) above and that the former loosely applies to exporters of manufactures and the latter to 'small' primary exporters, but in any case to try to think out what happens on the import side and the export side separately under whatever elasticity conditions are likely to occur in the case under consideration.

What will the elasticities be like in the cases of interest to developing countries?

On the import side, elasticity of demand will in most countries almost certainly be well above zero (provided that, following the assumptions of the model, we exclude cases in which there are quantitative restrictions on imports, which could reduce the elasticity to zero), and elasticity of supply will probably be for practical purposes close to infinite; but, the more essential imports are (that is, the less domestic products can readily substitute for them), the less price-elastic will demand be, and it will be an important characteristic of many developing countries that their capacity to substitute for imports will be limited and their elasticity of demand for imports correspondingly low. The presence of quantitative restrictions on imports will be likely to make that elasticity even lower.

On the export side, much will depend on whether the exports are primary products (and therefore homogeneous with competing products) or manufactures and services. For manufactures and services, price-elasticity of demand may be fairly high because the goods concerned have reasonably close substitutes abroad, while for manufactures price-elasticity of supply may also be fairly high even over a shortish period. For primary products, unless the country produces a large share of the world's supply of the product, the elasticity of demand for *its* exports will approach infinity (like that of a firm selling on a competitive market), but, in the shortish term at least, the elasticity of supply will often be very low. (In the case of the tree crops, for example, it may well be impossible to increase output in response to higher domestic prices within five to seven years.) However high the elasticity of demand, if the elasticity of supply is zero, the export receipts in foreign currency will not rise.

On the whole then, the more the country depends on primary products for its exports and the less diversified are its manufactures, the less effect devaluation will have on its trade balance in the shortish term *even under the background conditions assumed in the model*. The Marshall-Lerner Condition is very likely to be satisfied because there will be a high magnitude of elasticity of demand for the country's exports, so that under the assumptions of the model the impact of the devaluation on the balance of trade will be positive, but on the export side that impact may be negligible in the short term, and on the import side in an undiversified economy it may act rather like a spending tax, reducing imports largely because the associated price changes reduce real spending power.

However, for even this latter effect to work on import spending as the model supposes, we should have to be sure that the increase in domestic nominal income (and consequent nominal spending-power) that would arise through the higher export prices in domestic currency was neutralized; this is what is implied by the background assumption that nominal monetary variables are held constant: the increased money-income would have to be taxed or borrowed away; and politically this may be by no means easy.

Hence in practice any short-term benefit on the external balance may be quite overshadowed by the effect of the devaluation on domestic prices. (Where quantitative import restrictions mean that there is unsatisfied demand for most imports before the devaluation, the effect of the devaluation on import spending in foreign currency may be negligible, but the effect in raising domestic prices may also be very small or even negative.)

All this is not to deny that the *allocation* ('supply-side') effect of a devaluation may be highly valuable where it is necessary to set a true social value on foreign exchange. It does, however, take some time for such benefits to be realized, and it is only too easy for them to be whittled away by other price changes if the exchange rate is pegged at its new level and other aspects of policy are not under careful control.

Even in the case of countries that export manufactures, any favourable impact on export earnings in foreign currency may be delayed, and indeed the initial response may be adverse. This effect has often been recognized empirically and is known as the **J-curve**: export earnings in foreign currency initially fall in response to the devaluation, apparently because producers reduce their prices in foreign currency and there is a lag before this results in increased orders.

However the really important doubts about the practical usefulness of the elasticity analysis arise *because the background assumptions of the model may not be fulfilled.* After a while, if not at once, the prices of non-tradables and domestic factors of production may rise in response to a devaluation; if wages are negotiated collectively, they may well be raised to take account of higher consumer prices. Moreover it will take some deliberate discipline for government expenditure not to rise in nominal terms to pay for the higher cost of tradables that the devaluation brings.

Also, as already mentioned, the monetary or spending-power effects of higher domestic-currency export earnings will raise import spending unless deliberately neutralized. These responses, sooner or later difficult to avoid, will tend to counteract any desired effects of the devaluation on the trade balance.

The absorption-injection approach

Strictly, this approach (stemming from Alexander, 1952) again concerns only the *balance of trade in goods and services*, but it can be extended to make statements about the 'basic' external account, as is done below. It rests on the definitional identity that the balance of trade is equal to the difference between domestic product ('injections') and domestic expenditure ('absorptions'). *Thus a deficit on the balance of trade can not be removed until product rises or expenditure falls enough to bring them into equality.*

If D = domestic product
Y = income, national product
X = exports
T = net domestic transfers to government
C = private consumption
M = imports
E = domestic expenditure
I = private investment
Ya = net factor income sent abroad
G = government expenditure
S = private saving
R = net international transfer receipts
B_T = surplus on trade in goods and services
B = basic external surplus,

by definition,

$$D = C + I + G + X - M \qquad (6.5)$$
$$D = Y + Ya$$
$$= [C + S + T] + Ya \qquad (6.6)$$
$$E = C + I + G \qquad (6.7)$$

From (6.5) and (6.7),

$$X - M = D - E$$
$$\text{but} \quad B_T = X - M$$
$$\text{so} \quad B_T = D - E \qquad (6.8)$$

Equation (6.8) is the identity on which the absorption approach is based.

This has implications for the relationship between an external and a budgetary deficit or surplus.

From (6.6), (6.7) and (6.8),

$$B_T = [C + S + T + Ya] - [C + I + G]$$
$$= (S - I) + Ya + (T - G) \quad (6.9)$$
$$\text{i.e., } B_T - Ya + R = (S - I) + (T - G) + R.$$

In other words, the external surplus on current account equals the private domestic surplus *plus* the government domestic surplus *plus* net international transfer receipts.

This implies that, if there is a fixed difference between domestic investment and saving (and foreign transfers are fixed), any change in government borrowing (the government deficit) will entail an equal change in the external deficit on current account.

Furthermore, if

$$I - S = F_P \quad (6.10)$$

where F_P is net inflows of capital for private sector,

(which is not an identity but may approximate to being true where there is little bank credit and little government borrowing from the domestic public), then, from (6.9) and (6.10),

$$B_T = - F_P + Ya + (T - G),$$

and so

$$B_T - Ya + R + F_P + F_G = T - G + F_G + R \quad (6.11)$$

where F_G is net government overseas borrowing

If F_P and F_G between them comprise all net inward movement of long-term capital, the expression on the left of the last equation is equal to the basic external surplus; and hence

$$B = T - G + F_G + R \quad (6.12)$$

In other words, if the assumption made in (6.10) is true, in the absence of international transfers (R) the basic external surplus equals net government domestic lending; to put it another way, the basic external deficit equals net government domestic borrowing.

This result depends upon the 'behavioural' assumption made in equation (6.10), which supposes that private domestic investment is equal to private domestic saving *plus* net inward movement of long-term private capital. But, *plus* net inward movement of long-term private capital. But, even if F_P is not *equal to* (I - S), still, as long as there is a *fixed difference* between them and international transfers are unaffected, any *change* in government domestic lending/borrowing will entail an equal change in the basic external surplus/deficit.

Though we can not guarantee that equation (6.10) will hold or even that the difference between the two sides of it will be fixed, yet its general plausibility, especially where changes in bank credit or in government borrowing from the public are fairly unimportant, points to the likely relevance of the fiscal balance for the external balance and hence for the movement of net international reserves, and suggests that the fiscal balance might serve as a critical instrument for control of the external balance. A conclusion of this form is the major policy lesson of the absorption approach. The less developed the economy's financial system and the more internationally dependent it is for investment, the closer some such conclusion as (6.12) is likely to come to being strictly accurate.

Reconciling the elasticity and absorption approaches

It follows from the definitions explored under the heading of the absorption approach that, whatever measures are used to reduce a deficit on the balance of trade, *they can not succeed unless they increase real output or reduce real expenditure or both*. Devaluation will not do the trick unless it has one or other or both of these effects. This is why, in the discussion of the elasticities approach above, it was necessary to be specific about the conditions required of the remaining policy and other variables in order for the Marshall-Lerner Condition to hold.

Under these conditions, devaluation will have a tendency to cause *absorptions to fall* (because of the contraction in real expenditure that follows from higher domestic prices for imports and possibly import-competing goods, and because of the switching of domestic product to exports as a result of higher domestic prices for exports), and also to cause *injections to rise* (because higher domestic prices for exports may expand supply, and because the switching of demand from imports to home products will tend to do the same).

If, however, the measures taken with a devaluation have the effect of leaving *real* personal disposable income and *real* government expenditure unaltered or raised, it is unlikely that absorptions (expenditure) will be reduced. The government might, for example, expand its own outlays in nominal terms to cover the increased cost of imports. Also, if the measures taken or not taken with the devaluation have the effect that the previous relationship between tradables' and nontradables' prices is quickly restored, there will also be nothing to generate the switching of demand on the import side, and the favourable price-cost-relationship change on the export side, that would have led to increased injections (output). What might easily happen is that nominal wages, the main component in non-tradables' prices, rise to cover the additional cost of imports. Once this happens, any relative-price effect of the devaluation soon disappears. Moreover, the rise in wages, coupled with unchanged percentage margins of prices over costs, would probably mean that real personal disposable income was restored.

The implication of this is that correction of a deficit on trade requires some sacrifice. The use of devaluation may perhaps involve less sacrifice from a social viewpoint than alternative measures such as straight fiscal contraction alone, because it entails less reduction, or even a rise, in output. But either consumption (or investment) has to fall or output has to rise. If many people are not working at their optimum levels of effort given the existing marginal rewards to effort, the increase in output may involve much less real sacrifice than a corresponding reduction in expenditure; after all, many people without wage jobs say they would like to have them. So, if devaluation can produce the necessary adjustment by a combination of increasing output and reducing expenditure, while fiscal contraction relies entirely on reducing expenditure (so reducing living standards or investment or both), then devaluation will have advantages.

The disadvantage of devaluation is that it raises the domestic price level. (If we are considering a situation in which prices are already continually rising, the corrective measure that we are discussing is an *increase in the rate* of devaluation, and this will increase the *rate of growth* of prices.) For policy purposes we have presumably to balance the *loss* entailed by the increased inflation against the *gain* that arises from the achieving of the necessary external adjustment at a higher level of output and employment. If there is very little switching effect, the gain is small.

The monetary approach

The monetary approach is commonly said to originate from an article of 1957 by J.J.Polak. The approach has been much used in recent attempts at modelling events. Apart from its other assumptions, which are explored below, it supposes that there are *no binding overall restrictions on capital movements* between the country concerned and the rest of the world: there has to be some channel by which money can move in and out in response to demand.

The monetary approach deals with *the whole of the external balance*, not only trade in goods and services. In the narrow form of the monetary approach, its implicit assumptions are (like those of the Quantity Theory) that real income and the income-velocity of money are 'stable', in the sense of not being affected (other than transitorily) by monetary measures. In its broader form, it can perhaps be said to suppose that real income is stable in this sense and that there is *some degree of stability in the demand function* for money.

We could then, while adopting a broad monetary approach, still assume that the demand for money was a function not only of income (as in the Quantity Theory) but also of interest rates and even of interest-rate expectations. But the policy value of the approach probably disappears if any variable on which the demand for money heavily depends is not reasonably stable, or not at least controllable independently of the money stock. Thus it might disappear if a measure increasing the supply of money could either increase real income or raise the demand function for money. To simplify, we shall first and mainly consider the approach in its narrow form.

The monetary approach thus depends on a behavioural assumption. It does, however, depend for its point on exploring the implications of a *definitional statement*. This is the statement that divides the money supply between (a) the part that is 'backed' by international reserves, and (b) 'domestic credit', which by definition means the part that is not so backed.

$$Mn = Rs + DC \quad \text{by definition}$$

where Mn is the money supply;
Rs is international reserves;
DC is domestic credit.

What exactly is meant by the money supply in this context is a matter of preference or convenience. Some interpret it to mean 'high-powered money' (M0), that is, to exclude commercial-bank credit and to include only notes and coins and the amount of the banks' other reserve assets. But there seems to be no particular logic in singling out high-powered money. The most suitable definition of money would be the one whose income-demand function was most stable. The definition of the money supply used will imply a corresponding definition of domestic credit. Domestic credit is by definition simply (Mn - Rs), whatever Mn is taken to mean. If the money supply includes certain bank deposits, then domestic credit may be increased by a rise in commercial-bank lending as well as by a rise in direct central-bank credit to the government or central-bank purchases of financial assets from the markets.

Since the demand function for money against income is assumed to be stable, any given level of income will imply a particular value of the demand for money. If payments are allowed to move freely in and out of the country, the demand for money will be precisely satisfied at equilibrium by the supply. Adjustment to this equilibrium will be achieved by the flow of money into or out of the country, whether for goods and services or for capital assets.

Then any increase in DC from an equilibrium position will raise the supply of money above the amount demanded. Demand is determined by income. Supply adjusts by the movement of money out. This movement of money out will reduce net international reserves.

How is this supposed to happen? The increase in DC makes the money supply higher than people want to hold. They therefore get rid of some of it, by exchanging it either for goods and services or for other assets. This extra direct spending and extra purchasing of less liquid assets (which raises their prices and hence reduces the yield on them) will inevitably have some effect in increasing outward payments, and this will continue to be the case until the supply of money has been reduced back to the level of the demand. Now it will necessarily be backed by less net reserves than before the change. And the amount by which the net reserves have fallen is the amount by which DC has risen. Thus, other things being equal, *increasing or decreasing domestic credit will decrease or increase respectively the international reserves by the same amount.*

At first glance this would seem to imply that the only variable relevant to control of the external balance is domestic credit. But, if we were to move on to a 'broader' interpretation of the monetary approach and to suppose that factors other than income could affect the demand for money, then in principle any variable that affected the demand for money might also thereby affect international reserves. *Increasing the demand for money* (for example, by lowering expectations of inflation or by creating expectations of a rise in interest rates) *will increase international reserves.*

It is also quite consistent with the monetary view to suppose that reserves may change for reasons unconnected with changes in the demand for money or the supply of domestic credit, for example, a rise in export prices or in inward investment, but unless there is an accompanying rise in nominal income or contraction in DC as measured in the foreign-exchange medium, the potential rise in net reserves will not be realized: the extra export receipts or extra inward investment will turn out to be matched by extra imports or other outward payments that cancel the effect on reserves.

The effect on international reserves of devaluing a pegged exchange rate is interpreted in the monetary approach as due to the effect of the devaluation in raising the domestic price level and correspondingly reducing the real value of domestic credit. So long as the *nominal* amount of domestic credit is not increased and *real* income is not reduced, the rise in prices has the effect of reducing the supply of money in relation to the demand for it. This, acccording to the logic of the approach, leads to an inflow of money and thus an increase in international reserves.

Open-economy Monetarism: IM and MA

Both the 'international monetarism' outlined in Chapter 5 (IM) and the 'monetary approach to the balance of payments' (MA) can be described as open-economy Monetarism. How do they relate?

They arose in different periods, originally to answer different policy questions. MA originated in the 1950s and 1960s to consider influences on the external balance under pegged exchange rates. IM originated in the 1970s and 1980s to consider the control of the domestic price level under flexible, probably floating, exchange rates. Both reflect the 'Classical' assumption that real income is not responsive to monetary events and to that extent oppose Keynesian views. However, MA relies in practice on some usable definition under which money will have a stable demand function, whereas IM, responding to the practical difficulties of using a Friedman-type money-supply rule, does not depend on having any particular definition of money or liquidity. Instead it sets much store on other 'Classical' assumptions: flexible prices and the 'law of one price'.

Though the MA agrees with Friedman-type Monetarism in supposing a stable demand function for money, the mechanism that it postulates for the adjustment between money supply and demand is different. Friedman supposes that demand does the adjusting through changes in price; the MA supposes that supply does the adjusting through international flows. IM adopts, and the MA is consistent with, a more active approach to the exchange rate than Friedman favours.

The mechanisms supposed by both MA and IM are impeded by restrictions on international trade and payments.

IM is not inconsistent with the fundamental MA view that expanding liquidity from domestic sources will favour increasing external deficit under a fixed exchange rate. The MA is not inconsistent with the fundamental IM view that using the manipulation of domestic liquidity to target a floating exchange rate at an appropriate level may stabilize domestic prices.

Reconciling the absorption and monetary approaches

How does the monetary approach fit with the absorption-injection approach? In a situation in which government domestic borrowing automatically becomes domestic credit, it is fairly easy to see how the absorption approach and the monetary approach fit together. To simplify we might first assume, as in the discussion of the absorption approach above, that there is no commercial-bank credit and no borrowing by the government from the domestic 'public'. Then government deficit and domestic-credit creation will be of the same amount. The monetary approach tells us that reserves will fall by this amount. The absorption approach tells us that, provided (I - S - Ya) is fixed, there will be an additional deficit of this amount in trade in goods and services, and by implication in the basic balance. These results are consistent with one another. If we assume that there are no *resulting* changes (apart from the official monetary movements themselves) in foreign transfers or in the capital account, the two results are identical under the simplifying assumptions about the economy that have been cited.

Now remove some of the simplification by allowing for some secondary credit creation by banks (BCC) and for government borrowing from the domestic public (DB). As stressed in the absorption approach, it follows by definition that

$$B_T = (S - I) + Ya + (T - G) \qquad (6.9)$$

But by definition,

$$B = B_T - Ya + R + F_P + F_G \qquad (6.13)$$

and it follows from behavioural assumption (6.10)

$$B_T - Ya + R + F_P + F_G = T - G + F_G + R \qquad (6.11)$$
$$\text{i.e.,} \quad B = T - G + F_G + R \qquad (6.12)$$

(We are assuming that there are no short-term monetary movements other than the official monetary movements themselves that represent the changes in reserves, but short-term capital movements could be brought in, necessitating only a distinction between basic and net balance.)

From (6.9) and (6.13),

$$B = S - I + R + F_P + [T - G + F_G]$$

So

$$B = S - I + F_P - DB + BCC + [T - G + F_G + DB - BCC + R]$$

But the expression in square brackets is the negative of domestic credit creation (DCC). So

$$B = [S - I + F_P - DB + BCC] - DC \qquad (6.14)$$

It follows that the basic balance will fall by as much as domestic credit rises, *if the expression in brackets in equation (6.14) equals zero or a constant.* Thus the absorption approach leads to the same conclusion as the monetary approach if it can be supposed that

$$S - I + F_P - DB + BCC = 0 \quad \text{or a constant}$$
$$\text{i.e., that} \quad I = S + F_P - DB + BCC \qquad (6.15)$$

or that the two sides differ by a constant;

in other words, that domestic private investment equals (or differs by a fixed amount from) domestic private savings *plus* private inward investment *minus* the amount borrowed by the government from the domestic private sector *plus* the increase in domestic bank credit to the public.

It is not implausible that this condition (6.15) should be roughly fulfilled in certain circumstances. In fact the two sides of (6.15) would be equal unless there was net 'hoarding' or 'de-hoarding' of money; and the two *would be equal or differ by a constant* unless there was *a change in the rate* of net hoarding or dehoarding of money. Equation (6.15) would seem to have the same implications within the definitions involved in the absorption approach as the assumptions about the constancy of real income and the stability of the velocity of money have in the monetary approach. It seems to follow that, if a change in one of the policy or behavioural variables is such as to cause a rise or fall in spending which would conflict with the assumptions of the (narrow) monetary approach (for example, if the demand for money falls or rises as a result of changed expectations of inflation), it will also cause (6.15) to be falsified.

Summary

The elasticity and absorption approaches deal only with the balance of trade in goods and services; the monetary approach deals with the whole of the external account. All three approaches are based on deductive reasoning, not primarily on observation. They are not inconsistent with each other and can be reconciled provided appropriate assumptions are fulfilled. The important message of the absorption approach is contained in a definitional statement with clearly defined terms. The other two approaches depend on a number of behavioural assumptions, including the absence of binding, comprehensive restrictions on international payments.

Part 3
Models for Developing Countries

7 Relevant differences among types of economy

The main macroconomic models devised since the 1930s for purposes of stabilization were developed in Europe and North America. Are they applicable to the developing countries?

As we try to answer this question, we must remember that there are disputes about how far any particular model applies even in the industrialized countries (ICs) and that the whole subject is very much in a state of flux. There are Keynesian models and Monetarist models, and within each of these categories a number of variants. There are closed-economy models and open-economy models. There are equilibrium and disequilibrium models. There are rational-expectations models and adaptive-expectations models and models that suppose a high degree of unpredictability in response to economic stimuli.

There is also a great variety among the so-called LDCs. Generally the term has been applied to countries of relatively low average income. Yet a few very-high-income countries, such as Kuwait, have often been included in the class, not because of their average income level but because of other features of their economic structure. Others which as recently as the 1970s were included by general agreement, such as Singapore and Hong Kong, have grown so like the industrialized countries, in average income and also in other respects, that there is little sense in classifying them any longer in any other category; in these two cases the World Bank no longer does so.

If there is any structural feature common to all or most of the LDCs, it is probably best covered by the vague word 'dualism': there are large sectors of any one national economy that contrast more sharply with one another than any correspondingly important sectors within the industrialized world. What this appears to reflect is that the institutional and productive changes associated with the 'industrial revolution' have come to these countries from outside rather than as a natural outcome of their own internal development. Such statements are of course matters of degree. The technical inventions and modes of organization that we associate with the beginnings of industrialism started in Britain, and it could be argued that everywhere else they were brought in from outside. But the Low Countries and some other parts of Western Europe seem to have had much in common with Britain in their receptiveness for the new modes of life, and settlers from Britain and Europe in the comparatively empty lands of North America and Australasia readily carried or borrowed the new approaches as well.

But in all those countries that have in the last thirty years been classified as LDCs modern industrialism came with a greater degree of foreignness, often brought and pursued by foreigners in the first place and sometimes not really indigenized for long periods. They have tended to retain sectors that are little influenced by modern industrialism in their modes and techniques of production.

At the same time the term 'LDCs' covers societies that differed fundamentally from each other before the advent of industrialism. The most important differences seem to have been related to population density over the preceding centuries. Those with a history of dense population and settled agriculture were often the seats of ancient civilizations, with specialized crafts, literacy and scholarship, a long commercial tradition, and territorial government. At the other extreme were communities of hunters, pastoralists and shifting cultivators, necessarily much thinner on the ground, often with political units no bigger than a village or a small clan, and with little or no trade or occupational specialization. The position has been complicated, since the early modern period, by European settlement of areas with substantial non-European populations, as in tropical America and southern Africa. There are also many variants between the extreme types.

For understandable reasons it has tended to be the countries of relatively low population density, both rich and poor, that have been most dominated by primary exports.

Thus, whatever the differences between LDCs and ICs relevant to stabilization policy, there is no reason to expect that they will be uniform over all LDCs. The characteristics listed below are respects in which *some* LDCs in each case might be expected to differ from the economies simulated in *some* of the Keynesian and Monetarist models.

Low internal integration and extreme structural openness

In some countries exports make up a large part of monetary-sector production and imports a correspondingly large part of expenditure, and there is little substitution between domestic production and imports or between domestic absorption and exports. An imaginary extreme case would be one in which the cash economy simply consisted of the production and sale of exports to buy imports; in that case world prices would be the only prices. Similarly, in some real-world cases (where international trade and domestic wages and prices are not under rigorous administrative control), it is likely that the domestic price level will be very largely determined by the world price level and the exchange rate. This is because the real values of wages and other domestic factor-payments (whether their nominal values are determined by indexing or bargaining or by a competitive market) will tend to be maintained in response to price changes, and, where import prices are a large component of total prices and export receipts of cash incomes, this will mean that they may readily rise by a large fraction of the rate of devaluation and continue rising as their initial rise raises domestic prices further. Though the lack of close substitutability would in itself tend to isolate the domestic component of prices from world prices, the dominance of import prices in the price index means that their influence on the domestic component through wages and other domestic-factor prices is likely to be strong. In the absence of strict and effective quantitative control of foreign transactions then, models of price behaviour of the closed or semi-closed type may be of little relevance.

Models of the 'small-open-economy' type are designed to fit this situation. These emphasize the importance of 'tradable goods', whose domestic prices are held to be set by their world price levels (as translated by the exchange rate), and their separation from 'nontradable goods'. In an extreme version of the open-economy family of models, such as that of King (1979), there may in effect be only one sector, and the pricing of tradables is then treated as if it covers the pricing of all goods. Or there may be two sectors, tradables and non-tradables. The term 'small-open-economy' (SOE) will be here applied to models in which it is supposed that importable goods are not produced domestically and exportable goods are not consumed domestically, and there are no domestic influences on the prices of tradables. There is then no question of *competitiveness* between home and foreign goods. While depreciation of the exchange rate may decrease expenditure and increase output (if it maintains a changed price ratio between tradables on the one hand and nontradables and productive factors on the other), it can have no *switching* effect. No actual economy exactly meets this specification, but primary-exporting countries with little domestic manufacture may be close enough in structure for such a model to be useful.

The term 'large-open-economy' (LOE) can be applied to models which, though giving importance to external transactions, allow importables to be produced domestically and exportables to be consumed domestically, and for domestic events to influence the prices of tradables. (The term 'large' is used as a bit of technical jargon to indicate that home prices of tradables are not simply determined by foreign prices.) Such a model becomes more relevant, in relation to the SOE type, as the production, and especially the export, of manufactures becomes important. While primary products tend to be standardized, so that you can talk of a world price for a particular grade of a commodity, manufactures and tourist services are differentiated; if they are produced in the country, domestic prices for them will not simply reflect world prices, even under a liberal trade regime. This means that the question of *changing competitiveness* between home and foreign goods arises in response to changes in exchange rate or in duties and subsidies, and consequently the possibility of *switching*, that is substitution between home and foreign goods in use and between domestic sales and exports in destination. Since the prices of tradables will not necessarily move together in response to an exchange-rate change, the real exchange rate may be thought of as an index of the ratio of home to foreign prices rather than of nontradables' to tradables' prices (Collier and Joshi, 1989).

Whether a SOE or LOE model seems more appropriate, the prices of nontradables may be influenced by the prices of tradables. The importance of tradable goods in the consumer 'basket' has an inevitable influence on money-wages (even if those wages are determined entirely by the market), and hence on nontradables' prices. (See, for some implications, Montiel, 1987.) The speed of response will depend on wage-fixing institutions.

SOE models with three sectors may distinguish between importables and exportables, which of course in primary-exporter countries are often completely different types of good. Sometimes four-sector models are used to distinguish in addition between different classes of exportables, such as a dominant primary commodity on the one hand and other exports (possibly differentiated products with more market-sensitive supply, such as manufactures) on the other. The situation modelled might thus fit at least some elements of LOE models. Such four-sector models have been used (as in Kamas, 1986) to analyse the effect known as the 'Dutch disease': the depressing effect that a price boom in one dominant primary commodity may have on a country's tradable manufactures or on other primary commodities.

All actual economies are open. Closed-economy models, such as the original versions of Keynes and Friedman, are most nearly relevant in countries for which foreign trade is small in relation to GNP, or in which it is closely controlled. In the recent past the US and the Soviet Union, or the Soviet bloc as a whole, would be the obvious candidates, but less so (in both cases) as time goes on, and in fact the closed-economy framework has limited usefulness. LOE, rather than SOE, models would be applied to the industrialized countries, but the difference is not one simply of absolute economic size or of relative poverty. Mauritius, which is small, and Bangladesh, which is poor, both have structures that may make a LOE model appropriate, while Nigeria, which is large in population, and Saudi Arabia, which is rich, may fit reasonably well to SOE models.

Export earnings as a main source of instability

Exporters of primary commodities commonly suffer considerable instability in export earnings. Since (a) many (though by no means all) LDCs are mainly exporters of primary commodities, and (b) in some cases exports are very important in production, and (c) it is often difficult to adjust by 'switching' in response to a fall in export earnings, such export-earnings instability will often be the major source, and a very serious one, of instability in the economy at large. By contrast, early Keynesian models tended to assume that private investment was the major source of instability.

In an economy affected in this way by export-earnings instability, conventional 'Old' Keynesian fiscal or monetary policies to counteract its effect on real income may have correspondingly large effects on the external balance and may be ruled out, or of limited use, on this account. Taking action to expand demand when export earnings are low will aggravate any external-balance problem caused by those low earnings. Thus, even if one uses essentially Keynesian models of the economy (assuming that equilibrium real income may be subject to manipulation), traditional Keynesian fine-tuning by manipulating aggregate demand against the main source of instability may have to be recognized as impracticable, and alternative disciplines for real-income stabilization will need to be sought.

Lack of a domestic bond market

A domestic bond market may not exist or may be too small to serve as a useful source for financing government borrowing requirements or to make significant 'open-market operations' feasible. In this case a government would have to finance any budgetary deficit by borrowing either from the monetary authority or from abroad. In either case the money supply would be increased directly by the amount of the deficit (aside from any secondary increases that might arise from the bank-credit multiplier). Then a fiscal deficit or surplus would correspond closely to an increase or decrease of (base) money, and the distinction between fiscal and monetary policy would become blurred, the only separate monetary sphere being the control of bank credit.

Low weight of bank credit

The distinction between fiscal and monetary policy is further reduced if bank credit is relatively unimportant.

Elastic supply of unskilled labour

Both Keynesian and Monetarist models suppose that the supply of labour sets the capacity limit to output. The workforce, given its willingness to work, together with the non-labour resources of the economy, determine equilibrium output in the New Classical model, sustainable equilibrium output in the Friedman model, 'full-employment' or capacity output in the Keynesian model. It is questionable whether this is the most useful way of looking at the issue for many of the LDCs.

Arthur Lewis (1954) proposed that, for the densely populated LDCs such as India and Jamaica, the supply of labour to organized industry might be thought of as infinitely elastic: that is, at the existing wage far more people than were now employed would be prepared to work. These people would come out of traditional agriculture and from what we now call the informal sector, in which their 'marginal product', what their labour would add to production and their withdrawal would subtract from production, was very low. The wage, for various reasons, would be above the value of this marginal product, and hence households in traditional and informal-sector activities would gain if their members could switch into industrial wage-work. Thus any expansion of industrial activity that found it worthwhile to employ people at the existing wage would have no trouble in attracting workers, and (provided the activity concerned was unprotected and unsubsidized) would thereby add to output.

The implication seemed to be that the labour supply would set no immediate practical limit to the expansion of output. This reasoning readily suggested that, if only the necessary resources could be set aside for investment, rapid growth would occur: labour was an under-used resource which could become much more productive if the investment was there to activate it.

However, there are certain important reservations that have to be made. First, not all LDCs, not even all the relatively 'undeveloped', seem to display a highly elastic supply of wage-labour. Where there is a relatively prosperous subsistence or subsistence-cum-smallholder sector, marginal household-enterprise product may not be universally low, and in some cases workers may be interested in wage-work for only limited periods or for only part of their time, in order that their cash needs, which may be only a part of their total material needs, can be met. In any case, the supply function for wage-labour may be decidedly upward-sloping.

Secondly, talk of the need for investment may conceal the critical fact for many LDCs that expansion of output is likely to require expansion, often a much more than proportional expansion, of imports. Of course, inward foreign investment may bring the foreign exchange to buy some of the necessary imports, and domestic investment financed by domestic saving may correspondingly release foreign exchange from consumption to provide what is necessary for the industrial growth, but it is important to remember that the foreign resources for investment do have to come from somewhere.

The implication of this latter point is that perhaps we should think of foreign exchange, rather than undifferentiated labour, as setting the critical limit to capacity. Even where the supply of labour is much less than infinitely elastic, extra foreign exchange may allow real wages to be increased sufficiently to attract the extra labour supply. Efficient ways of generating or of conserving foreign exchange offer considerable possibilities for growth. It is the more regrettable that so many LDCs have for long adopted policies which strongly discourage the generation of foreign exchange through exports and have pursued highly inefficient measures for conserving and rationing it.

Beside foreign exchange, it may often be the case that skills, especially entrepreneurial and managerial skills, set a limit to capacity. In the 1980s skill shortages are increasingly being recognized in ICs too as a constraint on capacity that is more relevant than any shortage of simple undifferentiated labour. The fact that the rate of inflation in ICs is sometimes found to start increasing at a rate of production at which there are still considerable numbers of unskilled workers unemployed may be taken as support for this view.

Prevalence of administrative controls

Keynesian and Monetarist models, and the open-economy models loosely related to them, suppose by implication that markets are allowed to operate over wide stretches of the economy. LDCs have shown a strong tendency to operate through administrative controls, especially over access to foreign exchange and in the financial system.

If the price of foreign exchange is held far below the one that would equate demand to supply, foreign exchange must be allocated by controls, and access to it acquires a value above the price that must officially be paid for it. Foreign-exchange licences are thus a privilege and a source of patronage; they are in effect a present from the nation to the individuals lucky enough to obtain them. Usually some of the foreign exchange earned finds its way to the unofficial market where, unless there are serious penal risks attached to buying it, its price is likely to be *above* what it would be in the absence of restrictions.

Intervention in the capital market usually involves holding down the interest rates charged by officially sanctioned institutions and also the rates that those institutions pay. In inflationary conditions the real rates on both bank loans and bank deposits are often negative. General economic reasoning would lead one to suppose that this has the effect of reducing the inflow of funds to these institutions and producing an excess demand for loans from them. These effects have been confirmed in a number of studies. Reducing real interest rates paid *may* also have the effect of reducing the actual proportion of income saved, but figures for national savings rates are notoriously unreliable, and it is not clear how far the effect of reduced real interest rates on bank and similar deposits reflects a fall in savings and how far just a re-routing of funds to other channels. However, it is generally taken that 'intermediation' of saved resources through financial institutions is potentially an efficient way of allocating them and that anything that discourages such intermediation reduces the productive use, if not also the volume, of saving.

The implication of controls on access to foreign exchange is that it is not necessarily the case that changing the official exchange rate will have any effect on the quantities of imports or on the prices at which they are made available to their final domestic users. If the controls are really complete and so effective that there is no unofficial market in foreign exchange, the answer to the question whether there would be more or less or the same quantities of imports bought as a result of a devaluation would depend on whether the earnings from exports would increase or fall or neither. If export earnings of foreign exchange were actually to rise as a result of a devaluation in these conditions, imports would *increase* rather than decrease, and, because they had increased, it would seem likely that the domestic prices of the goods bought with the foreign exchange, or made from the goods bought with it, would actually *fall* (unless these prices too were closely and effectively controlled), since the goods concerned would have been rendered more plentiful. This result is the opposite to those that we should expect of the same policy measure in an economy with a liberal foreign-exchange regime. Let's put no bets on the result in practice, but at least this paradoxical outcome is a possibility.

The existence of an unofficial market complicates matters but does not greatly affect the general tendency of the analysis. If there is an unofficial price for foreign exchange, it will be above the official price. A raising of the official price (devaluation) in itself may be associated with a raising or a lowering of the unofficial price, depending on what the context of the devaluation is. If the devaluation is accompanied by liberalization of access to foreign exchange, there is a presumption that it will serve to reduce the unofficial price of foreign exchange, and this of course will favour the lowering rather than the raising of consumer prices. Complete liberalization with the devaluation, and the movement of the official rate to a level approximating a free-market rate, will remove the unofficial market altogether.

These assertions are briefly explained as follows. If the official price for foreign exchange is allowed to rise in the direction of where a free-market-equilibrium price would lie (as it would do with an official devaluation), the unofficial market becomes less relatively attractive to sellers of foreign exchange than before and the supply in the unofficial market is probably reduced. At the same time the unofficial market may become either more or less attractive to buyers of foreign exchange: more attractive if the price-rise in the official market occurs with little or no rise in quantities of foreign exchange made available; less attractive if this effect is outweighed by the fact that a greater quantity is made available to the official market. If the unofficial market in fact becomes less attractive to buyers, and if this reduced demand in the unofficial market outweighs the reduced supply, the unofficial price will fall; otherwise it will tend to rise.

The more the rise in the official price of foreign exchange is associated with an increase in its availability through official sources, the more likely is it that the unofficial price will fall. On the whole a fall in the unofficial price is probably to be expected if a raising of the official price is accompanied by increasing liberalization of access to foreign exchange, with free availablity for an increasing range of purposes; as the change proceeds, the two prices, probably though not certainly, become closer until (certainly) the unofficial market disappears when complete liberalization (at or about a market-equilibrium price) is reached.

If, however, the government were devaluing without intending to make any more foreign exchange available, its action would probably divert supplies from the unofficial market without diverting demand, and so cause the unofficial price to rise. (Some of these issues are discussed in Nowak, 1984.)

More reliable in practice perhaps is the effect of raising 'repressed' interest rates. Demand-side-only models might lead us to believe that raising interest rates will reduce investment; but, if raising interest rates brings more funds to financial institutions, and if there is an excess demand for loans from those institutions in any case, the effect will be to increase loans from those institutions and probably to increase investment altogether.

Endemic inflation

Several LDCs, most notably some in Latin America, have suffered long periods of very high inflation. Though high inflation appears to signify some want of control, and though no people or government would *choose* high inflation if other things could be held constant; yet high inflation does seem to be sometimes consistent with high rates of growth, as was shown by Brazil over a number of years. Can high inflation be in any sense held to be *chosen* for understandable reasons?

It seems clear that a there is no universal Phillips Curve: that higher inflation cannot be relied upon to increase output. Nevertheless it may be that, where there is a shock of some kind, accepting a rise in the rate of inflation may seem a preferable alternative to some other form of adjustment. This is not inconsistent with Brazilian experience in the late 1960s and 1970s. Admittedly it may be that the short-term gain from tolerating the inflation has longer-term costs, or that, with sufficient social discipline, there are non-inflationary ways of minimizing the pain of adjustment.

In high-inflation countries inflation comes to be regarded as normal, but high inflation seldom maintains a steady rate. There is a large element of uncertainty that accompanies it.

This is to some extent mitigated in several countries by extensive 'indexation', that is, the legal or conventional adjustment of particular prices in line with the changes in a general price index. Wages in the public sector are commonly indexed in this sense, and in several countries of South America (among them Brazil, Chile, Colombia) it has also been the practice to express some government or government-regulated interest rates in real terms. Indexation is discussed further in Chapters 14 to 16.

A country with endemic high inflation is doing everything as it were on a moving staircase. To keep its real exchange rate constant, Brazil has had continually to devalue its nominal exchange rate. The question has been simply (given inflation in the world outside) how much faster or slower devaluation should be than the rate of inflation. To have kept the nominal rate constant against any major currency or the SDR would for much of the time have involved drastic real appreciation unless that discipline had quickly brought the inflation rate down toward zero.

The faster and more irregular the rate of inflation, the more necessary it is, in studies conducted for policy purposes, to express macroeconomic aggregates in real terms.

No international market in the country's currency

This is pretty general among LDCs. They do not make their currencies convertible as a rule. This has been sometimes argued to make it impracticable to have a genuinely free-floating exchange rate, since there would be no source of stabilizing speculation to cover transient shortages and surpluses of the country's currency in the market. The rate, it is claimed, would therefore fluctuate unduly. Recent experience of 'independently' floating currencies, such as those of Nigeria and Ghana, may challenge this view, though it is hard to be certain how genuinely 'free' any particular 'independently floating' currency is.

Foreign debt

The heavy burden of foreign debt carried by so many countries in the 1980s is a factor which, while not rendering standard models any less applicable, raises a new dimension of the stabilization problem. (See Chapter 11.)

A typology of developing countries

The peculiarities outlined above suggest some questions that we might ask about any particular country when considering what stabilization regime would be appropriate to it.

(a) Is it 'primary-export-dominated', a country with very limited domestic manufacturing and its exports overwhelmingly of primary products? If so, then in the absence of close foreign-exchange controls, exchange-rate changes are likely to have small switching and output effects and large price effects. Also, stabilization of domestic output and expenditure will depend on medium-term disciplines that take into account, and compensate for, fluctuations in export earnings.

(b) Are the bond market and bank credit unimportant? If so, monetary and fiscal policy must be virtually identical and cannot be treated as separate policy instruments.

(c) Is there a 'labour surplus', a large excess supply of wage-labour at existing wage rates? If so, there are likely to be specially high increases in capacity output in response to increased foreign-exchange earnings; foreign exchange may be the most important short-term constraint on growth.

(d) Are the official price of foreign exchange and real interest rates held at well below market levels with corresponding administrative controls? If so, the direction of the effect on consumer prices of official devaluation will be indeterminate, and the effect of raising real interest rates will probably be to increase private investment.

(e) Is there long-standing high inflation and no plan to reduce it? If so, indexation of wages, interest rates, and the exchange rate, becomes an important policy issue, and there must be continual nominal depreciation of the currency to avoid real appreciation.

8 Structuralism: model or attitude of mind?

Since the late 1950s or earlier people have talked of the rivalry between 'structuralist' and 'monetarist' approaches to inflation in developing countries. The term 'structuralist' as applied to a view of macroeconomic policy originates in Latin America, and received much support from the UN Economic Commission for Latin America in Santiago. Chronically high inflation has been a longer-running story in certain countries of South America than elsewhere; but in the 1970s and 1980s various countries in Africa, and others such as Israel, have succumbed at times to the same disease, and the same debates are likely to be of interest.

The question of external deficits is not easily separated from that of inflation. Persistent external deficits may prompt currency devaluation and therefore feed inflation. Inflation without currency devaluation is likely to lead to a tendency to external deficit. So reducing external deficits is inevitably thrown in to the discussion.

'Monetarist' as the term is used in these discussions since the 1950s covers a rather broader range than the same term as used in US and British debates on macroeconomic policy from the 1970s and applied to the doctrines of Friedman and the New Classicals. Using fiscal or monetary restraint or any general exchange-rate policy, or some combination of these three, as the sole means of reducing inflation or an external deficit, would count as 'monetarist' in this context. Thus what is Monetarist in the North Atlantic sense would be monetarist also in this sense, but what is Keynesian in the other debate would probably count as 'monetarist' in this one if it confined itself to general, economy-wide measures, not discriminating among sectors and not directly regulating prices or quantities. To distinguish between the two uses of the word I shall use 'monetarist' with a small initial and quotation marks when it is opposed to 'structuralist'.

What then is structuralism? You do not have to read far to realize that it is not at all easy to define, and you may well come to the conclusion that it means rather different things to different writers.

Little (1982, pp. 20-1, cited Arndt, 1985) talks of *structuralism* and *neoclassical economics* as the two broad approaches to development economics. The idea here is presumably that neoclassical economics expects desirable adjustments to take place continually and gradually through price movements and therefore believes that many processes will work best when left to themselves without drastic intervention from a superior power. Structuralism, on the other hand, 'sees the world as inflexible. Change is inhibited by obstacles, bottlenecks and constraints.' Spontaneous price movements will not be enough to set things right. The price movements that would be needed are too great and interest groups in any case would resist them. Structuralism 'seeks to provide a reason for managing change by administrative action'.

Structuralism in this sense, a belief in **rigidity or unresponsiveness to market forces**, was very much the fashion in development economics, at least until about 1970, and many people in developing countries still regard the attitudes that it entails as almost axiomatically right. But by the 1970s it came to be questioned more generally than before. Evidence had accumulated from systematic studies that much of the deliberate action taken by developing-country governments for the sake of economic development, had been counterproductive, and on the other hand that a group of LDCs had achieved seemingly miraculous rates of growth which depended heavily on expanding supplies to the world market with more or less heavy reliance on market forces and in some cases even free trade.

A slightly different, but not inconsistent, interpretation of the meaning of structuralism in economics is that it puts emphasis on the importance of **the structure of the particular economy involved**, rather than relying on universal presumptions and working rules as 'neoclassical economics' has tended to do. Thus the Latin American structuralists stressed the peculiarities of the Latin American economies against the supposed characteristics of the industrialized countries. The tendency was to suppose that their own economies suffered from rigidities and bottlenecks to a greater extent than those in the countries where both 'Classical' (neoclassical) and Keynesian models had first been propounded.

A further emphasis that is regarded as an aspect of structuralism is the interest in **the structure of 'North-South' economic relations** (Jameson, 1986, pp. 224 ff.). Raul Prebisch, who is regarded by some as the founder and chief exponent of Latin American structuralism (though he did not coin the term), appears to have introduced the expressions *Centre* and *Periphery* to refer to Europe and North America on the one hand and the developing countries on the other, and, simultaneously with Hans Singer, to have developed the thesis that their relationship was not symmetrical. This was linked, rightly or wrongly, to a belief in the *secularly falling terms of trade* of the LDCs (considered as primary-product specialists), and the attempt to explain this through such apparent differences as the *different income-elasticities of demand* for the products in which the two groups of countries specialised, and *different degrees of monopoly of labour supply.* There was also a belief in the importance of *differences in access to new techniques.* From this mode of approach to world economic relations sprang 'dependency theory' (Frank, 1965) and the 'theory of unequal exchange' (Emmanuel, 1972), though each of these writers has his own view of the nature, and the implications, of assymmetry between Centre and Periphery.

The structuralist approach to macroeconomic policy

A set of macroeconomic policy rules can be said to work well if it can reduce inflation or external deficit with minimal immediate loss of output and employment and minimal reduction of allocative efficiency.

It is easy enough to think up policies, which, if they could be and were rigorously pursued, would reduce inflation and the external deficit to zero or less. If they were politically and administratively possible, and we did not have to count the cost, they would in this limited sense 'work'. A sufficiently repressive monetary policy, *if it could be followed without leading to a coup or revolution*, would do the trick. So would a system of rigorous administrative controls of prices and quantities, *if they could actually be implemented.* But, apart from the question whether such policies could actually be carried through, we should also consider the *losses in output and employment and the general disruption of people's lives* that might follow the measures for monetary repression, and we should consider *the inefficiencies, the stunting of growth, the irritations, the petty tyrannies, the corruption and cynicism,* that might follow from the controls. The more responsive the economy was to price signals, the less would be the costs of monetary repression and the more we should be inclined to favour it over the administrative controls. The less responsive it was, the more we should tend to favour the controls.

This is the core of the difference between 'monetarism' and structuralism in stabilization policy. The premiss behind the discussion is in either case that we are starting from a mess: inflation is too high or the external balance is too unfavourable. Some correction has to be made.

It is probably fair to say that the IMF has consistently favoured the 'monetarist' approach: reducing aggregate demand in money terms through fiscal or monetary restraint or both, with or without some switching of demand and supply or fixing of the price standard through respectively shifting or pegging the exchange rate.

The structuralist reply has been to say that relying on such measures is too costly in the developing economies of Latin America. More sector-specific administrative measures should be used: duties, subsidies, quantitative controls, price-fixing. Indeed structuralists have sometimes said that inflation (or chronic external current-account imbalance) is an inevitable accompaniment of growth in certain countries, and that there will be less loss in permitting the inflation to continue, or in seeking foreign accommodation for the external imbalance, than in trying to change these tendencies by reducing aggregate demand or attempting to fix or to alter price relationships through the exchange rate.

Seers (1962) attempts to develop a formal structuralist model of an economy in which certain relationships are fixed. I shall attempt here not to reproduce his model or his argument strictly but to use it as a starting point to explain the message of this first insight of structuralism.

The five key features of his model are that there is a (more or less) **fixed income-propensity to import**, that **export earnings are determined exogenously**, that the

growth rate of food output is exogenous or subject to quite low limits, that **income-elasticities of demand vary greatly** from one kind of good to another, and that **national-income growth must take place at no less than a certain rate** (determined by population growth and consumption expectations) in order to be politically tolerable.

The *fixed income-propensity to import* is related to the supposition that there are certain things, particularly certain types of engineering goods important in capital investment, that the economy cannot itself produce. This propensity may in fact rise as the growth rate increases, because of the increased relative importance of capital investment; the point of calling it fixed is that, given a particular growth rate, the import propensity is also for the present given, though in the longer term it may be reduced by measures for import-substitution. The reason for treating *export earnings as exogenous* seems to be that exports are assumed to be concentrated on a few primary products, whose quantity can not be altered by any policy measure except after long delay, and whose prices are determined in the world market. The rate of growth of export earnings, over which the authorities have little control, will thus limit the rate of importing, and thus of the income growth that is possible, without an external current-account deficit. Yet, unless growth takes place at a certain rate or more, the expectations of the growing population will not be met.

To meet the required growth rate, the authorities may find it necessary to run a current-account deficit, relying on international loans or investment to make this possible. Alternatively they may let the exchange rate depreciate, and thus promote inflation. Rising income may also lead to a rising demand for food, and domestically produced food supplies, like export earnings, may also be unresponsive (inelastic) to price changes and will certainly be so in the short term. Food prices may thus rise considerably in response to a comparatively small proportional change in income. Food and primary exports thus provide examples of the 'bottlenecks' of which the early structuralists made much. If, as we have supposed, their supply is unresponsive to price changes, and if their growth does not happen to equal what is needed to match the required growth rate of the economy, attempting to achieve that growth rate will entail some combination of external current-account deficit and price-inflation.

This does seem to express a dilemma in which LDCs commonly find themselves. One way of putting it is to say that there is a **foreign-exchange constraint**, and possibly also a **food-production constraint**, on development. No one probably denies that these constraints exist in the very short term. The difference of opinion is over whether market responses have the potential for reducing them. But growth that does not relax these constraints leads to difficulties with the price level or the external balance.

To make faster growth possible eventually, there must be structural change of such a kind as to reduce the import-propensity; and structural change itself will have inflationary tendencies for reasons that may be related to the systems of property and power. So some of the structuralists have said that **satisfactory growth in certain economies, without radical change in property or national management, entails inflation.** (It was often supposed that the special difficulties would disappear if there could be such radical changes as land reform, better education, more equal distribution of income, or more deliberate national planning.)

What lessons does this insight hold for stabilization? The negative answers seem stronger than the positive ones.

Structuralists agree in opposing 'monetarist' prescriptions for reducing inflation or external deficit. If inflation is an unavoidable accompaniment of growth under existing institutions, then taking action to suppress inflation by repressing demand is an anti-growth response. The same applies to attempts to suppress external current-account deficits by the same means, if it is true that such deficits are also an inevitable result of growth.

So what should be done in the way of strictly short-run stabilization measures? Seers's answer is probably representative: maybe inflation does not matter greatly; after all, some countries have lived with it for a long time without collapsing; overseas loans and investments should be procured to cover the external current-account deficit. By implication there is an appeal to the rest of the world to be generous and tolerant: to provide the accommodating loans, not to assume that the policies that have brought on inflation and the deficit are irresponsible.

In the medium term, the structuralists say, **change the structure**. The structures to be changed may or may not be those of property and power, but at least include the commodity structure of industry. There has been a tendency for those reading the structuralist lessons to think of this as entailing mainly or exclusively **import-substitution**. But at the time that structuralist views emerged this was already beginning to seem a dead end, as exponents such as

Prebisch realized. There are two other possible ways of reaching the same objective of faster growth through relaxing the foreign-exchange constraint.

One way is to **expand exports**: over much of the last twenty-five years, the East Asian 'newly industrializing countries' have managed to do this with manufactures, the Ivory Coast with agricultural commodities, Brazil with both, a number of others less dramatically with one or other or some combination of the two, and many for shorter or longer periods with metals and fuels. Policy has played a part in many of these achievements; an LDC's exports are not as firmly fixed and given as structuralists and many other development economists around 1960 were inclined to assume.

The other way is to **switch demand to nontradable goods** with comparatively little imported input. This was done consciously and deliberately in Colombia in the early 1970s, and, deliberately or not, in Singapore for many years, by diverting demand to housing. In Colombia there turned out to be, as Currie (1971, 1974) expressed it, a 'latent' demand for housing which required only appropriate financing arrangements to be turned into an actual demand. Diverting demand to housing would reduce the income-propensity to import and so, like increasing exports, relax the foreign-exchange constraint on growth. (These ideas are explored further under the heading 'Demand, structure and the growth of capacity' at the end of this chapter.)

But the 'monetarists' would reply that these measures, important as they may be, will not work quickly enough to deal with the short-run problems. IMF advisers themselves now frequently recommend 'supply-side' adjustments, such as price alterations to reflect relative values more closely, but they generally insist at the same time on restrictive demand-side measures in order to make the adjustments between income and expenditure in the meantime. The structuralists also want supply-side measures but generally of a different kind: those that set less store on the benevolent operation of markets. Their opponents would claim that some of these measures involving detailed allocative intervention have been tried and spectacularly failed to deliver. Structuralists also generally resist the simultaneous demand-side adjustments that the 'monetarists' consider part of the recipe.

It may be argued that the structuralists are really asking to avoid altogether the immediate short-term adjustments toward external current-account balance and stable prices which the 'monetarists' consider necessary and are requiring in effect that the rest of the world should provide more generous accommodation in the form of loans and grants in order to give them time for the supply-side measures to take effect.

Structuralist insights on inflation

A summary of the major theoretical insights of structuralism into the mechansims of inflation is given by Luis Bresser Pereira (1987).

What Bresser Pereira treats as the first major insight ('paradigmatic moment' in his words) of structuralism, dating from 1958, is the view that **in the course of growth developing countries will be subject to sectoral shortages, 'bottlenecks', which will lead to the raising of prices in the sectors concerned.** These price rises will be passed on to other sectors, presumably by such practices as constant percentage markups and the tendency of workers and profit-makers in one sector to try to keep up with income advances in other sectors.

The second set of insights of structuralism, which he attributes to Rangel (1963), include first a recognition that **changes in the money supply may be 'endogenous'** to the system, that is to say that they are not readily and simply controllable by the government, but spring from other forces at work in the economy. The money supply after all depends largely on what banks will lend and their customers will borrow, and that depends on such variables as interest costs and business prospects. Restrictive policies that raise interest rates may actually increase the need of firms to borrow and to that extent increase the money supply rather than reducing it. This has in fact been one of the difficulties of applied Monetarism (in the more restricted sense), as attempted in Britain in the early 1980s. The possibility had been recognized as far back as the 1930s by Keynes and others, and has been stressed as an argument against Friedmanite Monetarism since 1971 by Kaldor (e.g., 1986). (For a summary of the issue, see Desai, 1989.)

Rangel stressed secondly the **oligopolistic elements in inflation:** that the pricing decisions are not taken in perfect markets and hence that price rises need not always reflect shortages in the markets concerned but may rather result from the moves by groups with market power (trade unions and such powerful producers as public utilities) to restore their income positions, as, with money uncontrolled or uncontrollable, each group is temporarily able to do.

This helps to explain the means by which inflation in one sector is spread to others.

Thirdly, inflation might be **a necessary response to a fall in external demand for a nation's products.**

Bresser Pereira's third set of structuralist insights is the recognition of **'inertial inflation'** due to the fact that, once inflation is under way, people will expect it to continue. (This is incidentally in line with Friedman's assumptions that lead to his model of adaptive expectations.) Inertial inflation comes about through what he calls 'informal indexation': all price setters tend to raise their prices regularly in line with what they think the prevailing rate of inflation is; real income will tend to be redistributed from those who raise them more slowly than the average rate to those who raise them faster.

In conditions of very high rates of inflation, he says, these adjustments happen very rapidly so that real distributive gains and losses on account of the inflationary process are minimized. At this point, no one can reasonably expect to gain at the expense of the rest through the continuance of inflation; on the other hand no one likes inflation in itself and it introduces some *general* losses of welfare that arise from the less efficient working of the monetary system; so, if there is some means of declaring a truce and keeping the price level fixed, everyone, it seems, should be pleased. This was the hope of the 'structuralist' experiment in stabilization attempted by Brazil in 1986 and of similar projects in 1985-86 on the part of Argentina and Israel.

Inertial inflation means once again that inflation of prices need not be related to shortages or 'over-heating' of the economy. There is excess demand as measured in last month's prices but not in this month's. The *inertial* component in inflation may be distinguished from the *inflationary shocks* that may arise from increases in real demand, or from structural shifts in demand that produce sectoral bottlenecks, or from decisions by government agencies or trade unions or other oligopolistic or monopolistic elements to try not just maintaining but shifting upward the trend path of their real incomes.

Is structuralism relevant only to developing countries?

Here we refer to some of the points made in Chapter 7. There is a contrast between many developing countries and most of the industrialized countries of the 'Centre', such as

Sweden, West Germany and the US. This lies in the relative importance of **primary products within the nation's exports**, and the relative importance of **intra-industry trade**. (Primary products comprised 60 per cent of merchandise export earnings in 1985 for 'developing economies' compared with 24 per cent for the industrialized market economies, according to the 1987 *World Development Report*, pp. 222-3.) Intra-industry trade refers to the fact that each of two countries may be buying the one type of product from, and selling it to, the other: Sweden sells refrigerators to Italy and also buys them from Italy.

However, just as not all developing countries are predominantly primary-exporters, so not all industrialized countries are overwhelmingly exporters of manufactures of kinds which they also import. Some, such as Australia, New Zealand, Norway, Denmark, the Netherlands and Canada, have a fairly high concentration of primary products in their exports. Indeed, for the UK, even before it became (after 1978) an important primary-product exporter, there was an influential stabilization-policy model propounded that was essentially of structuralist type. This was the model of the Cambridge Economic Policy Group, known as the 'New Cambridge' model, which saw the light in 1973 and has had an appeal for the non-Marxist left because of its interventionist elements. (For an exposition, see Cuthbertson, 1979.) This assumed that earnings from UK exports and amounts of UK import spending would be rather unresponsive to changes in exchange rate. For this reason it argued that a rate of economic growth that would prove adequate to satisfy workers' income expectations and hence avoid a spiral of inflationary wage and price increases would require a general system of duties on manufactured imports in order to reduce the propensity to import. It has to be said that the suppositions of this model have been questioned both on detailed empirical grounds and on grounds of logical consistency.

The typical differences between the industrialized and the small-open type of developing country are relevant especially to the use of the exchange rate in influencing the external current account. They do not for any obvious reason apply to the use of aggregate fiscal policy or monetary policy to the same end. However, the fact that the simultaneous use of the exchange rate *to mitigate the depressing effect of fiscal-monetary restraint* on output and employment seems also less likely to be effective in many of the LDCs is relevant to the general reluctance of the structuralists to accept such methods of restraint there.

What about the use of fiscal and monetary measures to restrain domestic inflation? There are clearly likely to be differences in the cost and pain of such restraint according to how high the rate of inflation is and what degree of price stability is aimed at. One might suppose that the more established high inflation is, and the more therefore it is likely to have become 'inertial' and unrelated to current shortages or excess demand, the more difficult and painful it will be to eradicate by fiscal and monetary restraint. This is a factor therefore likely to differentiate countries according to past experience rather than discriminating between rich countries and poor, but more poor countries than rich happen to be in the difficult class.

In the case of certain LDCs, those with little internal economic integration and relatively liberal external policies (such perhaps as Botswana, Papua New Guinea, and, at least until the mid-1970s, Malawi and Kenya), domestic prices may tend to move in fairly close relationship with world prices divided by the exchange rate. If that is the case, it follows that fiscal-monetary restraint, provided it does not have the effect of altering the exchange rate, may not be in an immediate sense very relevant to the domestic price level, and indeed that the exchange rate will probably be a more appropriate instrument for controlling the price level in the short term. However, this statement must be qualified by saying that, if fiscal-monetary expansion under any given exchange rate reaches the point at which foreign-exchange has to be rationed administratively, the exchange rate begins to become less relevant, and fiscal-monetary policy more relevant, to the domestic price level.

Demand, structure and the growth of capacity

What will be attempted here is to to give an approach to growth and stabilization that to some extent reconciles the insights of structuralists, Keynesians and 'supply-siders' (who would often be counted as 'monetarists'). It returns to ideas that have been mooted in this and the previous chapter.

The Old Keynesian framework supposes that at any time a 'capacity' level of output and income can be defined for an economy and that the level of aggregate demand will determine how far that capacity output and income is realized. That is a simple enough idea, and many people regard it as having been an extremely important and fruitful one when it was first propounded. However, without rejecting this notion entirely, we can recognize its limitations. The Old Keynesian models of the textbooks treated capacity as being reached when there was full employment of labour. But what we often see in both poor and rich countries is large numbers of workers who appear to be unemployed and ready and willing to be employed, while at the same time we have good reason to believe that simply taking measures to increase aggregate demand will either increase the rate of domestic inflation or increase the external deficit. Correspondingly, the simple use of reduction in aggregate demand to reduce the rate of inflation or the external deficit is likely to increase unemployment.

Whether or not we accept the Monetarist dogma that all unemployment in a market economy is in some sense voluntary, we should probably regard the limit to capacity as being set not simply by the supply of undifferentiated labour but, at least in large part, by foreign exchange or the supply of certain skills or a combination of the two.

But the capacity level of output will depend also on the structure of final demand and the pattern of techniques used. Shifting of demand and techniques so as to make fuller use of the resources that are plentiful will increase capacity. So will a greater degree of technical efficiency, (including 'X-efficiency', that is, efficiency in organization and motivation).

Where inflation or an external deficit has to be reduced, both structuralists and supply-siders are saying: let's not just reduce aggregate demand; let's also increase capacity; then we can achieve the goal of equating supply to demand at a higher level of output. Structuralists have tended to see the way to do this as through administrative direction or improved infrastructure or the redistribution of assets. Neoclassical supply-siders have tended to see the way to do it as through getting prices right: avoiding the 'distortions' that come with administrative controls and some other forms of government intervention. Yet both must be aiming at altering the pattern of demand or techniques or the degree of technical efficiency. Both sides are concerned with changing structures and see this as a necessary, or at least very helpful, element in attempts to equate demand to capacity at stable prices.

As mentioned earlier in the chapter, experience suggests that the sustained 'miracles' in the growth of capacity in developing countries have come about either by expansion of exports appropriate to the country's factor endowments or by redirection of domestic demand to goods with a high unskilled-labour component such as housing. Both these results have normally been achieved by removing obstacles to the working of market forces rather than through administrative direction. Where it has been necessary to change the structure of demand for home-produced goods, this has been done most successfully by releasing the price mechanism, or by changing the institutional arrangements under which it operates, rather than by obstructing it.

Summary of enduring insights from structuralism

Controversially, I suggest that the most useful lessons from structuralism are mostly in the understanding of high inflation.

(a) Imperfect competition in the markets for goods and labour makes it possible for price rises that occur in particular sectors because of temporary shortages or external shocks to be passed on into other sectors.

(b) Once expectations of continuing inflation are established, inflation will proceed through inertia, without the need for further shortages or external shocks to maintain it, as sellers of goods and labour, operating in imperfect markets, raise prices and wages to maintain their shares of real income.

(c) Attempts to reduce inflation by restricting the money supply may be unsuccessful because money supply may respond to demand for it and hence not be controllable by tampering with money supply alone.

(d) If the authorities do succeed by fiscal or monetary measures in suppressing the growth of nominal demand for goods well below rates recently experienced, this may have a large effect in reducing employment, output, and growth, and a comparatively small effect in reducing inflation, as long as expectations of inflation persist and oligopolistic producers and workers' organizations have some freedom to set their own prices.

(e) Removing expectations of inflation, simultaneously with any measures reducing nominal demand, is thus critical if an attempt to eliminate high and chronic inflation is to succeed without serious damage to the real economy

(f) Appropriately changing the structure of demand and output may increase the growth of capacity. This may reduce the loss of output, the suffering, and the political opposition, entailed by measures to equate supply to demand at stable prices.

Part 4
International Approaches to Stabilization

9 Commodity-price stabilization

The international context of instability

Instability in LDC economies has been more acute since the early 1970s than before. Fluctuations in primary-commodity prices have been particularly large, and downward movements in earnings force a country to make painful adjustments in real living standards, to redistribute real income as some of those employed lose their jobs, and often to impose or to tighten restrictions in such fields as foreign exchange which have the effect of reducing the efficiency of economic life. In a number of cases this has been aggravated by the **debt crisis** which became evident towards the end of 1982 and was still running at the turn of the decade.

The debt crisis itself was precipitated by the 1981-2 world slump, which led to large falls in the prices of many primary commodities. Its origin lay in the enormous aggregates of loans that private banks had made to the governments of certain middle-income countries from the mid to late 1970s. These governments had tended to rely on further borrowing to service their debts. In late 1982 banks, seeing the earnings of debtor countries declining, began to think the unthinkable and to wonder whether the borrowers would be able to go on servicing larger and larger amounts of debt. They then became hesitant about the further lending needed to turn the existing loans over. This response, which may have seemed prudent for any bank individually, immediately threw on the debtor countries burdens on which they had not counted, and did so at a time when most of them were less able to bear them than before, with oil prices still high and many other commodity prices particularly low. The banking system began to seem under threat because of the possibility that a number of borrower governments might default.

To avoid formal default the IMF encouraged the governments and the banks to negotiate rescue operations that involved 'rescheduling' of the debt, that is, retiming the servicing obligations so that they would proceed more slowly or more evenly. The conditions attached to these agreements often involved severe austerity in the debtor countries: reduction in real net government outlays (other than for overseas-debt servicing) and hence in employment and income.

It will be unnecessary to stress the implications of such instability for welfare. The debt crisis aggravated the effects of the instability to which many primary-exporting countries are subject on account of fluctuations in world markets for their exports. Export earnings are sometimes heavily dominated by one or a small number of products (copper in Zambia, cocoa in Ghana, oil in Nigeria, sugar in Cuba and Fiji), and common sense suggests that this concentration makes them particularly susceptible to fluctuations in earnings.

Those LDCs now relying on *manufactures* for about half or more of their exports (such as China, India, Pakistan, South Korea, Taiwan, Hong Kong, Singapore) seem to be much *less* affected by fluctuations in their export markets. When they do encounter a fall in export demand (as Singapore did in 1985), they seem more readily able to restore their position (as Singapore did in 1986), and there are fairly clear reasons why this should be so.

A full treatment of remedies for instability in developing countries would consider the reasons for the world slumps of the 1970s and 1980s and the high real interest rates that have prevailed in the latter decade. This would take us into the topic of macro-policy co-ordination among the main industrial countries. The slumps of 1975-6 and 1981-2 can be fairly attributed in large part to mismanagement among the rich, and the high real interest rates particularly to mismanagement in the US, as is widely recognized; but the political and technical problems of finding remedies are great. These are matters out of the hands, and largely beyond the influence, of LDC governments, and, at the cost of glaring incompleteness, they will not be discussed here.

'Exogenous' instability in LDC economies arises principally from

(a) instability of export prices, but also from
(b) instability of export volumes, as a result of weather or pests, and
(c) disturbances to staple-food production.

Export-price instability, however, with the disturbances to export earnings and to the incomes of export producers and government revenue that arise from it, receives the most attention. We consider export-earnings instability, but recognize that much of it arises from instability in export prices.

Export-earnings instability

With some commodities (such as copper, sugar, copra, cocoa) real world-price variation within a couple of years may be as great as four to one or even ten to one. Zambia is a prime example of a country that found its government revenue from copper, which provided at certain times the greater part of its total government revenue, virtually disappear in the course of two years. Copper's share in revenue fell from 59 per cent in 1969 to 19 per cent in 1972 and from 53 per cent in 1974 to 3 per cent in 1976. It is estimated (Helleiner, 1986, pp. 905-7) that changes of quantities demanded and prices in world trade, together with changes in world interest rates, would by themselves have had the direct effect of reducing Sri Lanka's external current balance, failing adjustment, by 66 per cent of GNP between 1978 and 1982. This is not quite the same as a reduction *of GNP* in this proportion, but it must be fairly closely related: increased payments for imports as a result of higher import prices, increased interest payments as a result of higher interest rates, and reduced export receipts as a result of lower export prices, all represent changes in real income. Sri Lanka in this period was an extreme case, but a number of other countries were also severely affected.

Why do these variations occur, and is there anything that can be done about them?

Broadly they can be attributed to supply or demand factors.

With the **metals**, it is largely the level of *demand* in industrialized countries (ICs), as reflected in world boom and slump, that seems to be critical, though often there are surprisingly long lags between the peak of a boom and the peak of say copper prices.

With the **foods and beverages**, which tend to have stable world demand conditions, it is mainly variations in *supply*, due to the weather or pests in a key producer country (Brazil for coffee, West Africa for cocoa, US or USSR for wheat), that affect the price.

With **agricultural raw materials** (wool, sisal, coconut products), *either demand or supply* variation may be important. A drought in Australia will raise the wool price, reducing the incomes of sheep farmers there but raising the incomes of those in Argentina. A world slump will lower the incomes of both.

Price-inelasticity of supply in the short to medium term aggravates instability. Agricultural products usually have inelastic supply; actual production is often almost zero-elastic for up to a year after the price stimulus occurs, but in the case of tree crops for up to seven years. Metal production may be unresponsive to price in the short term because of the importance of fixed costs in mining and the long delay between decision and production in the opening of new mines. Both types of commodity contrast in this respect with manufactures in general, for which there is often, somewhere in the world, excess capacity that can readily be brought into use, and for which variable costs are often high in relation to total costs.

World demand for primary commodities too is often **inelastic to price**. This is the case with the staple foods and beverages and with those metals and other raw materials that (unlike rubber and most fibres) do not have synthetic substitutes.

Eagerness to stabilize prices springs from a desire to stabilize earnings and income (both in aggregate and for the producers concerned). So, with any price-stabilization scheme, we have to consider whether it serves to stabilize earnings from the product. In addition, it is relevant to ask whether the stabilization scheme has any expected cost in revenue and net income for the producers and their countries.

1. **International price-stabilization agreements**

The main political demand for means of stabilization from LDCs has been directed to international commodity agreements between importing and exporting countries. These must be distinguished from cartels, set up by producers or producing countries only. Quite a number of intergovernmental exporter-importer schemes of this sort have been projected, but few have worked for long. (See for details: Morton and Tulloch, 1977, Appendices; Gilbert, 1987, from the latter of which many of the factual assertions here are drawn.) In 1976 the UN Conference on Trade and Development agreed to set up what was called the Integrated Program for Commodities (which was supposed to include a set of stabilizing agreements for eighteen commodities that would make use of buffer stocks) and a Common Fund for Commodities to help finance it, but the richer members of the UN were not keen at the time to subscribe to the Common Fund. The agreement to set it up did not come into force until July 1989, when the Governing Council for the UN Common Fund for Commodities met for the first time. Funds of over $500 million were committed to help finance buffer stocks and for other purposes connected with advancing the primary-commodity industries. The US was the only major industrialized country not to ratify the agreement at that time (*Keesing*). An IMF Buffer Stock Financing Facility has also been authorized (*IMF Annual Report 1989*). The only new commodity to be subject to an exporter-importer stabilization scheme since the UNCTAD 1976 initiative has been natural rubber, in the agreement of 1979 (operative from 1982), renewed in 1987 with a new agreement to come into force from 1989.

Are producer cartels an option?

A producers-only scheme, in other words a **cartel,** is possible, but, in spite of, or perhaps because of, the OPEC experience, it is not at all clear that a commodity cartel, even if it succeeds in raising the price of the commodity, is likely to operate in the ultimate interest of its members. If in the short term it can push the price up by limiting supplies, it will be tempted to do so, and the effect may be, as in the OPEC case, that competing production is eventually expanded and demand for the commodity reduced, so that in the end the price crashes (as oil's did in 1986), and the result of the exercise turns out to be the very reverse of stabilization. In 1983, ten years after the first great oil-price rise, the OPEC countries were selling roughly half as much petroleum as in 1973.

Moreover, there is only a limited number of commodities for which conditions seem favourable for an LDC-exporting-nation cartel of the OPEC kind that can at least for some years control the price (Radetzki, 1976). The LDC producers must provide a large share of world supply of the commodity; there must be no close substitutes; and it certainly helps if a small number of producing countries account for most of the output. **Coffee, cocoa, and tea**, score well on the first two tests, but coffee particularly is weak on the third. The coffee cartel of 1977-80 operated in a period in which prices were exceptionally high because of unusual weather in Brazil. **Copper, tin and bauxite** are others that might appear favourable. The International Bauxite Association has something of the character of a producing countries' cartel in an industry that has a very small number of extracting firms. After the collapse of the tin buffer stock in 1985, the producer members of the International Tin Council formed the Association of Tin Producing Countries, which has operated a cartel that uses export quotas, with the two major non-member producing countries, Brazil and China, agreeing from 1987 to observe quotas themselves (*Keesing*). However, the attempt of CIPEC, the copper-exporting LDCs' association, to impose a cartel in the mid-1970s in order to support the copper price failed because of lack of the necessary co-operation and discipline for achieving control over supply.

Experience with price-stabilization agreements

There are at least two coherent principles on which an international price-stabilizing scheme may be set up:

(a) export controls (quotas);

(b) buffer stocks.

Six commodities have been subject to such agreements (at least on paper) over substantial periods since 1945. Two (coffee and sugar) have used solely export quotas; one (natural rubber) has worked entirely by buffer stock; two (tin and cocoa) have in principle used both (though cocoa's export quotas applied in its first two agreements only, both of which were ineffective). The **wheat agreements** have lacked powers of enforcement since 1971 (Gilbert, 1987, p. 592), but before that time they depended on neither principle but on the willingness of the US as the biggest exporter to regulate its sales in order to maintain the agreed price range (rather as the OPEC cartel relied for some years on Saudi Arabia and Kuwait to make the necessary reductions in their sales in order to support the oil price).

The course of the agreements involving both exporting and importing countries has been by no means smooth. The wheat agreements as they now are can be ignored for the present purpose. The **cocoa agreements** (the first made in 1972) have been only fitfully active; buffer-stock operations have been suspended for much of the time and have not (1990) operated since mid-1987. The International Cocoa Organization was in financial difficulties at the end of the 1980s with disputes over the members' levies; the US and Ivory Coast (biggest user and biggest producer respectively) had not ratified the 1980 agreement by mid-1986; the latest extension of the agreement (1990-2) has no mechanism for regulating prices or quantities (*Keesing*). The four **sugar agreements** (active 1954-63, 1969-73, 1978-83) and four **coffee agreements** (active 1963-72, 1980-9, with a period in 1977-80 in which producing countries ran their own cartel) have been in suspension for quite long periods; though the 1983-9 coffee agreement was formally continued for a further two years in 1989, quotas were suspended from July of that year, essentially because of disagreements between producer and importer members over the interpretation to be put on quotas in the proposed new agreement (*Keesing*). **Tin** had the longest continuous run under a working agreement (1956-85), though the tin price frequently went through the ceiling fixed by the members. In October 1985 the fund was unable to stop the price from falling through the floor, and the system collapsed, with enormous debts incurred in the process of trying to support it.

The International Tin Agreement was often rated successful until its collapse in 1985. One advantage that it had was that the international market in tin was heavily dominated by a small number of exporting countries, most of them LDCs and all of them members; for much of the time seven countries accounted for about 90 per cent of world exports; this advantage was whittled down in the 1980s with the advent of Brazil as an important exporter but outside the International Tin Council (ITC). A complication was the US stockpile of tin which was gradually disposed of over the years, but eventually there seems to have been a degree of co-operation between the US and the ITC (Gilbert, 1987, p. 611). It has been suggested (ibid.) that export controls were more important than the buffer stock in controlling the price. Gilbert maintains that the controls were effective in keeping the price above the floor but that when it was necessary to go into reverse they reduced the scheme's capacity for pushing the price down. Hence, he says, the arrangement was more effective in maintaining the floor than the ceiling. Helping in this process, it is sometimes claimed, was a 'natural' tendency for the market price to rise, at least in money terms; but it is difficult to be sure how much of this apparent natural tendency was in fact due to the controls.

Buffer-stock schemes have intervention rules and arrangements for updating these rules. In the tin, rubber and cocoa schemes there has at any time been a price band within which the manager tries to contain the world price. In the tin agreements, the band was divided into three equal parts. The manager was obliged to buy at the bottom of the range and to sell at the top. Within the bottom third he might buy at his discretion, and within the top third he might sell at his discretion, but within the middle third he might buy or sell only with the consent of the ITC.

Export-quota schemes also generally have an agreed price range at any one time. They usually have some more or less automatic trigger rule, related to either the price or the stock level of the commodity, which determines whether the controls are tightened or loosened. Floors and ceilings in the coffee agreements have been moved several times in a year.

In the **coffee agreements** the importer members agreed to buy from the exporter members up to the quota amounts before buying coffee sold outside the agreement. The exporter members agreed to make supplies available to the importer members within the agreed price range up to their respective quotas before selling outside the agreement. There was also a free market in coffee in which importer countries which were not in the agreement, such as Japan, operated. Amounts produced by exporter members outside their quotas could be sold on the free market. The dispute in 1989 appears to have been over whether in future the exporter countries should be allowed to sell outside their quota limits at all. The existence of the agreement probably stabilized prices for its members. It probably had the effect of destabilizing them in the free market, but this conclusion admittedly depends on *a priori* reasoning. Probably the agreement tended to raise prices generally, both for its own members and for non-members.

Most of the **sugar trade** not covered by the international agreements while they were in operation came under the Commonwealth (now EC) or the US preferential agreement or Soviet-bloc purchases. These other arrangements have dealt with a large part of world output. It is probable that this large measure of intervention helps to make the free market outside any agreement highly volatile, whether or not the international agreement itself is in force.

Difficulties with both types of scheme

Both types of scheme require some agreement on **target price ranges.** Exporters tend to want them higher than importers, and this is cause for disagreement. Even if both sides were committed to approximating the long-run trend price, it would be very hard to agree on what that price should be. Where restriction of supply was possible, producers would be tempted to push price above the long-run trend level, even if they knew what it was, and if (as is always the case) they did not know it for sure they would tend to err on the upward side, since, if the demand for the commodity is inelastic in the short term, that error would be immediately more advantageous to them than one on the downward side. In 1987 the coffee agreement had fifty exporter and twenty-four importer members. All of these had to be satisfied with the price range, and all the exporter members with the distribution of quotas.

Critics of the schemes in fact say that there will always be a tendency to turn them into devices for *price raising*. As suggested above, a case can be made for saying that this happened with the tin agreements. It may also be the case with the coffee and the sugar agreements.

Difficulties with export quotas

Export controls impose an administrative burden, especially with a smallholder crop. Quotas have to be allocated to individual producers. There is likely to be disagreement between countries over their quota sizes, and there are temptations for the smaller producer countries to break the rules, especially if they see that they have resources for an increase in production of an attractive crop, as was alleged of some of the newer coffee producers in Africa in the 1960s.

Difficulties and doubts with buffer stocks

Buffer-stock schemes are attractive on several grounds. They do not require decisions on quotas, or depend on good behaviour, though the one with the longest record of apparent success was backed by export quotas. It would seem that they need not disturb the general tendency of market prices but would simply iron out fluctuations, accomplishing what private holders of stocks would achieve between them if they behaved with 'rational expectations' or in a perfect market.

However, it is not as easy as it sounds. The buffer-stock manager needs to be able to predict the future with a certain degree of accuracy. Also there need to be substantial resources in the hands of the manager: to hold as cash when he is keeping the price down and to hold as stocks of the commodity when it is necessary to support the price. The less resources he has, the more accurate his predictions need to be if the price is to be kept within the agreed limits.

Buffer-stock schemes are also open to the objections (in principle) that, if they succeed in stabilizing prices, they may not stabilize (indeed may destabilize) earnings for producers, and that they may actually reduce producer earnings over the cycle (even after the net earnings of the buffer stock itself are thrown in). How do these last disadvantages occur, and are they important in practice?

On admittedly somewhat simplified assumptions, such as that price stabilization entails always changing the price to the mean of two extreme prices and that shifts of supply and demand curves are parallel shifts of straight lines, it can be shown geometrically that:

(a) where fluctuations are **demand-determined**, price stabilization will **stabilize earnings but will tend to reduce them;**

(b) where fluctuations are **supply-determined**, price stabilization may **stabilize or destabilize earnings but will tend to increase them** (Johnson, 1977; for a different but not inconsistent statement, see Nguyen, 1979).

These statements about the effect on the expected amount of earnings refer to the sales revenue going to the producers, the expected gain or loss made by the buffer stock itself being disregarded. On the simplifying assumptions, the buffer stock would receive as much cash in the high-price case as it would pay out in the low-price case, provided that its activity served to keep the price continually at the mean or target level, but, if instead it bought or sold only enough at any one time to approach the target price gradually, as it would surely do, rather than to reach it at once, it would gain somewhat, through selling when price was high and buying when it was low. So, if any costs of storing the commodity and costs of the capital involved could be ignored, the buffer stock itself might make some gains. If the net gains made by the buffer stock are ultimately distributed to producers and the net losses ultimately met by them, the overall effect on them will thus be if anything more favourable than would appear if the gain or loss made by the buffer stock itself were disregarded. All this of course supposes, as is implied in the simplifying assumptions already made, that the buffer-stock manager always makes the right decisions for achieving the fund's objectives.

A brief explanation of these assertions follows, with the help of Figures 9.1 and 9.2. In each case the market price in the absence of intervention is supposed for simplicity to oscillate between P_1 and P_2, spending equal time on each. The mean or expected price is thus P_0, midway between the two. The buffer stock and its fund are supposed to be used for raising or lowering the price to P_0. Insofar as supply responds to price, it is supposed here to respond immediately. (Alternatively, if this assumption is abandoned and supply is assumed to respond with a lag, it is probably reasonable to suppose that stabilizing the price will tend to reduce fluctuations in supply rather than increase them, and that 'perverse' supply responses can be ignored.)

In the **demand-determined case** (Figure 9.1), fluctuations in demand, indicated by movement of the demand curve, D, move revenue in the same direction as price. Thus stabilizing the price (represented here by restoring price in any period to the mean price) will **stabilize earnings.**

So long as the supply curve, S, has positive price-elasticity, that is, so long as it is upward-sloping (as in the diagram), the tendency in the absence of intervention would be for the producers to sell more when the market price is high and less when it is low. The price-stabilizing intervention counteracts that tendency and leads them to produce the same amount whether the free-market price would be high or low.

This is the reason why the intervention reduces producers' earnings more when market prices would be high than it increases producers' earnings when market prices would be low. So the effect over the cycle will tend to be to **reduce earnings.** This is probably evident if you look at the diagram: at least if the curves approximate to straight lines and move roughly in parallel, as in the simplifying assumptions. The outer L-shaped area, $P_1P_0BQ_0Q_1A$, is larger than the inner L-shaped area, $P_0P_2CQ_2Q_0B$.

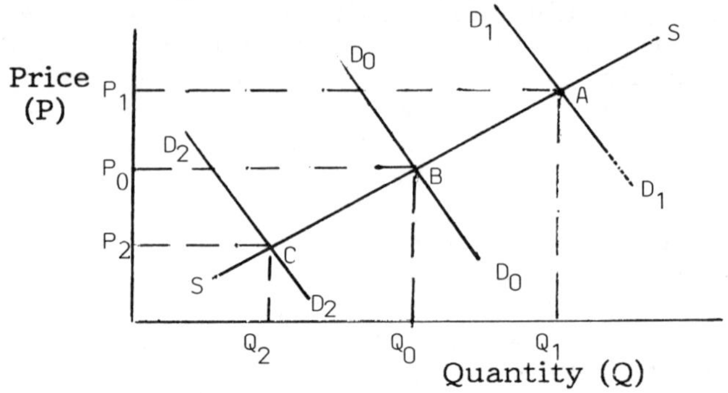

S is the supply function for the commodity. D_1, D_0, and D_2, are high, middle, and low, demand functions, giving high, middle, and low, prices, P_1, P_0, and P_2, respectively, in the absence of intervention.
The buffer stock is supposed to be used to stabilize price at P_0.

Figure 9.1 Effect on earnings of price-stabilizing intervention where instability is demand-determined

Nevertheless, if the supply were zero-elastic to price, that is, if the supply curve were vertical, the loss in earnings over the cycle would disappear, as can probably be seen from Figure 9.1.

In the **supply-determined** case (Figure 9.2), the result is not quite so easy to pick up from the diagram.

If the **demand is elastic** as in Figure 9.2(a), there are (in the absence of intervention) less earnings when price is high (P_1AQ_1O) than when it is low (P_2CQ_2O). Stabilizing the price reduces earnings (to $P_0FQ_1'O$) when they would otherwise be low and increases it (to $P_0EQ_2'O$) when they would otherwise be high. Thus, when demand is elastic, the effect of stabilizing price must be to **destabilize earnings.**

If the **demand is inelastic** as in Figure 9.2(b), then (in the absence of intervention) earnings are high (P_1AQ_1O) when price is high and low (P_2CQ_2O)when price is low. The effect of price-stabilizing intervention in reducing earnings (to $P_0FQ_1'O$) when they would otherwise be high and increasing them (to P_0EQ_2O) when they would otherwise be low will thus stabilize earnings *unless* earnings become so small in the high-market-price case and so large in the low-market-price case that the gap between 'corrected' earnings in the two cases is greater than that between 'uncorrected' earnings. This earnings-destabilizing result is possible in principle if the *supply* curves are sufficiently elastic. So, when demand is inelastic, stabilizing prices may **either stabilize or destabilize earnings.**

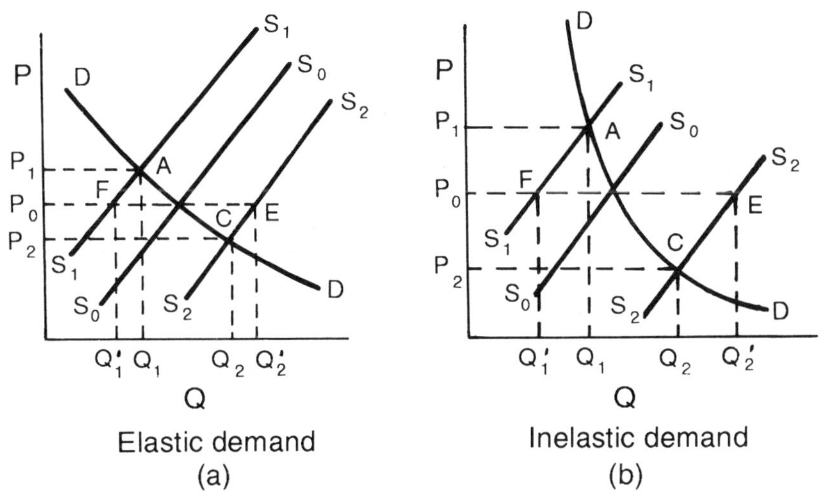

D is the demand function for the commodity.
S_1, S_0, and S_2, are low, middle, and high, supply functions for the commodity giving high, middle, and low, prices, P_1, P_0, and P_2, respectively.
The buffer stock is supposed to be used to stabilize price at P_0.

Figure 9.2 Effect on earnings of price-stabilizing intervention where instability is supply-determined

It will probably be clear that, when the demand is inelastic as in Figure 9.2(b), for any given elasticities of supply, the earnings-destabilizing effect is less likely to happen **if the price-stabilization is only partial** and not complete as supposed in the diagrams. This is argued formally by Nguyen (1980).

Under the assumptions that we have made, including **completeness** of price-stabilization, it can be demonstrated that, in the supply-determined case, price-stabilization through a buffer scheme will stabilize, rather than destabilize, earnings *provided the sum of the magnitudes of supply and demand elasticities is less than a half.* (A geometric proof can be given on the simplifying assumptions made here. A somewhat obscure algebraic argument is given by Johnson, 1977.)

This sounds exacting, but it may well be fulfilled in many cases since world demand for most primary products is apparently inelastic and, within the period relevant to stabilization, supply-elasticity may be zero or very close to it. Add to this the fact that in practice price-stabilization will be only partial, and *we must doubt whether the earnings-destabilizing possibility is of much practical importance.* (Indeed it appears possible 'in principle', which here means 'with sufficient knowledge of the supply and demand conditions', to devise a scheme of part-stabilization of prices, in the supply-determined demand-inelastic case, that would keep sales revenue completely stable. At least this can be demonstrated for models in which the free-market price can take only two values. How far this could be translated into practice under imperfect knowledge, in a world in which the conditions are constantly changing and free-market prices can take many values, is another matter.)

The tendency, in the supply-determined case, **for earnings to rise** as a result of price stabilization depends on the fact that there is more of the good supplied in the low-market-price phase (for which price-stabilization raises the price and the earnings) than in the high-market-price phase (for which price-stabilization lowers the price and the earnings).

Verdict on buffer-stock and export-quota schemes

This may seem complicated. To simulate the real world at all closely we should need to make it even more so. As with so many pieces of analysis of this type, probably only the people who have to give lectures or write textbooks on the subject (and temporarily some of those who see fit to learn them up for examinations) are aware of the precise details of the analysis even at the simplified level presented here. What we need to be aware of for practical purposes is that potential flaws in buffer-stock price-stabilization exist, what their general character is, how serious or trivial they are likely to be, and what methods of analysis may be used to judge their relevance in a particular case.

Altogether maybe we should not take these *a priori* earnings-destabilizing effects of buffer schemes very seriously. The important difficulties are, I believe, first the *political* ones of keeping the producer and importer countries satisfied and the stock adequately financed and second the *technical* one of correctly estimating the trends of supply and demand and the responses of prices.

Quota schemes similarly face political problems of reaching agreement on price ranges, and among exporters on size of quotas.

In assessing prospects, we cannot ignore the fact that so few commodities have been covered by international producer-consumer agreements to stabilize prices, and that in 1990 only one of any significance is effectively in operation.

2. Using hedging contracts to stabilize export prices

This is not strictly an international approach to price stabilization, but is perhaps most naturally considered after, and in contrast to, international price-stabilization agreements; and support from international institutions might help to make it work. The idea has been discussed for some years but has recently been advanced in a particular form by Powell and Gilbert (1988), on whose paper this section is largely based. There are three types of market contract relating to future prices, each of which may be used either for **speculation** (in which an operator takes risks for the sake of expected gain) or for **hedging** (in which he is prepared to accept a reduction in expected worth in order to reduce risk). Often one party to a contract is speculating and the other is hedging, though sometimes both are hedging (and the contract seems advantageous to both because they have different obligations outside the market concerned) or both are speculating (and taking different views of the future).

Three types of contract that can be used for hedging are: **forward purchases**, where the parties agree to trade a certain quantity of the commodity at a specified time in the future for a specified price; **futures**, where the forward arrangements are standardized, certain rules are observed to ensure that the contracts can be fulfilled, and there is a clearing house to ensure observance; and options. The buyer of an **option** buys either a right to sell (a 'put') or a right to buy (a 'call'), in either case to do so at a specified price and on a specified date. He pays a price also for the right. The buyer of the put option will exercise it if the market price is below the 'exercise' price (the price specified in the option contract); the buyer of the call option will exercise it if the market price is above the exercise price.

Powell and Gilbert argue that for various reasons it is likely to be impracticable for governments to stabilize their producers' export earnings adequately by the use of forward or futures contracts (though the use of futures may have some value), but maintain that options are more promising. Not all writers on the subject agree in preferring options for this purpose over the other types of contract, but an explanation of how this might work with options gives an idea of the approach and its possible difficulties.

The exporter government or other body that wants to stabilize the net price received should simultaneously, they suggest, buy a put and sell ('write') a call with the same date attached to both. It would thus be *able* if it chose to sell at *no less* than a certain price and *obliged* if required to sell at *no more* than a certain price. The former price would thus set a minimum and the latter a maximum to the price it would receive.

The two contracts might be made on the same quantity but with different exercise prices chosen so that the cost of the put contract would be exactly matched by the proceeds of the call contract. This would mean that the put exercise price would be below the call exercise price, and these would set the minimum and maximum prices respectively that the exporter government would get for the whole quantity. If the market price turned out to be between the two exercise prices, the government would trade at the market price.

Alternatively, the exercise prices might be the same while the quantities differed between the put and the call option so as again to make the cost of the put equal to the proceeds of the call. If, as we should expect, the exercise price were below the expected market price, the quantity specified in the put contract would be greater than that specified in the call contract; that is, the whole quantity covered could be involved in the put but only part of it in the call. The exercise price (the same for both put and call) would then set a minimum to what the country would receive, but the country would in addition earn a share of any additional sales receipts if the market price were above that price, the share being the proportion that the call quantity bore to the put quantity. (This is an attempt at paraphrase from Powell and Gilbert, 1988.)

The alleged advantage of this solution over commodity-price-stabilization agreements is that 'the market' would set the relevant stabilized prices. There would be no need for a political forum and a stock manager to make judgements. Also the risks to those contracting in effect to stabilize the producer prices would be spread across the market rather than concentrated on a single entity, such as the ITC's buffer stock. The particular producer government would also, Powell and Gilbert point out, be able to choose the risks that it was prepared to accept rather than having a choice imposed internationally.

The problem, however, might be the scale of the risks to be borne. The market might not be prepared to provide the necessary cover for the whole crop of a producer country except at exercise prices that were too unfavourable to the producer governments to be attractive. This is partly because of the risk that governments might default on the option contracts that they had 'written' and the difficulty of bringing them to account if this happened. Alternatively, to remove this risk, the governments or other hedgers of commodity receipts might have to put up guarantee funds that were too burdensome. This, Powell and Gilbert suggest, is the case for an international agency to guarantee the governments' obligations and so reduce the risks to the other parties and the costs to the governments of the hedging contracts. The World Bank or IMF might play this role.

3. Domestic producer-price stabilization

Here again we are dealing with what is really a domestic device; the pretext for considering it here is that it again has analogies with the international devices discussed in the earlier part of the chapter.

The country exporting a primary commodity may itself set up an organization with a certain amount of finance to stabilize the commodity prices received by producers. This is generally applied to agricultural crops. It requires a marketing board or equivalent that has monopsony powers to buy the commodity within the country before export.

The board gives producers less than the world-equivalent price when that price is high, and more than the world-equivalent price when that price is low. Thus the country's producers' own prices are stabilized to some extent. Will their earnings also be stabilized? If their output is not systematically and negatively related to the world price of the commodity, it seems likely that on the whole price stabilization *will* stabilize their earnings. In a country that is heavily dominant in the world market for a commodity, however, (as Brazil is for coffee) there may be such a negative relationship. (The reason for marked rises in coffee prices is usually that the Brazilian crop has been damaged.) For most producers of most agricultural commodities, however, such a relationship is not very likely. Most of the coffee-producing countries have too small a share of the total world market in the commodity, or else their own supply is too regular, for a negative relationship between their own supply level and world prices to be important.

In most cases, then, it would seem that producers' earnings *are* likely to be stabilized by a scheme of this sort provided that it succeeds in stabilizing prices.

Stabilizing the disposable income of the primary producers doubtless helps to stabilize their expenditure. Hence, through multiplier effects, the stabilizing impact will spread to income and expenditure generally, as well as reducing instability of disposable income for the producers.

Marketing boards, especially in West Africa, have come in for a large amount of disapproval. It is undoubtedly true that they have often paid the producers at prices that are not symmetrically above and below world-price equivalents but consistently below them. This is one reason convincingly given for the marked decline of cocoa production in Ghana while its neighbour, the Ivory Coast, was expanding production. Marketing boards have been an easy prey for what are really taxes on export producers. They may need to have formal rules written into their constitutions that will limit their use as a source of state revenue to the detriment of production. A device that has sometimes been used is to give producers' organizations strong representation on the marketing board or other stabilizing body, where they can look after the interests of the producers.

Note

Information and ideas, not all referenced, have been taken from Gilbert, 1987, from Powell and Gilbert, 1988, and from *Keesing's Contemporary Archives*.

10 Earnings compensation and insurance

The difficulties and doubts associated with commodity-price stabilization have led to the notion of export-earnings compensation. It is, after all, earnings rather than prices that we should like to stabilize; and we have seen that it is possible in principle for price-stabilization through buffers actually to destabilize earnings. So why not deal with earnings directly by some form of 'insurance'? In return for an insurance 'premium' or equivalent, a country or its commodity producers as a body could receive, out of an internationally held fund, a compensatory payment whenever earnings fell by more than a certain proportion below, say, a trend value. The 'premium' might take the form of a payment into the fund when earnings were more than so much above some trend level. Or a donor country or group of donors could in effect pay the premium by financing the compensatory payments themselves. If the insurance-policy analogy were followed, the compensation would come automatically to the affected country on condition that certain objectively defined events had occurred; it would not be a matter for discretion on the part of the fund-holder or of some international authority.

1. International earnings-compensation schemes

There are in fact two international schemes that operate on something like this principle, though one of them has moved farther from the ideal since it was originally formed. One of them, known as **Stabex**, is run by the **European Community** (EC) for its African, Caribbean and Pacific associates (the ACP States), of which there were recently sixty-six. The other is run by the **IMF** for the world at large and is now known as the **Compensatory and Contingency Financing Facility** (CCFF). The two schemes are different and depart in different ways from a simple insurance principle.

(a) Stabex

Stabex was established in 1975 under the first Lomé Convention (Lomé I) which set out arrangements for EC aid to, and co-operation with, the ACP States. It has been renewed in successive Lomé Conventions and modified slightly. It is administered by the European Development Fund.

The Stabex scheme deals only with the ACP countries' exports *to the EC*. Such trade is treated *commodity by commodity*, with no account being taken of the country's export picture as a whole, or even its picture of commodity exports to the EC as a whole. It covers, moreover, *only certain commodities*; these recently numbered forty-eight and are now exclusively biological (they include timber, crustaceans, and hides as well as agricultural products in the strict sense); iron ore was originally included but taken out in the third Lomé Convention; sugar is not covered but is dealt with under a separate arrangement. Minerals are not included; there is an EC-ACP 'Mining Products: Special Financing Facility' ('Sysmin'), but Sysmin is apparently not comparable to Stabex (Hewitt, 1987); this means that the ACP countries that are mineral exporters without significant exports of tropical-crop products (a group currently including Nigeria, Zaire, Zambia and Zimbabwe) can not use the scheme.

When earnings from a country's exports to the EC of one of the commodities fall by more than a certain percentage below a 'trend' value, payments are made to the country's government. According to the rules, these will eventually be paid back if the relevant earnings subsequently go high enough in both volume and value terms. But the 'least developed countries' (LLDCs) are formally exempted altogether from the obligation to repay. This means that, according to Hewitt (1987), only twenty-three have any obligation to repay, and some of these are not likely to be recipients since they do not export the relevant commodities. In fact, repayment appears seldom to have been required for *any* of the ACP members; only 6.4 million ECUs was repaid in the first five-year period, and the repayments in the second period were solely in the form of deductions from transfers that were otherwise due to be made to the countries (Hewitt, 1987). No interest is charged on the receipts. So there is no revolving fund as was originally envisaged, and *de facto* the payments are virtually aid in the form of grants.

The payments on account of shortfalls in export earnings are made automatically if the criterion is met for some commodity, but they are made after the end of the year concerned: generally within twelve to eighteen months.

In nominal terms slightly over a billion ECUs were transferred to ACP countries under the scheme between 1975 and 1984 inclusive (Hewitt, 1987, p. 621; an ECU has been worth somewhat more than a US dollar.) More than three quarters of the amount was in respect of just three commodities: groundnuts, coffee and cocoa. Of the ACP countries, forty-eight received Stabex transfers in the first ten years. Senegal, Ivory Coast, Ghana and Sudan were the largest nominal beneficiaries, receiving between them nearly 40 per cent of the total.

A study (Herrmann, 1983, cited Hewitt, 1987), conducted in nineteen sample ACP countries, of whether the effects of the Stabex transfers were predominantly stabilizing or destabilizing to the economies concerned, found that in a majority of cases they were rather destabilizing than the reverse. That this should be possible probably has to do with the lag in receipts after the year of shortfall and with the fact that Stabex is based on commodity-by-commodity exports to the EC only, which may not be related closely to a country's total export earnings, let alone its external current-account balance. Hewitt judged that in the first five-year period supply factors predominated among the reasons for the transfers (most prominently failures in groundnut crops in West Africa), and in the second period demand factors.

A certain amount is budgeted for each five-year period and there is an allocation for each year within the period. If the fund runs out before the period is complete, in principle no further payments can be made, but in fact payments have sometimes over-run what is budgeted.

Judged by the standard of a hypothetical insurance policy against external economic shocks, Stabex conforms by making the payments automatic (so long, at least, as there is cash in the fund allocated for the purpose); and the payments are not loans in any normal sense of the term. There is, however, no equivalent of an insurance premium. Furthermore the circumstances in which the payments are made relate only to certain very limited shocks (nothing from mineral or processed or service exports, or from exports to outside the EC, or from changes in interest rates or import prices).

(b) The IMF Compensatory and Contingency Financing Facility

What was originally called the Compensatory Financing Facility (CCF) has been in existence since 1963, but in 1983 changes were made in its administration which are claimed by critics to have assimilated it more closely to other 'higher-tranche' (that is, less automatic) drawing rights from the IMF. The name was changed to the present one in 1988, when the scope of the occasions for which drawings could be made on the facility was widened somewhat. It applies not only to LDCs, but in recent years LDCs have done most of the drawing from it. Quantitatively it is far more important than Stabex. Hewitt cites peak years of disbursements for both, which show the ratio of CFF to Stabex payments as varying from five to nearly fifty. Dell (1985) shows that in three of the seven years ending in 1983 drawings under the CFF amounted to a third or more of all drawings from the IMF. They fell greatly after 1983, and indeed total IMF disbursements annually at the end of the 1980s were of the order (in nominal SDR terms) of the CFF disbursements alone in 1983. (CFF drawings in the peak year ending April 1983 were 3.7 billion SDRs.)

The scheme allows payments to be made to cover falls in export earnings (including from 1979 earnings from tourism and worker remittances) below trend; rises in import prices for basic foods above trend (from 1981); and 'contingencies' (the new element introduced in 1988), which are sudden movements of export or tourism earnings, worker remittances, import prices, or international interest rates, from the levels projected in any adjustment programme agreed with the IMF. The contingency element is a potentially important concession, which in part answers one of the criticisms previously made of IMF agreements. There are rather complex provisions limiting the amount (as a proportion of the drawing country's IMF quota) that can be drawn on account of each form of need (40 per cent for export earnings, 17 per cent for food-import prices, 40 per cent for contingencies), with an extra 25 per cent that can be drawn for any one of them, the aggregate upper limit being therefore 122 per cent of quota.

To draw under the CFF/CCFF has required three additional conditions to be fulfilled: there must be a balance-of-payments need; the need must be temporary and largely beyond the country's control; and the country must co-operate with the IMF to find appropriate solutions to its short-term payments problem (Hewitt, 1987). From 1983, the tests of co-operation have been tightened and codified, with further codification in 1990. Fund staff accept that it was much easier to meet the conditions up to 1983. It was intended thereafter that the very high drawings under the CFF in the wake of the world slump and the onset of the debt crisis should be reduced, with greater reliance on other IMF facilities.

The criteria for drawings under the compensatory part of the facility are now (1990) complex. The requirements become stiffer the higher the proportion of quota the member intends to draw, and the less evidence there is of 'co-operation' from the member in the past. Only those whose balance-of-payments position, apart from the shortfall identified under the scheme, is satisfactory may draw up to the full 82 per cent of quota that may potentially apply to the compensatory part. For those not in this category, even drawings up to 65 per cent of quota require an 'arrangement' (an agreement on policy measures) with the IMF (or else policies that would be regarded as meeting the conditions of an arrangement); and, if the member has not been a co-operator in the past, a review indicating good performance under an 'arrangement' (or equivalent policies) is required in addition. This is, rightly, said to involve what is known as 'conditionality' in many cases. The approach has been argued to convey the presumption that changes in policy are needed, though the 1983 statement of the policy (Dell, 1985, pp. 247-8) and the 'contingency' provision of 1988 imply that this is not necessarily so.

The CFF had in fact moved in a more and more liberal direction until 1979-83. The amount drawn by any country that could be outstanding at one time rose by successive decisions from originally 25 per cent of the country's IMF quota to 50 per cent in 1966, 75 per cent in 1975, and 100 per cent in 1979, when also limitations were removed on the *gross* amount that a country could draw within any year.

Until 1983, *readiness to co-operate in the future* was the condition of a CFF drawing so long as the country's liability to the IMF would after the drawing still be within 50 per cent of its quota. In those conditions, says Dell citing Goreux (1980), there would be only about a month between the application and the drawing if it were approved. Kumar (1989) finds an average delay of 3.85 months between the end of the shortfall year and compensation payment for all the CFF purchases from 1975 to 1985.

In the same study (covering 79 countries and 192 purchases) Kumar finds that simple average percentage 'reductions' in export-earnings instability by various indicators range from 3.4 to 5.4 per cent if each CFF 'purchase' (drawing) is added to export earnings in the relevant shortfall year or distributed between the shortfall year and the year of purchase. In most cases taking into account CFF 'repurchases' (repayments) reduces these reduction percentages slightly. G.Langlands (unpublished, personal communication, 1991), in a study of nine developing countries making purchases between 1978 and 1987 in which he uses a wider foreign-exchange-availability variable and adds each CFF purchase to this variable in the shortfall year to which it refers, finds a simple average reduction in instability of 3.4 per cent, which falls to 2.3 per cent if repurchases are included.

So how does the CCFF compare with the ideal of an insurance policy against external shocks?

Clearly payments out of the facility are not automatic, though until 1983 they went closer to being so than they do now. They are not grants as of right, like insurance payouts. Interest is charged on the amount drawn, at about 10 per cent in 1990. It is a loan repayable in three to five years, and whether to give the loan or not is a matter for IMF discretion; the statistical evidence is a necessary but not a sufficient condition. There is no insurance premium unless the IMF quota itself can be regarded as one, but interest is charged on outstanding drawings. The external shocks to which the IMF can respond through the CCFF are much wider and more rationally defined than those that permit claims under Stabex, but of course the fact that the payment is a shortish-term loan with a discretionary element makes it very different from an insurance payment.

***

Thus both the schemes depart from normal insurance principles that might seem on the face of it desirable. There can be little doubt about the deficiencies of Stabex, even though it may still be thought worthwhile. About the present state of the CCFF, opinions may differ according to how salutary one considers IMF policy pressure to be. Those who consider that the IMF generally intervenes for the country's good may not want a system of automatic compensation. Those who have doubts about the IMF's prescriptions may consider that it would be better to move to a more automatic response to requests under the compensatory part of the facility. It may be that shocks of all kinds exogenous to policy could be measured accurately enough to make the degree of exogenously generated shock the objectively defined criterion for payment.

If we start from Stabex, there seems to be a case for extending it in two ways: to expand the list of countries covered so as to include all LDCs, and to extend the part of export trade covered to include exports other than to the EC and products other than biological primary commodities, pooling export earnings from all the commodities for purposes of deciding eligibility. Extending the commodity list to minerals, especially petroleum, would admittedly open new dimensions of instability which might take very large resources to mitigate. Cover might also be extended to cover disruption due to changes in import or interest costs, or to failures of staple food production, all of which will have their effects on the external balance and on real national income.

If there were to be an ambitious system of automatic compensation, it would very probably be necessary to make it rather more like either insurance or liberal bank credit than Stabex now is: there would need to be either regular contributions or repayments. Any repayments need not be tied to a preset timetable but might be linked to a reversal of the shock that prompted the credit: the principle supposed to operate with Stabex but scarcely enforced.

If the CCFF is to be developed to make its payments more nearly automatic, or if Stabex, whose payments are already automatic, is to become much more comprehensive in dealing with exogenous shocks, there will need to be an objective way of distinguishing disturbances due to factors outside the control of the government concerned from those that follow from internal policy. International organizations can not be expected to give any government a permit in effect to increase absorption without limit in the expectation that the resulting external-payments difficulties will be mitigated by compensation.

Helleiner (1986), drawing on work by Bacha, applies a method of measuring the effects of certain external shocks (through export quantities demanded and prices, import prices, remittances from workers abroad, debt levels, and interest rates), and correspondingly of measuring the extent of the country's adjustment. If such a method could be accepted as sufficiently objective, there might be some hope that a comprehensive and automatic compensation scheme should become acceptable.

Various schemes for expanding and reforming Stabex or the CCFF are outlined and discussed in Hewitt, 1987. Alternative approaches, some of which could be regarded as reforms or extensions of Stabex or the CCFF, are discussed below.

2. Mineral-revenue stabilization funds

What is outlined here is a domestic device, but it is convenient to include it because of a similarity in purpose and concept with some of the international measures and because its effectiveness would be greatly enhanced by international support.

Minerals are generally extracted by large multinational companies who do not really have to be protected from market fluctuations and whose own expenditure within the country is unlikely to be closely related year by year to their earnings from their local mineral interests. Thus the two main reasons why marketing-board stabilization is set up for smallholder agricultural export goods (as discussed in Chapter 9) do not apply to extractors of minerals.

Instead, the important task is to prevent the fluctuations in mineral prices from disturbing public expenditure. Probably the most efficient ways of taxing mineral projects (provided certain mistakes can be avoided) are those that relate the amount taxed closely and by a rigid formula to the profitability of the project. Such methods of taxation, however, cause revenue to be particularly irregular. If government expenditure simply follows the course of revenue, it too will be highly irregular. If it is high when revenue is high, there will be great difficulty experienced in reducing it sufficiently to match revenue when revenue subsequently falls, and the effect of the irregularity may introduce a bias to over-spending.

Thus it is extremely desirable to make the course of expenditure independent of the fluctuations of revenue. This can be attempted by arranging for all the mineral revenue to be put into a specially created fund, with rules that provide that it will be paid out into ordinary government revenue only in accordance with longish-run estimates of average revenue levels. The responsible official might be required to make estimates of this average according to certain principles, to make the estimates public, and to authorize payments accordingly.

The rules will of course have to be devised so that cash is accumulated in the fund when earnings are high and the fund runs down when earnings are low. Foreign reserves will correspondingly tend to rise when mineral earnings are high (because not all the earnings are spent) and to fall when mineral earnings are low. Since it is the external balance that represents the most important constraint on spending, the method involves accumulating external balances in good times so that they can be used up in hard times.

The policy can be regarded as anti-cyclical in something like the Keynesian sense. There are budgetary surpluses and deficits deliberately incurred. But, by contrast with conventional Keynesian fiscal fine-tuning, government expenditure is set on a steady course and is *not* responding to short-term events. The approach is generalized in Chapter 13 below.

Devices more or less along these lines have been adopted by Botswana in 1973 and Papua New Guinea in 1974, in each case early in a mineral bonanza, but in the case of Botswana there are apparently no clear anti-cyclical rules controlling payments out of the fund (R.R.T.Tatedi, personal communication).

It is probably obvious that either stabilizing smallholder disposable income through a marketing board or stabilizing government expenditure through releasing mineral revenue at a steady rate is the more likely to be smoothly and successfully implemented if there is international support of an insurance type to smooth the country's aggregate-revenue fluctuations. One possible form of international support, of a comprehensive kind, is that discussed below under the heading 'inverted conditionality'. But any form of export-earnings-compensation scheme that really served a stabilizing function would help.

3. Food-supply insurance

It would be good to have a greater degree of formalization of international responsibilities in case of serious failures of staple crops, so that the response can be automatic and prompt. The FAO's early-warning system now appears to be quite effective in alerting the world to the likelihood of famine in particular places, but there is no regular arrangement for ensuring a commensurate response as soon as the warning signs are out. The government of the affected area still, it seems, has to take the initiative in asking for help, and it may postpone doing so as long as possible. Any country faced with the prospect of overall shortage is likely to benefit from the assurance of ready cash to help purchase additional food from abroad before domestic supplies become scarce. International and local transport and distribution arrangements may also be critically important, but the ready availability of cash would encourage prompt action and reduce the destabilizing effect of famine on the rest of the economy. This at any rate is an area for consideration.

4. Comprehensive shock insurance

The insurance principle might be applied to cover in an automatic manner as many as possible of the kinds of shock outside the control of policy-makers. This would represent an extension of the CCFF, with a return to a more automatic pay-out. If this is regarded as building from the present (1990) CCFF, all the kinds of change covered in the contingency part of the CCFF could be included also in the compensatory part, which would then include changes in international interest rates and in import prices in general (not only those for foodgrains, which are already included). In addition an allowance for domestic foodcrop harvest fluctuations could be included. As now applies to the individual compensatory components, there would need to be an agreed way of calculating the total effects of these changes against a base representing the average of so many past years. Because the base would thus be changing, the authorities would still have an incentive to encourage movement out of activities in which supply or demand was moving unfavourably; in addition, compensation would make up only partly for any shortfall.

There could certainly be an argument for making the protection provided by such an equivalent of the CCFF more like an insurance policy. An insurance pay-out is automatic rather than discretionary, and also non-repayable. If the cover were to be more generous than under the CCFF, contributions, corresponding to insurance premiums, would presumably have to be made. At the moment the deposit of the first tranche of the IMF quota is probably the nearest thing to an insurance premium that a country whose own currency is not in demand internationally provides as a payment for the right to draw on the IMF's facilities, but, as this is a single deposit rather than an annual contribution, it is perhaps natural that the right based upon it is simply that of shortish-term borrowing. Something a bit more like a regular insurance arrangement could be provided if the country made payments to a fund when the net effect on it of the various exogenous events counted was favourable in relation to trend and was able to draw out when the reverse was the case. If this were done, the effect would be to shift income risk from the countries covered.

There is no reason to think that any other party would bear additional risk as a result; in fact, if such a device transferred cash net to and from primary-exporters as a body when primary prices were low and high respectively, and transferred them respectively from and to an international fund otherwise held in liquid form, it would tend to reduce risk for both primary-exporters and the rest of the world. The reason for this is as follows. Insofar as payments were made to participating countries when primary prices were low *because of world recession* (and the reverse in the case of world boom), and these payments and receipts represented issue and withdrawal of SDRs or corresponding net payments from and into a fund, the device would have an anti-cyclical effect on the world economy, that is to say, it would tend to reduce fluctuations in world activity and would thus be of general benefit. If the cause of the payments in and out were variations in harvests or interest rates or prices of manufactured imports, the effect on the world economy at large would admittedly be less obviously desirable, but such an effect is in any case unlikely to affect large numbers of primary-producing countries *at the same time*, and there is no reason to think that the effect overall would be *destabilizing*. When there is a *widespread* fall in primary-export earnings, *covering a number of commodities*, as over 1974-6 and in 1980-2, this is likely to be a result of world slump rather than bad weather, and the corrective flows are likely therefore to be anticyclical. (Primary-commodity *price-stabilization* through a buffer stock is less likely to be anticyclical in that it would simply transfer spending power during a world slump to primary-exporters from primary-importers, but again there is no reason to think that it would be *destabilizing* overall on that account.)

Since what is being suggested here is a device run on different principles from the IMF's facilities, a separate institution (though not necessarily dissociated managerially from the IMF) might be set up, financed initially by international contributions, or else perhaps given the right to draw SDRs if ever inflows did not suffice to cover outflows. In principle, the administering agency could make payments, and collect dues, on objective criteria, but, as with insurance policies, the operating body might set initial conditions before the member could be enrolled. If that were the case, this device would shade into the one described below under 'inverted conditionality'.

5. Inverted conditionality

'Conditionality' is the term used by the IMF for policy conditions with which a government drawing under one of its facilities agrees to comply. The government comes to the IMF after it has got into difficulties, and the conditions imposed are supposed to be remedial.

But why wait until things have gone wrong and then impose (probably painful) correctives? Prevention is better than cure. Why not agree with the government of the country, when it is *not* in trouble, that it will abide by disciplines which, on projections from recent past experience, have a reasonable likelihood of maintaining stability, but then, if exogenous events should go wrong beyond the extent supposed in the projections, allow the country to draw freely and automatically so that it can maintain a fairly stable path of real income?

What is intended here is an arrangement with purposes that include those of the 'comprehensive shock insurance' described in section 4 above. The aim is, as there, to protect the country concerned from all forms of exogenous shock, but at the same time it is more deliberately to encourage the country's government to follow a prudent course during good times as well as bad in the face of the changes and uncertainties that it is likely to encounter. Financing might be arranged somewhat as in the outline of 'comprehensive shock insurance' above, but the cues for payments out would be not exogenous events that were to a certain degree unfavourable in relation to trend but exogenous events that were outside the limits projected when the policy rule had been formulated. (Payments into a fund might be made in correspondingly favourable circumstances.) The cues for payments out would therefore be more like those for the contingency element of the CCFF than those for the compensatory element; and it may be argued that the IMF has taken a step along this road in adding the contingency element in 1988.

The government would present a proposed policy discipline to the IMF or other administering authority for its approval. The kind of rule envisaged is principally a fiscal one, in which, for example, government expenditure is to be related to an estimate of 'permanent' revenue (as outlined in Chapter 13 below), but there might also be agreements about the exchange-rate and the overseas-payments system and about wage-adjustmemt formulas. If the authority agreed that the rule was a reasonable one, giving an 'expected' value of net inflows of reserves that was not less than zero, it would 'underwrite' the policy rule in the sense of agreeing to make whatever advances might be necessary for the rule to be maintained without serious disturbance. In ordinary circumstances the policy discipline itself would be expected to provide the stabilization required, but, if something much out of the ordinary occurred, or if the country started the process with low reserves or at the bad phase of a cycle, international support would be forthcoming.

A very modest form of what is intended in this proposal does seem to be available and has been practised recently in one or two cases by the IMF, for example with Nigeria. An 'arrangement' is made, and a precautionary standby credit is offered, to be drawn upon if certain events occur.

The effects on the world economy at large would be similar to those outlined under 'comprehensive shock insurance', and would be if anything anticyclical. As in that case, there would be a strong presumption that the effect would be to reduce the income-risk for individual LDCs while not increasing it significantly, and possibly even reducing it, for other countries and persons.

Note

As well as making much use of Hewitt, 1987. I am indebted to discussions with staff of the Commodities and Exchange and Trade Relations Departments of the IMF in August 1990.

11 Debt and borrowing

Until 1982 both governments and financial institutions seem commonly to have believed that the level of a government's international debt could be no cause for concern. If this was a reasonable position at all, it was reasonable only so long as it was generally believed. Once its truth began to be doubted, it ceased to be even arguably true. As in other similar cases in which a vast structure of claims has been built up upon confidence without provision for guarantees in case confidence falters, the end was sudden. As confidence collapsed, so did the inflow of resources. Net inflow of capital and property income to Latin America, which had averaged about 16 per cent of the region's exports of goods and services from 1973 to 1981, averaged about *minus* 25 per cent of exports from 1982 to 1986 (Griffith-Jones, 1988, p. 12).

To deal with this international problem we naturally look to the ways in which similar difficulties have been met domestically by countries with developed central-banking systems: through rescues, guarantees, last-resort lending. Is it really true that similar remedies and safeguards could not be applied internationally?

But it is worth asking first what is wrong with the present (1990) position, and what corrective or preventative action might aim to achieve. If we leave aside the view that there is no crisis and that nothing fundamentally is wrong, opinions cluster round two poles.

One is that the real trouble is the **collapse of confidence** which has virtually stopped the flow of new voluntary private lending to a number of countries. This hampers their growth. The task is principally to restore and then maintain confidence. Prime importance must therefore be given to preventing default.

The other typical opinion is that the disaster is the immediate burden which the switch to a large **outflow of resources** puts upon the debtor countries, reducing growth to about zero in many cases and increasing mortality, malnutrition, and general poverty. The task is to make whatever adjustments are necessary with the minimum disturbance to the level of consumption and investment expenditure.

These two views are not totally at variance with one another, but they differ over priorities: avoiding default in the one case, and avoiding disturbances to national expenditure on the part of the debtor countries in the other.

Eight years of remedies have prevented formal, open, permanent default, but confidence has certainly not been restored to the point of causing the voluntary inflow of private capital to resume in most of the heavily affected countries; and **negative growth**, with the inevitable suffering that accompanies it, has been the lot of many of the debtor countries for much of the 1980s. There has been an enormous loss of potential output: for Latin America as a whole, GDP per head in 1985 was almost 10 per cent *below* its 1980 level (Griffith-Jones, 1988, p. 12). No 'act of God' can be blamed for this waste. It must be put down to bad management, and inevitably we ask how things might have been, and might still be, done better.

The peculiar features of the way in which the problem has been handled are analysed by Griffith-Jones (1988). She points out that *the debtor governments have had considerable potential bargaining-power which they have failed to use.* (See below under 'a debtors' cartel'.) This is because the **rescheduling** conducted under the aegis of the IMF dealt with the debtor countries one by one. The banks, on the other hand, have formed a steering committee to deal with each major debtor country. They have acted in concert, while the debtors have been isolated. The IMF, though it has put what pressure it can on the banks for rescheduling loans, has made its own financial support to the debtors dependent on the agreement of the banks. Her argument is that these arrangements heavily biased the outcomes in favour of the creditors, who would otherwise have been in a weak position. In addition there was no representation of the many interests in the industrialized countries who stood to suffer from the depressing effects on world trade of the kind of conditions imposed on the debtor nations.

To expand or paraphrase this account: the debtors failed to understand and exploit the intrinsic strength of their position and failed to invoke their potential allies in the affluent world. The creditors' home governments were only too glad when the IMF appeared to be relieving them of the necessity of rescuing failing banks. The result was a set of arrangements disproportionately favourable to financial institutions and financial prejudices and doing little to sustain world trade and output, let alone protect the poor in the indebted nations.

This chapter deals first with possible ways of avoiding similar debt crises in future and then with possible expedients for overcoming the unmanageable indebtedness of the present. For both present and future the objective is taken as *both* to restore confidence *and* to minimize the disturbances to expenditure.

1. Relating debt-servicing obligations to commodity prices

This suggestion is taken from Powell and Gilbert (1988) and is one possible way of helping to prevent a recurrence of the traumas of the debt crisis of 1982 and since. The proposal is that loans to primary-exporter-country governments should be contracted in such a way that the servicing obligations of a debtor government are related to prices of relevant commodities.

Since this would transfer some of the risk from the debtors to the creditors, it would at first glance seem likely that the **expected true rate of interest** on such loans would be somewhat higher than the rate of interest on loans of the conventional type. However the result might well be better for both parties, as Powell and Gilbert argue; for it is improbable *a priori* that a position in which one side takes all the risk and the other none is a 'Pareto-optimum' for the parties, that is to say that there is not some bargain that would be better for at least one of them and no worse for the other. There is likely to be some **risk-sharing** deal that is better for both, just as it is likely, if one party on a desert island has all fish and no coconuts while the other has all coconuts and no fish, that some improvement for both by mutually advantageous exchange will be possible. It is likely, in other words, that there will be some combination of transfer of risk and rise of interest rate that represents an improvement for both parties from the typical loan of the present.

Furthermore, relating the servicing to commodity prices would reduce the probability of default; this in itself would reduce the risk *to the lender* and might imply that the overall increase in risk to the lender and hence in the expected price to be charged for the loan would be small or even negligible, while there were real gains in risk-reduction to the borrower. This is a further and stronger reason why the switch in the form of servicing obligations, with any associated change in the cost of borrowing, would be likely to make possible a 'Pareto-improvement' (a gain to at least one with no loss to the others).

The international institutions might in various ways encourage this form of contract.

2. Guaranteeing and moderating debt

This is a further way of seeking some protection against a recurrence of debt crises.

An international organization might act as **guarantor** for certain loans to LDC governments. It should guarantee loans up to a level, and for purposes and on terms, which it considers prudent for the borrower. Its refusal to guarantee loans would be a warning sign to both prospective lender and prospective borrower. The device would thus provide some check on excessive borrowing and some standard of what was excessive. If **unguaranteed** loans were nevertheless made and there were some fear of default on them, such fear could affect only the unguaranteed loans. The international organization concerned would have the opportunity to maintain confidence, at any time when that seemed necessary, by becoming more ready to support refinancing loans. It is worth noting that an international body, the Multilateral Investment Guarantee Agency, exists to provide similar guarantees for international direct investment.

The obvious candidate for the role of guarantor is either the IMF or the World Bank. Giving such discretion to either might not be universally popular, but they have clear technical and political qualifications for the role. Either may borrow in private capital markets (as the Bank extensively does); the obligations of either are considerd as safe as any can be; and both would have influence over LDC governments which they could exercise against any threat of default that appeared irresponsible. However, the guarantee system would of course be designed to ensure that default on the guaranteed loans was extremely rare. An advantage might be that governments could come to understandings with the IMF or the Bank about following prudent policies *before crises arise*. If they followed those policies and still got into trouble, they would then be in a strong position to seek IMF support, as under the 'contingencies' part of the CCFF, without the objectionable strings that normally go with a rescue. This possibility is obviously related to that developed in Chapter 15 under 'inverted conditionality'.

3. An international debt-management agency (DMA)

This proposal, concerned mainly with relieving the burden of existing debt to the borrowers and its insecurity to the lenders by substituting securities of lower value, has been put forward by various writers from early 1983 (listed Corden, 1989, p. 151 note; also ACFOA, 1987; Sachs, 1989) and has been discussed and analysed (e.g., by Corden, 1989). A 1988 Act of the US Congress recommended the idea for study. The DMA could in principle be a World Bank or IMF affiliate with a new brief, and it could embody also the guarantee function suggested in the previous section.

Since 1982 there has been much **part-defaulting** by governments, either explicitly (as notably by Brazil, Bolivia and Peru) or more quietly. A certain amount of LDC-government debt has been **re-sold at heavy discounts** because of doubts about how much of the servicing will actually be paid; some has been sold directly to the debtor-government itself, as in the case of Bolivia (Sachs, 1989). There have also been **debt-equity swaps**, under which a firm first buys the debt at a discount from the creditor-bank, and then sells it back, also at a discount, to the debtor-government, on the understanding that the proceeds will be invested in the debtor-country. Schemes have also been proposed (such as Feldstein, 1987) by which the burden of debt on an economy expected to grow at a reasonable rate may be much mitigated if it obtains extra funds for an initial period, sufficient, for example, to prevent its debt-servicing net of new borrowing to rise above a certain proportion of GNP. The rescheduling that took place under the aegis of the IMF, at least in the early 1980s, was much more modest than this, deferring repayments (which of course does imply additional borrowing), eventually over quite long periods, but apparently without always having any medium-term plan to minimize the sacrifice by relating servicing to annual capacity to pay, and without limiting interest rates or discounting the debt or converting it to equity.

The quest for a DMA is for an intermediary that could give the debtor countries the benefit of the low value that the market sets on their debt by **selling it back to them at a discount**, while, by avoidance of actual default, spreading the cost equitably among a particular country's creditors. Paradoxically, the creditor-banks may write down the value of their holdings without reducing the obligations of the debtors. This is a 'deadweight loss' due to uncertainty: the creditors lose without the debtors' gaining. A creditor bank acting alone will not simply tell the debtor to treat the loan as 40 per cent of its previous outstanding amount, even though it may have written the loan down to 40 per cent in its books. This is because, by so doing, it would not greatly reduce the risk of default. There might still seem to be only about a 40 per cent chance that the reduced loan would be fully serviced. The reduced loan might then have to be written down in the books to something like 16 per cent of the original value outstanding. What is required is some operation that will reduce it from a shaky loan of $100 to a secure loan of $40. The DMA, because it can deal with all of a government's debts together and, as one of the network of multilateral agencies, has considerable bargaining power with the debtor governments, might be able to make that transformation.

The DMA could also, by being itself an extremely reputable borrower, find where appropriate the funds necessary for medium-term (say five to fifteen years) **rescheduling** and adapt its lending so as to spread the burden better over time. To fulfil these functions it would probably need to have only a moderate amount (ACFOA suggests $3 billion) of paid-up capital from member governments, provided there were larger amounts of guaranteed capital (so that total capital was, say, $30 billion) that could be drawn on if necessary and there was a capacity to borrow in the markets. (ACFOA suggests that a total capital of $30 billion would make possible borrowing of $300 billion. This is the principle on which the World Bank has been financed.) It would be essentially a financial intermediary which, because of its intergovernmental status, would be able to raise capital more easily, and to take greater risks with individual acts of lending, than any private institution.

Corden (1989) considers the possible **gains and losses** to various parties arising from the establishment of an international facility which would buy LDC government debt at a discount from the financial institutions and offer it, also at a discount, to the debtor governments concerned. Precautions would be needed to prevent debtor governments from running down the value of their debt by spreading rumours of default, and to ensure that other debts were not put at a disadvantage to those reconstituted. Corden examines the possibility on various assumptions of how it would operate and what would have happened in its absence. He observes that (a) if participation by debtor governments is voluntary, they are hardly likely to lose; that (b) the same is true for the creditor financial institutions if they participate voluntarily, so long as it is provided that debt not purchased by the agency is not subordinated to debt that has been so purchased and that the price at which sale takes place is fixed in such a way that the debtor government can not reduce it by rumours of default; but that (c) the governments and institutions that guarantee the facility would be accepting risks at best if not actual expected net outlays. Sachs (1989) argues more forcefully for the establishment of a facility of this kind.

Whether those governments and institutions that represent the world community in such matters should be prepared to accept risks, and indeed expected costs, in order to relieve the debt burden on so many LDCs, as well as providing some increase of security to a number of banks, is largely a question of political values. If the question were an analogous domestic one, there would probably be much less doubt about what risks and sacrifices the community through its central bank should accept.

The **Brady Plan** of March 1989 (named after the then US Treasury Secretary) is directed at reducing the cost of debt servicing by Latin American governments. It involved in mid-1989 (*Economist*, 24 June 1989, pp. 16-17) $28.5 billion of actual contributions envisaged from governments and multilateral bodies. But it was essentially a hope or aspiration, rather than a fund or institution.

4. Multilateral discretionary lending

Mention should be made of the lending of the IMF, and also the stabilization-directed lending of the World Bank. As a development from its standby credits related to 'tranches' of a country's quota, the IMF has introduced a number of **facilities** and **funds**, from among which the CFF/CCFF has been mentioned in Chapter 10. IMF loans are usually 'conditional' (except the first, and to some extent, the second, tranche of the quota, and, until 1983, some of the borrowing under the CFF), which means that they are discretionary and that the borrower has to accept certain conditions. Generally they are short-term (until the 1970s most were for only a year); the Extended Fund Facility (EFF) of 1974 was so called because loans under it could last up to three years. The conditions, which often include certain standards of performance in the economy measured in macroeconomic aggregates, may have to be fulfilled quickly if the loan is to be renewed.

In 1980 the World Bank introduced its Structural Adjustment Loans, running from three to five years, which broke with its normal (though not exclusive) tradition of *project* lending and were designed to encourage and to make possible allocative changes considered necessary in response to various shocks, and so to mitigate the pains of stabilizing measures. These SALs are conditional, and the conditions are policy measures rather than standards of macroeconomic performance. For the first few years at least, they always followed the granting of an IMF loan to the country concerned (Körner, 1986, p. 146).

The IMF set up its own Structural Adjustment Facility (SAF) in 1986. This was designed to supplement World Bank SALs to 'low-income' countries, and allowed for repayments over up to ten years (ACFOA, 1987, p. 68). The total resources available to the SAF were SDR 2.7 billion at the end of 1989. The Extended Structural Adjustment Facility came into operation in 1988 for the lowest low-income countries, allowing drawings up to 150 per cent of quota, or in extreme circumstances up to 350 per cent of quota, and expected to command resources of up to SDR 6 billion.

Thus, while the IMF in the 1980s, with its emphasis on 'supply-side measures', has moved increasingly towards a concern with allocation, the Bank has concerned itself more and more with stabilization. The **terms of loans** for essentially stabilizing purposes have also become longer.

In the **rescheduling of debt**, the IMF has acted as a kind of broker and catalyst, not as a financial intermediary. Its total disbursements under all heads in the year ending April 1989 amounted to only SDR 2.7 billion (in striking contrast to SDR 10.3 billion at current prices six years earlier). The function of an *intermediary* in rescheduling and in reducing debts, in order to render them less burdensome and more secure (as discussed in the previous section), is not fulfilled by the IMF or the World Bank.

Critics of the Fund's objectives of quickly reducing expenditure and imports and expanding export quantities complain that the measures which it favours increase the tendency to recession in the world economy and to slump in primary-product prices, that their effects on the most vulnerable sections of the poor are usually bad, increasing for example the mortality and malnutrition of children (an assertion documented in Cornia *et al.*, 1987), and that they are often politically disruptive. This dissent from the IMF approach is at least partly over values, though the values may be set by the scope of the formal functions and the level of funding of the IMF rather than by any policy decision on the part of those administering it. This difference over values should not be confused with differences of technical judgement over whether the trade-oriented and market-oriented reforms imposed by the Bank and Fund (and abhorred for example by Körner *et al.*, 1986, pp. 169 ff.) are favourable to current income and growth.

5. A debtors' cartel

Should the large-debtor governments combine to threaten that they will default completely on their debts unless acceptable forms of discounting and rescheduling are offered to them? To paraphrase a saying: 'If someone owes you a hundred dollars and can't pay, he has a problem; if he owes you a hundred billion dollars and can't pay, you have a problem.' The Latin American and OPEC debtors, say, and the Philippines, Côte d'Ivoire, and a few others, might direct their threat of default against the private creditors only. Morally they might argue that the debt crisis is at least as much the banks' fault as their own; or more generally that it is the fault of those who run the world financial system and gave them bad counsel, and that therefore the financial system or the world should pay the cost; after all, there was little if any advice to discourage what now seems crazily excessive borrowing.

If the threat had actually to be brought into effect, no penalty that most of those governments would suffer, in the form of lost access to financial markets, would be likely to outweigh the gain from being relieved of debts that may exceed their own annual GNPs. You can afford to finance an awful lot of three-month trade credit out of repudiated debt that is larger than your annual import bill. The prudential and moral case for concerted debtor action that might extend to default is made by Griffin (1988). But what might be hoped for is that, in the face of such a threat, final default would not be necessary. An adequately financed debt-management intermediary, of the kind outlined above, might be set up by the rich nations to make tolerable and equitable rescheduling deals and so save the face of the system.

It is not out of the question that one debtor country acting alone should be able to carry through a policy of deliberate default, in desperate self-protection or in order to bargain for better terms. Indeed Bolivia could be regarded as a case in which this happened (Sachs, 1989, pp. 20-2). Bolivia in 1985 had been regarded as one of the most unpromising of debtors. In its stabilization programme of that year (see Chapter 19), it refused to service its debt to the banks. Its refusal was eventually tolerated by the IMF, to which its other stabilization measures were generally welcome, and which made an arrangement with it on the supposition that its debt arrears would continue. In 1988 the government managed to cancel about half its debt by direct purchase from the creditors at 11 per cent of nominal value. Costa Rica (Sachs, 1989, p. 22) also defaulted with impunity while it was undertaking an orthodox stabilization propgramme. Other countries, however, such as Peru under Garcia, have limited their debt-servicing in a half-hearted way, only to be pushed back into line later by IMF and other international pressure. The comparison suggests that it pays to default single-mindedly and to do so in conjuction with other policies of which the IMF would approve.

A credible joint threat of *general* default might still be made, but the fact that it has not done so eight years after the debt crisis first broke is not a favourable sign.

Part 5
Domestic Instruments of Stabilization

12 Stabilization targets and instruments

As macroeconomic policy became a subject of systematic analysis in the wake of the Keynesian revolution, it was recognized that there were several different objectives or **targets** of concern and several different kinds of **instrument** that could be used to attain them.

Targets were commonly thought of at one stage as two: internal and external balance. 'Internal balance' meant full employment without inflation, and 'external balance' meant a sustainable balance of external payments. Later it came to be accepted that internal balance was better seen as two targets: full employment ('internal balance' in the sense used in this book) on the one hand, and stable prices on the other.

In the 1970s, after some countries (though not at first many LDCs) had ceased to control their exchange rates directly to the extent of pegging them against some other currency, the balance of payments in itself could cease to be a matter of great concern in such countries, but it became recognized as important to influence the behaviour of the exchange rate in order to contribute to price stability or to the steady maintenance of the employment and income target, or alternatively later to a particular *pattern* of output and employment. In place of the external balance, the exchange rate itself might be thought of as a target variable.

Any one of the instruments used (such as fiscal policy) was quite likely to have a bearing on all three target variables. Tinbergen (1952) began to sort out the general relationship of the **target variables** (variables in which the targets were expressed) and **instrument variables.**

Where the target variables had to be manipulated separately to reach their target values and the instrument variables could be thought of as being controllable independently of one another, Tinbergen propounded the rule that there must be at least as many instruments as targets if all targets were to be attained. In Chapter 5, esaw some of the implications of this rule with the help of the IS-LM-BB diagrams. The relationship can be thought of as a series of equations:

$$Y_1 = a_0 + a_1X_1 + a_2X_2 + a_3X_3$$

$$Y_2 = b_0 + b_1X_1 + b_2X_2 + b_3X_3$$

$$Y_3 = c_0 + c_1X_1 + c_2X_2 + c_3X_3$$

where Y_1, Y_2, Y_3, are the target variables;
X_1, X_2, X_3, are the instrument variables;
a, b, and c, coefficients are constants.

In order to achieve any given set of values for Y_1, Y_2, and Y_3, we shall have to set particular values for each of X_1, X_2, and X_3. In other words, we shall need to control three instrument variables in order to achieve three targets.

If it is believed that one of the three target variables will set itself at the right level without intervention, then we are in effect requiring the system of control to determine only two target-variable values, and two instruments may be enough.

To get any set of target values, it would seem that we need simultaneously to set appropriately the values of the required number of instrument variables.

Assignment

Because this adjustment of everything simultaneously demands knowledge of all the coefficients (which we shall almost certainly not have) and may not fit well with the legal rights and obligations of various government agencies or with the power structure, it may seem convenient to 'assign' one target variable to one instrument variable, so that those managing the one instrument simply pursue the one target, by trial and error if necessary.

The possible deficiencies in 'assignment' where more than one target variable has to be controlled are illustrated by Swan's (1955) exposition of the conditions for obtaining internal and external balance under pegged exchange rates.

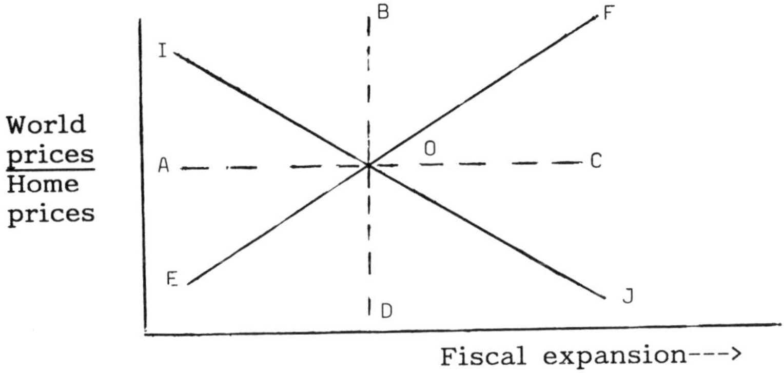

Figure 12.1 Two targets and two instruments: internal and external balance through fiscal and exchange-rate manipulation

In Figure 12.1, the instrument variables, represented on the axes, are the exchange rate or tariff level on the vertical axis (in fact it is probably more satisfactory to think of it as the *real* exchange rate) and the fiscal stance on the horizontal axis. IJ represents the locus of combinations of these two instrument variables that give internal balance (the employment target and price stability), and EF represents the locus of combinations that give external balance (the desired external-payments position).

The economy may find itself off one or both of EF and IJ. To reach O, the position of both internal and external balance, there is at any time a unique pair of values of fiscal stance and real exchange rate required.

When the instrument variables and underlying conditions set a point upward and to the right of IJ, there is excessive inflation; when they set a point below and to the left of IJ, there is excessive unemployment.

When they set a point upward and to the left of EF, there is excessive external surplus; when they set a point below and to the right of EF, there is excessive external deficit.

Thus IOF gives inflation and external surplus;
FOJ gives inflation and external deficit;
IOE gives unemployment and external surplus;
EOJ gives unemployment and external deficit.

Suppose that internal balance is assigned to fiscal policy, so that the finance ministry is instructed to expand when the economy is in unemployment (below and to the left of IJ) and to contract when it is inflationary (above and to the right of IJ).

And suppose that external balance is assigned to exchange-rate policy, so that the central bank is instructed to devalue the exchange rate when the economy is in external deficit (below and to the right of EF) and to appreciate when it is in external surplus (above and to the left of EF).

Since both instruments should be moving the economy in the direction of O in every case, this assignment would give the right directions of response when the economy was in each of the areas BOF, COJ, DOE, and AOI, but the wrong direction of response of one or other instrument when the economy was in any of the other four areas, IOB, FOC, JOD and EOA.

The closer IJ is to the vertical and EF to the horizontal, the less important the areas of wrong response are likely to be. With IJ vertical and EF horizontal, these areas of wrong response disappear, and the assignment under consideration would seem to do exactly what is required. Similarly, if EF had been vertical and IJ horizontal, the reverse assignment to the one we have considered would be precisely right. But these cases assume away the problem of multiple relationships among the variables.

Assignment, it would seem, is inevitably a less-than-ideal response where these multiple relationships exist. But, given its political and administrative convenience and the conceptual simplification that it introduces to thought about stabilization issues, it may nevertheless be worth adopting, provided the right (that is, the least wrong) assignment can be found. The right assignment would presumably be one in which each target variable was fairly highly responsive to the instrument variable to which it was assigned and relatively unresponsive to others.

As this problem has begun to be realized, various investigators have tried to explore analytically and empirically which target seemed most responsive to which instrument.

King's model: an assignment, based on the monetary approach, for a liberal, small-open economy

For example, J.R.King (1979), in his study of Kenya in 1963-73, sets against each other two models.

One (the 'Output Determination Model', ODM) is a version of 'Old Keynesianism' in which real output (and hence employment) could be influenced by fiscal surpluses or deficits, by the interest rate through its effect on private investment, and by the exchange rate through its effect on real export and import flows. Excessive fiscal deficits or monetary expansion or an unduly low exchange rate would be inflationary. The external balance in this model would also be affected by fiscal and interest-rate stance and by the exchange rate.

The second model ('Model of Financial Flows', MFF) is primarily expressed in money terms. It assumes that real income is generally determined by underlying real resources, not by short-term policy. The implication of the model is that, *under a pegged exchange rate*, domestic-credit expansion (i.e., monetary expansion not covered by net inflows of money from abroad) has a direct effect on the external balance (but not on the domestic price level or on real income), and that the changes in exchange rate have a direct effect on the domestic price level (but not on the external balance or on real income). *Without the pegged exchange rate*, and on the assumption that the external balance would have adjusted itself to the necessary extent through market-determined floating, the model would indicate that domestic monetary expansion, instead of producing an external deficit, would cause the exchange rate to fall and hence the domestic price level to rise.

King's attempt to project the implications of the MFF to Kenya from 1963 to 1973 and to see how closely they fitted with what actually happened suggests a close association between domestic credit expansion and external balance and (for given world price levels) between exchange rate and domestic price level, as the model would suppose, but they suggest none of the associations that might be expected from the ODM. King says that this may indicate that the domestic component of the money supply can be used effectively to control external balance and the exchange rate to control the price level. Real income is assumed to look after itself, except in the very short run when it can be disturbed by sudden shocks such as moves that would require big general-price-level changes; and the only measures suggested for stabilizing income and employment are those that will avoid such sudden shocks (for example, one might guess, by providing for continuous, rather than spasmodic, adjustment).

If this assignment of instruments to targets is right for Kenya, it may be because of certain characteristics of the Kenyan economy at the time, such as a high degree of 'small-openness' in structure (in the sense that prices of both importables and exportables will be determined largely from abroad so long as markets are allowed to operate), a measure of liberalism in policy (permitting adjustment of many prices in response to market pressures and hence adjustment of domestic to world prices), and a fairly low level of labour organization (so that wages too respond downwards as well as upwards to market pressures). Other countries may not display the same responses; nevertheless a number would appear to be similar in structure (in being highly 'small-open') and in the weakness of labour organization, even if they are less liberal over foreign and domestic trade policy. The plausibility of the model, coupled with its apparent fit with Kenyan evidence in the period, suggests that it may have wider application among the more liberal of the LDC economies which are principally dependent for exports on primary commodities.

The emphasis on manipulation of domestic credit may seem strange in countries that have no very large bond market. In many cases the chief source of domestic credit will be money created to meet a fiscal deficit (and not covered by additional foreign borrowing). Domestic-credit expansion and fiscal deficit will in practice mean much the same in such a case. In terms of practical policy it may be decisions on *fiscal* expansion that increase or reduce external current-account deficits.

King's MFF model, with its policy implications, is based on the 'monetary approach to the balance of payments' expounded in Chapter 6.

A small-open-economy assignment emphasizing fiscal discipline and stabilizing real expenditure

Suppose that the background conditions for King's model apply: an approximation to the 'small-open' structure and a sufficiently liberal regime. This will mean that the external balance can be regulated by domestic credit, and the price level to a large extent through the exchange rate. Suppose it is also true that domestic credit is very largely dependent on the fiscal surplus or deficit. In that case the fiscal deficit can be taken as determining the external deficit.

In principle, then, fiscal balance will imply external balance. But fluctuations in export earnings may bring fluctuations in fiscal revenue. If fiscal balance is to be maintained year by year, this will mean reductions in government expenditure in years in which export earnings are low. In such years, however, disposable income and hence expenditure of the public are also likely to be low. So maintaining fiscal balance in a country heavily dependent on primary exports is likely to mean the acceptance of fluctuations in national expenditure and employment. (King's formal analysis ignores this problem by supposing that real output will return to full-capacity level through the adjustment of prices, though he recognizes that in fact measures that require a large price change will be disturbing to output.)

One possible way of countering this is to aim to balance the fiscal budget, and hence to balance the external account, *not year by year but over a longer term*, running surpluses when export earnings and hence government revenue and private spending-power are high, and running deficits when they are low. Government expenditure may be geared to some trend or 'permanent' 'expected' value of revenue, following the medium-term direction of revenue but along a smoothed path. Unless there is a sudden and permanent break between the past and the future, a rule to implement this principle should be attainable, making it possible both to keep nominal government expenditure stable and to satisfy the external-balance requirement. (Practical methods for helping both to do this and to stabilize the level of nominal private expenditure are discussed in Section 2 of Chapter 10 and Section 3 of Chapter 9 respectively.)

There remains the matter of stabilizing real output *at close to the full-capacity level*. This can in principle be achieved by controlling money-wages. Constant money-wages for a higher level of nominal expenditure, or lower money-wages for a constant level of nominal expenditure, mean a higher level of real expenditure.

Money-wages also serve largely to influence the domestic component of prices. The foreign component of prices may be controlled by the exchange rate.

The assignment that is emerging is therefore not quite as neat as we might like. Pairs of instruments seem to be combining to look after each target. There are two tasks that we might address: to make it formally consistent with the n-targets-n-instruments framework (which would seem to be required if it is to work), and to make it operable with comparatively simple administrative rules.

One way of seeing this assignment is that there are five targets, some of which may be treated as intermediate towards further targets. One is a **sustainable external balance** (over the medium term); this is achieved by a fiscal account which is balanced (over the medium term). A second target is a domestic component of prices that would maintain **full-capacity output at the trend levels** of private expenditure and fiscal expenditure needed to fulfil the first target; this is achieved by control of money-wages. A third target is the **foreign component of prices that will maintain price stability** given the domestic component of prices needed to fulfil the second target; this is achieved by control of the exchange rate. The fourth and fifth targets are to keep nominal **expenditure, public and private, on a smooth path**; this is achieved by following an appropriate time-pattern of government spending, and if necessary introducing devices to encourage smooth time-patterns of private spending, within the average limit set by the need to fulfil the first target. It will be seen that, if the second target has been fulfilled, this will also serve to maintain full-capacity output. Fiscal policy is therefore seen as three instruments: one setting the average *level* of government expenditure, a second setting its *time-path*, and a third instrument to *smooth private expenditure*. The third might be embodied in a producer-price-stabilization scheme or some other variable-tax-like device.

Provided each of these instruments could actually be manoeuvred, a fairly simple administrative arrangement could be devised to apply them. To take the fifth target and instrument first, automatic private-expenditure-stabilizing devices might be set up and left to function autonomously. The first and fourth instruments would be applied by the budgetary authority's relating nominal expenditure in each year to the trend or 'permanent' level of nominal revenue. Wages, the second instrument, would be controlled with a view to approaching a full-capacity level of output and, once it was reached, to keeping nominal domestic labour costs per unit output stable. The exchange rate, the third instrument, would be set at a level that equates supply and demand for foreign exchange, and then adjusted to keep the overall price level stable given the movement in the wage level. This is the assignment headed 'small-open fiscal' in the table of assignments on p. 180.

In practice it could not be quite as simple as this, even if there were no political and distributional problems in using the instruments in this way, and even if the SOE characteristics applied in extreme form to the economy concerned. As explained later, in Chapter 13, there may be reasons for modifying somewhat the fiscal rule. Furthermore, the country's import or export prices may rise or fall not only because of general changes in the world price level but also because of changes in the relative prices of particular imports and exports that happen to be important in its own trade. It may then be desirable for the prices of foreign goods in general within the country's trade basket to rise or fall somewhat, and the desire for overall domestic price stability and full-capacity output will therefore dictate correspondingly lower or higher rises in money-wages. Similarly, the domestic component of prices may need to change, temporarily or for longer, for reasons such as harvest fluctuations and natural disasters. But cognitively these are not particularly hard adjustments to make, whatever their political difficulties.

By contrast with King's model, this one may be described as Keynesian. It does not, like his, rely on rapid spontaneous wage and price adjustments to maintain real output at full-capacity level.

The transition to large-open-economy assignments

The important new element introduced as we pass from small-open economies to large-open economies is the relevance of the relationship between the exchange rate and the money-wage rate for international competitiveness, and hence for output in the short term and trade-related growth in the longer term. Co-ordination of the two instruments will be needed. Even if the initial relationship is right, it does not follow that manipulating each of them to keep its relevant component of prices constant *on average* will keep a right relationship *between the particular prices that are relevant for competitiveness.* If the import-price index has risen simply because the oil price has risen (where oil or a close substitute is not produced within the country), appreciation of the exchange rate to the extent necessary to keep average domestic prices constant (given the money-wage level) may unduly reduce the competitiveness of the country's export and import-competing goods. Furthermore, if control of wages and hence the domestic component of prices is less than perfect, the use of the exchange rate faces a dilemma between higher inflation and lower competitiveness. Holding the foreign component of prices constant, or lowering it, when the domestic component has risen is not necessarily the best choice.

With that major reservation, however, the assignment outlined in the previous section may remain a useful starting-point. Though fluctuations in revenue may not be as great as in the typical economy to which the SOE model is applied, it may still make sense to balance the expenditure to an estimate of 'permanent' revenue (with the modifications introduced in Chapter 13). But now wages and the exchange rate will have to be manipulated in a co-ordinated manner to maintain not only price stability but also competitiveness. It is now not only their average effect on prices but the ratio between them that is important. If it is not possible to achieve both price stability and competitiveness, some decision must be made as to which should take precedence. In practice, even those countries that come closest to fitting the SOE model may need to pay some such attention to the real exchange rate.

The assignments for economies to which LOE models are applied may happen to require further modifications for other reasons. First, there may be significant possibilities of domestic-credit creation independently of fiscal deficits; and this may require some direct or indirect targeting of monetary variables above and beyond the fiscal discipline. Second, the country's currency may be held by non-residents and internationally traded, so that the interest rate may influence the external short-term capital account. If both these features are present, the conditions for pursuing macroeconomic policy are similar to those for typical industrialized countries. Then, if the foreign-exchange regime is reasonably liberal, an assignment such as that designated in the schema below as Meade II, using fiscal, monetary and wage policy as the three instruments, may be appropriate.

Possible assignments of targets to instruments

Below is a schema of possible assignments of macroeconomic targets to instruments. (Note that the exchange rate may be either target or instrument.)

Target variables are denoted by:

- Y, output (and employment)
- P, domestic price level
- P_d, domestic component of price level
- P_f, foreign component of price level
- B, external balance
- E, exchange rate.
- G_t, time-path of output sold to government
- C_t, time-path of output sold to private sector

Instrument variables are denoted by:

- f, fiscal balance
- f_a, average level of fiscal spending
- f_t, time-path of fiscal spending
- m, money supply (or domestic credit)
- w, wage level (in nominal terms)
- e, exchange rate
- r, import tariff or restraint
- t, tax-like device to stabilize private spending

An arrow from an instrument to a target means that the instrument is assigned to that target. Arrows pointing two ways about a target mean that that variable is allowed to find its own level.

'Old Keynesian' is an attempt to stylize what would probably have been a fairly standard approach in the 1960s; for New Cambridge, the British version of structuralism briefly outlined in Chapter 7, see Cuthbertson, 1979; Meade I and II are attempts to approximate the 'New Keynesian' assignments implied in Meade, 1978 and 1983 respectively; 'Friedman' and 'International Monetarist' are outlined in Chapter 5; King, expounded in this chapter, is related to Polak, 1957, and fits the pegged-exchange-rate version of King, 1979; 'small-open fiscal' is described above and forms the initial framework used in Chapters 13 to 15 below for a primary-export-dominated economy, with modifications for large-open economies and other variants.

Old Keynesian	New Cambridge	Meade I	Meade II
f(m) --> Y	f --> B	f,m--> P	f --> P
e --> B	r --> Y	w --> Y	w --> Y
w --> P	<--P-->	e --> B	m --> E
			<--B-->

Friedman

m --> P

<--Y-->

<--B-->

International Monetarist

m --> E --> P

(E being an indicator of appropriate level of m)

<--Y-->

<--B-->

King

m --> B

e --> P

<--Y-->

Small-open fiscal

f_a ------------> B

e --> P_f -----> P

w --> P_d

f_t --> G_t -----> Y

t --> C_t

The upper row of four sets of assignments, and the last one, can all be described as Keynesian in that all take real income as a target variable and all use fiscal policy as an instrument. The other three can be called Monetarist; none of them takes real income as a target variable, and all use money supply or domestic credit as an instrument. They are generally inclined to be less interventionist, having only one or two target variables to be controlled. 'Old Keynesian', 'Meade I' and 'Friedman' could be described as closed-economy assignments. They do not ignore the external sector, but they treat it as separable from considerations of domestic prices and output. The other five are open-economy assignments. 'Meade II' is designed for an LOE. The remaining three (including 'International Monetarist', in spite of the fact that it has been applied in industrialized countries) can be classed as SOE assignments, supposing that the world price level affects the domestic price level but not domestic output. All, except 'Friedman', 'Meade II', and 'International Monetarist', are understood as devised for situations where exchange rates are either pegged or else managed other than simply by monetary policy.

A lesson from this variety of possible assignments is to keep an open mind: to recognize that there are a number of possible instruments and that each may have its effects on several target variables; and to try to choose a working system (not necessarily a pure and simple assignment of targets to instruments one-to-one) that best fits the structure of the economy and the political and administrative conditions in which policy is carried out. *Unthinking* acceptance of instability of expenditure, of inflation, or of external-payments crises, as inevitable, and of exchange or import controls, or 'the money supply', as the sole or essential instrument, is to be discouraged.

Stabilization is inevitably linked with the question of trade and exchange controls. Controls are often introduced in response to the failure of stabilization policy. Removing them may require some alternative means of doing the job (usually over external payments) to which they are supposed to be directed.

13 Fiscal rules

This chapter and the next three aim to build up a framework for stabilization policy that makes use of several of the main instruments that governments have available for the purpose: **government revenue and expenditure** (the 'fiscal balance'), the **exchange rate**, **wage policies**, and **interest-rate policies.** The existence of each of the four potential instruments demands some decision on how it will be used or not used. The aims are to stabilize the path of real expenditure, preferably under conditions of 'internal balance' in the labour market; to stabilize the general level of prices; and to maintain a survivable external account. These stabilization objectives must be obtained in such a way as not to be inconsistent with other economic objectives, such as an acceptable distribution of income and wealth, efficient allocation of resources, and growth. All must also obviously be consistent with the political constraints that happen to exist.

Chapter 12 showed the practical reasons why 'assignment' of particular targets to particular instruments is attractive, and why on the other hand it may easily give unsatisfactory results if practised in pure form. There were examples of a number of different assignments that have been recommended for various circumstances and under various beliefs about how the world works and various ideological preferences.

The problem of these next chapters is to propose an approach which is sufficiently flexible to take account of the diversity of developing countries while at the same time saying something reasonably precise and usable. Behind the discussion of each instrument is the fiscally-based SOE model (pp. 174-6, last scheme on p. 180) outlined in the previous chapter, but each proceeds from there to make adjustments for economies fitting better with LOE models or diverging in other ways from the simple initial assumptions.

In the case of each of the instruments, the preference is for finding an appropriate rule that can be followed in such a way as to reduce the operation of year-to-year and month-to-month discretion. The reason is partly that set out at the end of Chapter 5 in the discussion of what survives out of Monetarist approaches. There are intrinsic difficulties about responding satisfactorily to immediate events without a longer-term perspective. A sea pilot does much better with a chart that shows him where he is going than if he has to rely simply on avoiding those rocks that he can see. Added to this is human weakness. Rules that have been fixed independently of the pressures of a particular week or month may provide protection against the temptation to do what is temporarily convenient. However, any resilient rule must contain within it procedures for adjustment as the longer-term perspective changes. And there may be occasions when the best-framed rule will have to be abandoned.

The present chapter proposes an approach to a simple fiscal rule, but it has to be said that the simplicity of the method as it is first presented supposes a rather simple economy in which autonomous fluctuations in the domestically generated component of investment are unimportant. Nevertheless, certain features of the approach will be relevant in other circumstances as well.

For setting or routinely adjusting the exchange rate, Chapter 14 suggests several different procedures that might be applied in different conditions, mainly according to the type of economy and to how effective the control of other instruments is.

Chapter 15 offers the general outline of a rule for varying those money-wage rates that are under government control or influence. The details would have to depend on institutions and politics, but the approach, a compromise between a maintained and an adjustable real wage, may have general usefulness.

Chapter 16 considers interest rates, emphasizing their role in allocation and domestic stability and its possible conflict with their role in external balance, but touching only lightly on the difficulties over the domestic role of monetary policy in an economy with highly developed financial markets.

Treating fiscal balance first is appropriate. The fiscal variables are among the instruments that are most directly under government control. A lesson that seems to emerge in Chapter 18 below, from consideration of a series of failed and successful attempts at stabilization, is that fiscal control is crucial. Without it, stability is elusive. To view the matter another way: getting the external balance right is a prerequisite for the stabilities that are of direct importance to welfare: those of real expenditure and the price level. And it will be the fiscal balance that will have a direct and strong impact on the external balance.

Thus, if an instrument and a target have to be separated out as of first priority, it should probably be the fiscal balance and the external balance. This chapter deals with the external position as being 'assigned' to the fiscal balance, regardless of what the settings of the other instruments are. But it also attempts to suggest how, in spite of that assignment, real expenditure may be kept on a roughly stable path. The *value* of expenditure on that path and its rate of growth will be determined by, among other factors, the closeness with which the spectrum of real wage rates enables internal balance to be achieved, the closeness of interest rates to the marginal rate of productivity of investment, and the closeness with which the exchange rate reflects the marginal productivity of foreign exchange: all factors affecting the allocation, or the completeness of deployment, of productive resources.

A stabilizing rule for fiscal policy

The fiscal rule propounded here is most directly relevant to an economy heavily dominated by primary exports, which are as a result its main source of instability. In the rule's derivation, autonomous fluctuations in investment arising from within the economy are assumed away, and (for its more complex version) inward private flows of investment are treated as controllable or predictable.

We need first to explain the use of the term 'permanent' in this context. When we talk of 'permanent' revenue we mean the **expected or trend value of revenue** for any particular year. We imagine some kind of regression against time of past actual figures for revenue, from which a trend can be projected into the the year under consideration. This trend will be adjusted, for purposes of the projections, by the use of any knowledge of how it is likely to be altered in the future. For example, if there are new revenue measures for next year their expected proceeds will need to be added to whatever the expected figure would otherwise be. The 'permanent revenue' for next year is thus an 'average' estimate of what revenue could be expected next year if next year were normal or average: the projected revenue with purely cyclical and random factors eliminated. There is of course no one right way of estimating such a trend value, and judgement has to be exercised, but a fairly simple method of doing so that would probably be workable most of the time could be precisely laid down.

Mansfield (1980) propounds a norm for **budgetary neutrality** in what he calls an 'export economy'. He defines a neutral budget as one in which expenditure has a prescribed relationship to trend-revenue rather than to actual revenue. Tanzi (1982) similarly writes of fiscal equilibrium as a state in which there is equality between 'permanent' revenue and 'permanent' expenditure. In Mansfield's terms, larger expenditure than is consistent with a neutral budget would be regarded as **expansionary** and smaller expenditure as **contractionary.** In order to smooth the income level, as he points out, it may well be appropriate for expenditure to be expansionary precisely when actual revenue is below trend and contractionary when actual revenue is above trend: what seems like the reverse of a spend-as-you-earn balanced-budget rule.

What Mansfield describes as an export economy is apparently one heavily dominated by primary-export earnings and subject to instability principally because of variations in export proceeds, the condition mentioned in the first paragraph of this section. It is an economy in which there is no domestic capital market, so that government borrowing is either from overseas or from the official monetary institutions and there is negligible or unchanging commercial-bank credit. Hence it is reasonable to suppose that government borrowing from the institutions is the sole source of domestic-credit creation, so that monetary policy does not exist separately from fiscal policy.

Such a model probably fits *reasonably* closely to the reality of a number of national economies in Africa and the Pacific. It will be referred to here as a **PED (primary-export-dominated)** economy. The economies that fit it closely may also show similarities to the SOE model, but the features of that model are not immediately relevant to the concerns of this chapter.

Given access to resources from overseas, this economy can increase its income and domestic product by drawing into the 'organized' sector workers from traditional activities, or from underemployment and unemployment, and giving them things to do which are more highly rewarded and in which they are, statistically at least, more productive. Indeed, in spite of cynicism about what sometimes happens, there are generally socially useful activities, many of an investment character, to which such people can be led through government outlays. Because marginal supplies of so many kinds of good come from overseas in any case, and there are plenty of potential recruits for low-skilled activities in the organized sector at wages close to those currently existing, expansion of this kind may have little effect on the domestic price level so long as adequate claims on foreign resources and goods are available; the excess demand is in that case simply directed overseas.

The limit to short-term expansion in this kind of economy is therefore set very simply by its **access to foreign exchange**. What can really be aspired to by short-term stabilization policy is not a 'full-employment' level of output in the sense supposed by the elementary Keynesian textbooks, in which the limit is set by the size of the workforce, but a level at which full use is made of the foreign-exchange resources 'permanently' available. Realizing the real value of the output level that can consistently be achieved with these foreign-exchange resources, and the wage-employment needed to produce it, depends on the wage rate, the exchange rate, and other variables affecting allocation. Because the gross inflow of these foreign-exchange resources varies considerably from year to year, adjusting absorption year by year to these injections will produce an unstable path of real income and expenditure, with the well-known and politically important pain that goes with such instability. Stability requires leaning against the wind of year-to-year export earnings, necessarily using either accumulated foreign reserves or the capacity for accommodating loans from abroad in order to allow for periods of basic external deficit.

The model that follows relies largely on accounting identities to produce a fairly simple set of fiscal rules for stabilizing real national expenditure in this hypothetical, but for many cases fairly realistic, PED economy.

The **price level** is assumed to be constant, kept so if necessary with the help of small movements of the exchange rate which compensate for any general world inflation. So real and nominal magnitudes are identical. This assumption, however, could be abandoned: with a fixed exchange rate and the possibility of domestic inflation, we could use the same equations but they would refer to nominal magnitudes only, and the trend values used would probably have to be derived in real terms and converted to nominal terms by rates of inflation, known or assumed.

Domestic product is assumed to adjust rapidly in Keynesian fashion to an equilibrium in which it equals aggregate demand for value-added of domestic origin; income is simply domestic product *minus* net remittances overseas of property income; so that, at that equilibrium,

$$Y = C + I + G + X - M - Ya \qquad (13.1)$$

where Y is income
C is private consumption
I is private investment
G is government expenditure on goods and services and net government overseas interest payments
X is exports
M is imports
Ya is net remittances overseas of property income

Income is divided between private disposable income and the part of income withheld by the government. Private disposable income may be either privately consumed or privately saved. The part retained by the government may be thought of as government revenue (T); it is taxation, together with other tax-like levies such as net private contributions to stabilization funds, *plus* any profits of government enterprises not transferred to private people, *minus* net transfers (taken to include any net interest payments) from government to private residents.

$$Y = C + S + T \qquad (13.2)$$

where S is private saving
T is government tax, tax-like revenue, and retained government profits, *minus* net transfers from government to residents

The **external balance** is made up as follows:

$$B = X - M - Y_a + F_G + F_P \qquad (13.3)$$

where B is the 'basic' surplus on the external balance
F_G is net 'autonomous' flows to government of capital and transfers from overseas
F_P is net 'autonomous' flows to private residents of capital and transfers from overseas

It is assumed that **private investment** in the economy is the sum of private saving and net flows to private people of capital and transfers from overseas:

$$I = S + F_P \qquad (13.4)$$

This is a convenient simplifying behavioural assumption, reflecting the supposition that in this economy internally generated fluctuations in private investment are unimportant.

At the income equilibrium, from (13.1) and (13.2),

$$I + G + X - M - Ya = S + T \qquad (13.5)$$

From (13.4) and (13.5),

$$F_P + X - M - Ya = T - G$$

So,

$$X - M + F_P + F_G - Ya = T + F_G - G \qquad (13.6)$$

So, from (13.3) and (13.6),

$$B = T + F_G - G \qquad (13.7)$$

The left side of this equation is the **'basic' surplus on the external balance**; the right side is **net domestic government lending.** To put it the other way, the 'basic' deficit on the external balance will be equal to net domestic government borrowing. This result depends on the behavioural assumption of equation (13.4) and will be more nearly true the more true that equation is. On our other assumption that domestic government borrowing other than from the central bank is negligible, the right side of (13.7) is the 'cash surplus' in the government budget, and on the further assumption that there is zero or constant commercial-bank credit, this equals **domestic credit contraction.**

Stabilization in this economy will need to meet two requirements to which fiscal policy is relevant.

The first requirement is that **the basic external balance, B, should average zero over the longer term.** If the basic balance averages *below* zero, reserves will tend to disappear and there may be difficulty in obtaining the accommodating receipts from overseas that will often be necessary to cover particular periods of high basic deficit. On the other hand, though keeping the basic surplus at an average *above* zero could be useful for a while, eventually a satisfactory level of reserves would presumably be reached. There would then be no further reason for averaging a surplus, and to do so would waste income opportunities.

To keep B averaging zero, the right side of (13.7), namely net domestic government lending or borrowing, would also need to average zero. This means that the *trend* in G would need to follow in an absolute sense the *trend* in $(T + F_G)$.

One way in which G could fulfil this requirement would be simply to be equal each year to the trend value of $(T + F_G)$. This is the standard of fiscal neutrality in the sense in which Mansfield uses the term. But this possibility leads us into considering the second requirement.

The second requirement then can be taken as that of **stabilizing the path of national expenditure.** Stabilizing it does not imply keeping it level, with no growth. We would hope and expect that the path should be a rising one. But we want as far as possible a smooth rise, not one that from time to time goes into reverse or even suffers very radical drops in its rate of increase. It is probably a good enough approximation to say that we need to keep steady the growth-path of $(C + I + G)$.

From (13.4),

$$C + I + G \quad = \quad C + S + F_P + G,$$

so that the second objective will be fulfilled if we stabilize $(C + S + F_P + G)$.

How can this be done? $(C + S)$ is disposable private income. Any instability in $(F_P + G)$ will contribute to making $(C + S)$ unstable; so part of the instability in $(C + S)$ can be eliminated if we can provide a stable $(F_P + G)$. But there will also be a tendency of *disposable personal income* to fluctuate *with export earnings*, independently of government spending and foreign investment, because of both direct and multiplier effects. The source of this variation will be mainly the fluctuation in what may be regarded as the rents or surplus accruing to residents who hold property in the export industries.

Some of those holding such property will be foreign-based firms and the government. This is likely to be the case with property in mineral extraction. We consider below the effects of fluctuation in this segment of the rents. The government will take its share into account as part of 'revenue' (T). The private foreign firm may vary its investment in response to the level of returns, but if so that will be taken into account in F_P, which we also deal with separately below. The part of the rents whose variation will be directly important to personal spending is the part that accrues to smallholders and other resident personal owners of export-commodity-producing firms. These owners will probably be mainly in agricultural commodities.

Thus any device that can stabilize the earnings of resident smallholders, co-operatives, and other enterprises, in the export-crop industries will help to stabilize (C + S). The obvious device for doing this is that often adopted (though sometimes abused) of marketing boards (referred to in Chapter 9) that pay less than the market price in high-price times and more in low-price times. The net levies of such boards act in the same way as taxes and are positive items in T; the net payments out are negative items in T. If the boards aim, as they reasonably should, to balance their accounts with the producers over the longer term, their transactions should be assumed to have no effect on the trend value of T. Formulas for calculating levies and bonuses may be devised which make the expected effect on T's trend value zero.

Ideally we should like to stabilize not the producer-price of the commodities but the **disposable income** of those with property in their means of production. Where, however, the instability in receipts is mainly due to instability in prices for the products (together with any supply-response to prices), stabilizing producer prices will probably go a long way to stabilizing disposable income. Instability in income that is due to weather or natural disasters in cropping areas would of course need to be dealt with differently. For political reasons, producer-price stabilization is never likely to be complete, even in aspiration, but for the present purpose it would seem that the further such stabilization can go the better.

If, through such marketing institutions, disposable personal income of residents who have property rights in the export-commodity industries can be roughly stabilized, the further stabilization of the growth-path of expenditure reduces largely to stabilizing (F_P + G). If the latter comprises the main direct sources of instability *other than* export earnings, stabilizing its path will also complete the task of stabilizing residents' disposable income, that is of stabilizing (C + S). Stabilizing (F_P + G) *and* crop-producer receipts will thus go far toward stabilizing (C + S + F_P + G), which is the same by hypothesis as stabilizing national expenditure.

If F_P, that is foreign capital inflows to the private sector, could be assumed to be changing at a steady rate, then the problem would be simply to stabilize the growth-path of G, and this, by the rule set out above under the first requirement, would entail its following the trend value of (T + F_G), that is the sum of 'revenue' and net capital inflow and tranfers to the government. But F_P may well vary quite considerably, and sometimes quite reasonable estimates can be made, in advance, of a change in its value that is likely to take place in a particular year. Such will be the case if there is to be a major new mining project. The critical figures in incoming investment in such cases will be the investments of a small number of large companies, and there will be no great difficulty for the government to obtain, well before the event, some idea of the orders of magnitude of these investments and of their patterns over time.

If we stick to the objective of stabilizing domestic expenditure subject to the external-payments condition laid down in the first rule, then, if F_P in each year were at its trend value, G would have simply to adopt the trend value of (T + F_G). So, if we use an asterisk to denote the trend value of a variable for any year, the combined rule might be expressed as

$$G_t = T_t^* + F_{Gt}^* \qquad (13.8)$$

There are probably circumstances in which this might serve well enough as the stabilizing rule, and a government that had overcome the political obstacles to following such a rule might well congratulate itself. However, this might not always be the *ideal* rule for stabilizing expenditure, even in the comparatively simple economy of the model.

Insofar as F_P is *above* its trend value, G should in compensation fall to the same extent *below* the trend value of (T + F_G), and, insofar as F_P is *below* its trend value, G should rise to the same extent *above* the trend value of $(T + F_G)$.

So, with an asterisk again denoting a trend-value, the combined stabilization rule for government spending in year t could be written:

$$G_t = T_t^* + F_{Gt}^* + F_{Pt}^* - F_{Pt} \quad (13.9)$$

Note that government spending has been defined to include government's net overseas interest bill.

It is worth repeating that a further condition required by the reasoning for this rule to perform well in the PED economy is that there should be a scheme for stabilizing crop producers' earnings.

Practical application

Can a rule involving so much estimation of trends be useful? It is of course easy enough to estimate a trend from past information; the doubt must lie in whether the past is a good enough predictor of the future, and, if it is, what form of trend is relevant.

For the trend in government foreign borrowing, there is no great problem because the government itself decides what that will be. (It is of course deliberate long-term borrowing that is under consideration. The kind of short-term borrowing that might be needed to accommodate a temporary external deficit has been left out of the model, and the external balance is dealt with in its 'basic' form.)

For foreign private capital inflows, the authorities cannot hope to estimate a trend that gives a reliable forecast. But it may be of some value to take account of any major departure from normal that can be known in advance. The 'normal' may be quite small in relation to the differences that arise from major projects, and it is these differences that are of interest. Admittedly it may be impractical to make government expenditures closely responsive to these differences, but it does no harm to have the ideal rule explicit so that any reasonable nods in its direction may be made. Ignoring foreign private capital flows will not, it would seem, *create difficulties over the external balance*; its direct effect on output and expenditure, and hence on employment, is what matters. If not compensated for by inverse movements of government expenditures, it may have the effect that workers are drawn out of the traditional sector during an investment boom only to be thrown back when construction is completed. If compensatory action by government to smooth the level of construction activities is possible, that will probably reduce inconvenience and pain.

The nub of the practical difficulty, however, is over export earnings and the revenue derived from them. Governments of oil-exporting countries, estimating at the end of 1980 the real-purchasing-power trends in their oil revenues by any regression method known to man, would have derived projections that would turn out wildly wrong from 1982 onward and possibly to the end of time. Moreover, what has happened to oil prices since 1980 has been a surprise, not only to governments of oil-exporting countries but also to oil-company executives and other sages, whom, with the benefit of hindsight, we might expect to have known better. Economic wisdom, insofar as it existed, appears to have provided no adequate corrective to naive projection.

Reflection on this example suggests that the indicator described here as a trend-value should rather be an arithmetic average over a certain past period, in real-purchasing-power terms of course. The average would need to be corrected for every budget period. Alternatively the implied projection could be made by decomposing the past history of export earnings and the revenue derived from them into the part that is due to changes in **prices** and **transient supply conditions** (such as the weather), on the one hand, and the part that is due to changes in **productive capacity**, on the other. The use of a trend might be relevant to the latter part, and an arithmetic mean, for want of anything better, to the former.

Errors will undoubtedly occur. As with a business or household, however, it is better to act prudently on the best information available than to live as if there were no tomorrow.

It might also be hoped that a PED-economy government which adopted a reasonable fiscal rule and adhered to it within several percentage points might be given automatically whatever compensatory finance it needed from the international community in order to tide it over patches of large external deficit, whether or not these appeared with hindsight to be merely the swings below a correctly estimated trend (a version of the possibility discussed at the end of Chapter 10 under the heading 'inverted conditionality'). To this end, the staff of the IMF or relevant international institution might discuss with officials of PED-country governments what an appropriate fiscal rule would be.

Perhaps the preoccupation of recent academic writing with monetary variables has left too little attention for the fiscal rules that may have a much more direct and obvious message than monetary rules for the decisions that governments deliberately and consciously take. For the oil-exporting countries, Morgan (1979), in a study based on the period from 1972 to 1978, observes that fiscal policy is the primary determinant of domestic liquidity and aggregate domestic demand and concludes that it must be the primary instrument of demand management. For the six oil-exporting countries for which he has data, he finds a close relationship between the *domestic* component of budget deficits and domestic liquidity expansion.

Chapter 18 discusses the case of Papua New Guinea since the mid-1970s, which has to a point tried to apply a fiscal rule along the lines discussed here, supporting it with the kind of domestic stabilization devices discussed in Section 3 of Chapter 9 and Section 2 of Chapter 10.

Adapting the rule for wider application

How far should a similar rule be applied in economies which differ from the simple PED model?

A first possible difference is the existence of significant **government borrowing from the domestic non-bank public or variable commercial-bank credit.** Then the domestic government deficit, the right side of equation (13.7), will not correspond necessarily to domestic credit creation.

Where instability is still largely from export receipts and not from domestically generated investment, a similar government spending rule would probably be appropriate. If it were judged from experience that, through government borrowing from the public, saved resources that would not otherwise be deployed or that would be used less valuably in the private sector could be used for public purposes, the rule in equation (13.9) might be varied by allowing that government expenditure, G_t, might exceed

$[\, T_t^* + F_{Gt}^* + F_{Pt}^* - F_{Pt} \,]$

by an agreed proportion of trend national income, the agreed proportion being the amount by which domestic investment was expected to be (or was thought capable of being usefully suppressed) below the sum of S_t and F_{Pt}:

$$G_t = T_t^* + F_{Gt}^* + F_{Pt}^* - F_{Pt} + qY_t^* \qquad (13.10)$$

where q is the agreed proportion of trend income.

Such a rule still supposes that private investment of domestic origin is stable under stable domestic-savings rates. If that is not believed to be so, it would seem that an ideal rule would need to be more complex. In practice, to maintain the discipline, it might still be best to work on the foundation of a fiscal rule such as that expressed in (13.9), with the qualification of a further factor, which would require a reduction in G, or an increase in borrowing from the domestic public, in any year in which this domestic component of investment was thought likely (in the absence of additional government borrowing) to be above its trend relationship to ($S + F_P$) (and the opposite when it was thought likely to be below).

This begins to look more like fine-tuning and hence to border on the discretionary, with the attendant risks that discipline will be abandoned; but there is a difference between a purely discretionary regime and one that starts with a rigid formula but gives a certain margin of variation that (even perhaps by law) must be argued for on certain specific grounds.

An alternative, which in the early 1980s would have been regarded as orthodox, would be to use **domestic credit** rather than the fiscal balance as the instrument to be controlled. To act in a stabilizing and compensating way, domestic credit could be raised and lowered in inverse relationship to foreign reserves, so tending to keep the money supply, which is the sum of the two by definition, on a steady path. This is essentially an open-economy adaptation of the Friedman rule.

The difficulties and weaknesses of such a rule, however, have already been mentioned. There are several possible definitions of the money supply, and hence of domestic credit. If a base-money definition is used, this is not likely to solve the problem raised in the previous paragraph because it would seem *a priori* likely that, when the domestic component of investment is unstable, the relationship of base money (M0) to the money supply on any of its more usual definitions will also be unstable (bank credit, for example, will be unstable), and, for that if for no other reason, the ratio of base money to income will be unstable. Government spending would appear to have a more direct, immediate, and predictable, impact on short-run income than any operationally definable version of the money supply or domestic credit. So there does seem to be a good case for making the rule fundamentally a fiscal one.

Fiscal discipline: summary

This chapter cannot of course propound an operational rule that would fit every case. The reader might, however, ponder the five main points which it is trying to convey.

(a) Fiscal discipline is necessary.

(b) To be effective, that discipline needs to be embodied in a rule of some sort, with only a limited semi-discretionary element whose use is required to be justified by certain defined criteria.

(c) However, the rule should not necessarily involve the balancing of the budget (or the maintenance of a constant surplus or deficit) year by year, which would be destabilizing to real income and domestic expenditure in many circumstances, especially in primary-export-dominated economies.

(d) Hence the rule for government expenditure should be expressed in terms of the recent-average or trend levels of certain variables, with an additional element to allow for the projected departure of certain other variables from their average or trend values.

(e) Such rational and responsible fiscal policies are much more likely to be practised, and their desired welfare effects realized, if the international community finds ways of insuring or backstopping them.

14 Choosing exchange-rate regimes and policies

Main circumstances bearing on the choice

At least four characteristics of an economy may have a bearing on the choice of exchange-rate regime and policy: two relating to what might be called the structure of the economy and two to policy or institutions.

The first is **whether the country's currency is widely held and traded internationally.** This is not likely to be the case unless it is convertible, that is, unless at least overseas-resident holders of the currency are permitted to sell it for other currencies, at a declared or a market price, to the authority that issues it. *Most* LDCs do not treat their currencies as convertible, and most of their currencies are not held and traded internationally. This is important for the mechanics of exchange-rate fixing and manipulation. Changing interest rates on domestic-currency securities is not likely to be of immediate use for influencing the exchange rate in these circumstances. The condition under which 'sterilized intervention' in foreign-exchange markets may be effective (that securities in home currencies are not perfect substitutes for those in foreign currencies) will then be fulfilled, and in fact all such intervention in inconvertible-currency countries may probably be regarded as 'sterilized'. Where currencies are not widely held internationally, they have seldom (until the mid-1980s) been market-floated, and a common view has been that market-floating would in this case lead to very unstable rates through the lack of stabilizing short-term currency flows.

The second is **whether the economy conforms fairly closely to the small-open-economy model**, that is whether there is little substitution between imports and home-produced goods and between exports and home-consumed goods. The more this is true, the more important are the domestic-price effects, and the less important the shifting and competitiveness effects, of exchange-rate changes. If the economy approximates to the SOE model *and* non-tradable-goods prices adjust fairly quickly in proportion to tradable-goods prices, the effects on competitiveness and shifting may be disregarded.

The third is **whether the market for foreign exchange is liberal or regulated.** Where foreign exchange is allocated mainly by controls rather than price, the domestic-price-level and competitiveness effects of any change in the official exchange rate are likely to be reduced and may be 'perverse'; the less effective the controls in a regulated system (and hence the greater the prevalence of 'black' or 'parallel' markets), the less important the position of the official exchange rate will be.

The fourth is **whether fiscal and wage disciplines are effective.** Where they are not, the exchange rate may have to bear part of the burden (of adjustment needed to maintain competitiveness or the external balance) that ideally these other instruments might carry. This argues against a fixed rate and makes it hard or painful to use the exchange rate actively to control domestic prices.

Range and classification of exchange-rate regimes

There are various possible classifications of the diversity of exchange-rate regimes that has existed at the end of the 1980s.

IMF publications (see table reproduced with footnotes in Collier and Joshi, 1989, p. 98, and a more recent version, *IFS*, August 1990, reproduced as Table 14.4 at the end of this chapter) divide them primarily into 'pegged', 'flexibility limited', and 'more flexible'. Collier and Joshi (1989) divide them primarily into 'fixed exchange rate', 'intermediate regimes', and 'independent float'. Here we shall divide them between 'pegged' and 'floating'. 'Pegged', as with the IMF, here covers those having a published rate or band at any one time, but, unlike the IMF's 'pegged' category, includes those that allow the peg to move ('crawl') within low and published rates of change or according to published indicators.

We subdivide pegged systems into 'fixed', 'jumping' and 'crawling'; and floating systems into 'managed' and 'market'.

'Managed floating' covers regimes that are in fact being deliberately held at determined rates or within narrow bands at any one time, presumably with direct market intervention and generally with exchange controls, but do not have these rates or bands published (see Collier and Joshi, 1989).

<table>
<tr><th colspan="2">Here</th><th colspan="2">IMF</th><th colspan="2">Collier & Joshi</th></tr>
<tr><td rowspan="5">Pegged</td><td>Fixed</td><td rowspan="3">Pegged</td><td rowspan="2">Single</td><td colspan="2">Fixed</td></tr>
<tr><td rowspan="3">Jumping</td><td rowspan="5">Inter-mediate regimes</td><td rowspan="3">Adjustable peg</td></tr>
<tr><td>Composite</td></tr>
<tr><td colspan="2">Flexibility limited</td></tr>
<tr><td>Crawling</td><td rowspan="3">More flexible</td><td>Adjusted by indi-cators</td><td>Crawling peg rule-based</td></tr>
<tr><td rowspan="2">Floating</td><td>Managed</td><td>Managed floating</td><td>Crawling peg discret-ionary</td></tr>
<tr><td>Market</td><td>Indepen-dently floating</td><td colspan="2">Independent float</td></tr>
</table>

Table 14.1 Exchange-rate regimes classified

'Market floating' includes those in which the state intervenes in currency markets, or manipulates interest rates, with a view to influencing the exchange rate, and also those (if any there be) in which the state leaves the market to look after itself ('dirty' and 'clean' floats respectively).

The number of footnotes necessary in the IMF's table (as reproduced in Collier and Joshi, 1989) is a sign of how complex the picture has become and how hard it is to draw boundaries. Table 14.1 is an attempt to give equivalences across the three taxonomies. The distinction between managed and independent (market) floats is especially dubious. It seems possible that the IMF's division, followed here, is made at least partly by treating as 'managed' those with comprehensive controls for allocating foreign exchange.

The IMF's class 'flexibility limited' refers to the arrangements made by four Gulf states and by the members of the Exchange Rate Mechanism of the European Monetary System. Though both operate under special rules, they can probably best be treated as having jumping or adjustable pegs. Currencies that can be regarded as on fixed pegs are mostly or entirely pegged to a single currency and are thus probably a subset of the single-currency peggers, as Table 14.1 implies.

Pegged or floating rates

Our definition implies that **pegged** rates exist if an authority at any time declares a rate at which, or a range of rates within which, or a rule for setting the rate at which, it will buy and sell its currency against another or a basket of others. All other rates are **floating**. Because of the volatility of rates among the major currencies, the basket peg, rather than the single-currency peg, has become increasingly popular since the end of the Bretton Woods system.

On this definition, the distinction between pegged and floating rates is not the same as that between fixed and flexible rates. Pegged rates may be flexible (as with jumping or crawling pegs). Pegged rates are here divided into fixed, jumping and crawling. 'Jumping' is used to describe those fixed for longish periods and consequently likely to change when they do so by rather large amounts. 'Crawling' is used to describe rates which, though pegged at any time, are frequently changing by small amounts, within limits to the rate of change, or by rules, that are publicly known.

Pegged rates may be pegged to one currency or to a basket. They may be pegged within a more or less narrow range of rates. The peg may be a more or less stable or flexible one, and if flexible it may move more or less according to a known rule (as in the case of a crawling peg that is known to be adjusting in such a way as to keep the real exchange rate roughly constant). Moreover a number of countries run multiple exchange rates, with some kinds of transaction subject to one and some to another. Often in such cases the rates applying to government and food imports and those that exporters receive have been higher (more 'appreciated', that is more favourable to the government as importer and more unfavourable to the exporters) than those for other imports.

A **market-floating rate** may in principle be on a free or 'clean' float or on a 'dirty' float (which implies some deliberate government influence or targeting). In any apparently free rate, there is always room for doubt over whether targeted intervention is completely absent. A government (or central bank) must buy or hold some foreign currency itself, and it is impossible for outsiders to say whether its intervention in the market is completely unmotivated by a desire to limit movements of the rate. A completely free rate would make it impossible to use the rate to help stabilize domestic prices, a use which might be especially relevant in economies approaching the SOE pattern. A common view is that there are no really free market-floaters, other than for brief periods.

Commitment to a peg is potentially a restriction on an authority's freedom of action. This is extreme under a fixed peg, as discussed below. Under a jumping peg the authority may sometimes be faced (if it wants to maintain its reserve position without either the distortions introduced by restrictions or a reduction in expenditure) with the need to make a big change in the peg, especially if it cannot use interest rates to achieve temporary capital movements. On the other hand, if disturbances in the 'basic' (current-and-long-term-capital) balance are not extreme, a declared rate may help to stabilize the perceived environment for trade and discourage speculative capital movements that might be destabilizing. So a jumping (or even a fixed) peg may be of advantage over the crawling variety in some circumstances (reasonable fiscal and wage discipline and a fairly stable external environment) and not in others.

In principle a market-float, if it is free, would allow a government to forget about the balance of payments and its reserve position. But then the effects of exchange-rate movements on the domestic economy would need to be considered, and, if the rate fluctuated unduly, this could be disturbing: to trade, to output and to the price level. A really free float, or any market-float, has been widely held (work reviewed in Wickham, 1985) to be unworkable for most LDCs, on the ground that, because their currencies are not widely traded, there is no scope for speculative capital movements of a stabilizing kind to steady the rate in case there should be temporary fluctuations in the basic external account. This may or may not be a serious objection in practice; black-market ('parallel') rates do not appear to be specially volatile, as we should expect to be the case if this argument were valid; but, be that as it may, market-floats in LDCs seem to have been rare before 1980. However, by 1990, the IMF (see Table 14.4) listed fourteen developing and seven industrialized states as 'independently floating'. Most of these floats have probably been far from completely free, however. The UK, for a time in the late 1980s was manifestly aiming at a particular exchange rate against the mark, and the large depreciation of the dollar against the yen and mark over 1985-7 followed concern about America's current-account deficit and its competitiveness in tradables.

One potentially free-floating device is that used in Ghana and Nigeria from 1986 (and briefly tried by Uganda and Zambia) by which *a large part* of the country's foreign-exchange receipts is auctioned to the highest bidder. By the end of 1987 both countries were using the auction to allocate all the foreign exchange going from the monetary authorities to the private sector and were treating the auction rate as the official rate. It is clear, however, that in Nigeria there was some deliberate phasing of the amounts sold to help stabilize the rate, and indeed it could scarcely have been otherwise (information from Lee Geok Lian, personal communications). Increasing the proportion sold in this way might be a means of moving toward a fairly clean float and finding out, before too much had been committed, whether it was likely to prove unduly destabilizing to the rate. Since these do seem to be market-floats in the usual understanding of the term, the fact that these experiments and others have persisted for several years does throw doubt on the conventional wisdom.

In spite of the increasing number of developing countries that have come to be classified as independent (market) floaters over the 1980s, we are generally dealing with either pegs or managed floats. In either case some decision has to be made about the appropriate level of the rate at any time. The fixing of the rate may, under a peg or managed float, be market-led: it may in other words be fixed at a level which is believed most likely to equate the 'permanent' supply and demand for foreign exchange, and be changed as that level appears to change; but that is still a policy decision rather then 'letting the market decide', and even the market-float, as the term is used here, may be deliberately influenced, with rate targets or ranges in mind.

Managed floating is followed by quite a large number of developing countries (20 or more in 1990), many of them exporters of manufactures fitting the LOE rather than the SOE model. It has the advantages and the disadvantages of flexibility. It does not preclude the use of the rate to influence domestic prices or indeed as an instrument for any of the possible macroeconomic purposes. In principle, it allows action against undue rate fluctuation, while permitting whatever rate changes help to achieve external balance. On the other side, it does not give the element of certainty to traders and investors offered by fixed pegs, and within limits by crawling pegs, and for much of the time by jumping pegs. Also it does not itself supply any discipline; some principle would need to be devised to fix *how* the rate would be managed.

Pegs: fixed, jumping, or crawling?

At the opposite extreme to a free float is a **peg intended to be fixed for all time.** Provided the intention is believed, this provides many of the advantages of operating in a single currency with that partner. The uncertainty due to currency fluctuations is taken out of trade and investment involving the partner country. Needless to say, this is most valuable when the partner is overwhelmingly important in the country's own overseas trade and investment. Keeping a fixed peg is also administratively simple. A number of developing countries maintain fixed pegs against the US dollar, and a number in West Africa, the CFA (Communauté Financière Africaine) countries, against the French franc. The CFA states are treated for many purposes as having a single currency with France, and some countries such as Panama have actually used US dollars as currency. As the relative importance of the US in world trade falls and the CFA countries diversify their trading connections, whatever advantages there are in these arrangements diminish.

A further potential advantage is that the inflation rate in the pegged-currency country is to a large extent tied to that of the country or group to whose currency it is pegged, but this is so only as long as trade barriers are not interposed; and the fixed peg is often likely to make the erection of such barriers inevitable as a compensation for reduced competitiveness or an escape from external-payments difficulties.

This leads us to the disadvantages of a fixed peg. It means that one instrument of possible adjustment is removed. Any change, 'real' or 'monetary', that raises domestic costs in the country in relation to those of the partner has the potential for reducing its competitiveness internationally, so depressing its output and moving it towards external deficit. All this is likely to inspire trade restrictions, and, where the arrangement permits, exchange restrictions, the politics of which work like a ratchet to prevent their coming down later.

The strongest case for a fixed peg, either to a single currency or to a basket, would exist where the economy fitted the SOE model fairly closely, and institutions existed (such as wage-fixing practices) to make the prices of nontradables responsive to the prices of tradables. Then the fixed peg to an appropriate currency would help to stabilize prices without raising the need to worry about its effects on competitiveness. Where sufficient internal discipline existed, however, for this benefit to be realized, there could be a case for allowing crawling appreciation to counteract the effect of imported inflation.

A **crawling peg** (or a managed float) has the advantage over a fixed peg that a rate which seems to have been wrongly fixed or to need adjustment can be moved, and over a jumping peg that it can be moved without (a) the embarrassment attending a major change of policy, (b) the disturbance to trade and production arising from a large relative-price shift, and (c) the speculative losses that the authority may incur from a large devaluation that the market is expecting. A crawling peg, as propounded by John Williamson (1965), is a peg that is allowed to move frequently, but with each move so small, say over the course of any week, that any speculative gain to a member of the public that might come from correctly predicting a jump would be outweighed by the cost of switching from one currency to another and back. (Williamson recognizes that, if the exchange-rate movement in any one direction that has to take place each week, or whatever the period is between shifts, is above a certain amount, a crawling peg on these terms is not workable.) Provided that the condition specified for its success holds, a crawling peg would also seem to have advantages, in reducing the risks of trade, over an attempt at a managed float (which by definition would have no declared rate). It has been thought especially relevant in a country of moderate to high (but probably not 'hyper') inflation, when considerable depreciation is necessary to retain competitiveness under liberal or semi-liberal trade policy.

Finding the best rate

For any given (a) pattern of productive capacity and of expenditure, (b) set of world prices for imports and exports, (c) level of the domestic component of prices in home currency, and (d) level of net inward long-term capital movement, we can suppose that there is an exchange rate which will, in the absence of duties, subsidies or restrictions on trade, equate 'permanent' supply of foreign exchange with 'permanent' demand for it when output is at the highest level consistent with say 'non-accelerating inflation'. The standard liberal view is that it is an exchange rate defined in some such terms as these that will be best as a means of guiding allocation within the economy, and that distribution objectives, and certain particular allocation objectives (such as that of providing for public and merit goods), are best pursued by other measures. Those other measures will of course themselves help to fix the background conditions (the pattern of expenditure for example) that determine which exchange rate is optimal. The use of the term 'permanent' signifies, as in Chapter 13, that short-term capital movements, and seasonal or cyclical or extraordinary variations in trade and long-term capital flows, are to be ignored.

The reason for defining the optimum exchange rate in such market-clearing terms is that, if the rate is above one so defined, so that there is unsatisfied demand for foreign exchange, there is a presumption that **foreign exchange is being allocated to uses in which it is less productive than in some of those to which it is not allocated**, and also that **domestic resources which could more productively be directed to exports or import-competing goods are being directed to non-tradable goods and services.** It is true that, in case of such under-pricing of foreign exchange, illegal markets provide a part-corrective, but the correction is only partial (unless *all* ultimate purchases and sales proceeds of goods traded internationally go through illegal markets), and in that case it still seems highly undesirable both (a) to dissipate national income as rewards to 'rent-seeking' individuals whose only claim to gratitude is that they have privileged access to foreign exchange and (b) to outlaw activities which are useful and which, if the official exchange rate were rationally fixed, would be perfectly legal. Added to this is the fact that a rate which is markedly 'non-market-clearing' **requires political and bureaucratic decisions on allocation** which, even if they were attempted as conscientiously as possible, could not be made without delay and administrative cost or with more than a fraction of the knowledge needed for determining what allocation is efficient, and which are open in fact to favouritism and corruption: in other words, for exploitation of the masses.

Probably a market-clearing rate can only be found by trial and error, and the conditions that make it the 'right' rate may be constantly changing. Small errors, however, may not matter greatly, and a rate that has served consistently with tolerably liberal policies may not be too far wrong. Where liberalization is being attempted from a position in which the rate is clearly too high, as is probably the case with many LDCs today, the Ghana solution of auctioning a part of the foreign exchange may serve to give guidance. The part auctioned may be gradually increased, and perhaps the official rate brought ever closer to the auctioned rate, until a single rate is reached.

This kind of trial-and-error procedure may be appropriate in the course of a major restructuring of prices across the economy. Such adjustments are never without their short-term costs, however. Hence the resistance to attempting them.

Varying the rate

It is a different question what rule should be adopted for varying the rate in more normal times when it has not been obviously far wrong in the past but various kinds of shock impinge. The answer depends to a considerable extent on the source and permanence of the shock (Lipschitz, 1984), and on the extent to which it is believed that moving or fixing the exchange rate is likely to move or to fix the prices of nontradables (which is in turn related to the character of the economy, SOE or LOE, and to the degree and mode of control exercised over wages).

The shock may be a 'real' one, which can be taken to mean that it is a change in productive capacity, or in the pattern of demand within the country, or in world prices of its imports or exports. The alternative is a 'monetary' shock, which is taken to cover a change of demand in money terms. Either kind of shock may be permanent or temporary, though inevitably it is difficult to decide which.

As regards the effects of the exchange-rate change, there are two extreme possibilities.

Case one is that the change effected in tradable-goods (T) prices produces **a prompt and equal change in nontradable-goods (NT) prices.** In such a case the exchange rate would be an ideal device for price stabilization. An *appreciation* would depress the price level, and, provided the real value of expenditure was held constant (the nominal value appropriately falling), there is no reason to think that either real output or the external balance would be adversely affected by the change. *Depreciation*, however, would not in this case make it possible to achieve a given objective in the external current account at any higher level of output than could be obtained by simple fiscal or monetary contraction, since there would be no resultant switching effect. If real expenditure were maintained, the only effect of the devaluation would be to raise the price level. This supposed response of NT prices could be regarded as the implied assumption behind the assignments in Chapter 12 labelled 'King' and 'International Monetarist'.

The other extreme assumption, case two, is that the **NT prices are unaffected** by the exchange-rate change. In this case *appreciation*, with constant real expenditure, would depress supply of, and increase demand for, T goods, pushing the external current account towards deficit. Unless expenditure in real terms were increased (which would worsen the external current account further), output would also probably be depressed, the outcome depending on a Marshall-Lerner-type elasticity condition. In this case, however, *depreciation* would tend to raise supply of, and to reduce demand for, T goods, and as a result any desired level of output could be maintained at a lower level of real expenditure than before, and therefore at a 'better' position in the external current account.

Case one seems likely to be more nearly true in a country approaching the SOE model, with indexation of wages to the price level, or, even more so, to the *projected* price level. Where this is approximately true, a fixed peg might be acceptable for long periods, and indeed crawling appreciation might be a useful weapon for suppressing the domestic inflation that might otherwise come about in response to rises in world prices.

Case two will be more nearly true in a country fitting the LOE model (with exports including significant manufactures or tourism, and with domestic substitutes for manufactured imports), especially if foreign trade forms a small proportion of national output (as in India or the US). Then depreciation might be used to prevent or reduce a fall in the external balance arising from increased real demand, or alternatively to prevent or reduce a fall in output that would otherwise arise from measures taken to reduce domestic expenditure for the purpose of supporting the external balance. It would in this case be all the more relevant if the domestic component of prices or government spending was out of control and there was no available method for curbing it.

Indexing for a constant real exchange rate

What has been said has a bearing on the question **whether the exchange rate should be routinely adjusted ('indexed') to keep the *real* exchange rate constant.** Such a rule might be justified on the ground that its application would serve to keep constant the degree of competitiveness of domestic exports and import-competing goods. This rule has been criticized, however, on the ground that it removes the 'nominal anchor' from the price system (Adams & Gros, 1986). That objection is relevant in case one, but less so the more the real situation approximates to case two (perhaps in Brazil or Korea or a liberalized India). Through much of the 1960s and 1970s Brazil in fact followed such a rule, apparently in recognition of the fact that the domestic component of prices was indeed likely to be out of control and that an attempt to use the exchange rate as an anchor for prices would depress output and worsen the external balance. By contrast, Argentina, Chile and Uruguay, within the period 1978-82, did try to use the exchange rate as an anchor for prices at a time of substantial inflation to which no other promising remedy was applied. The resulting depression of output and loss of credibility of the policy led to its abandonment in each case.

Lipschitz (1984), generally supported by Adams and Gros (1986), implies moreover that a rule for appreciating or depreciating to maintain a constant real exchange rate is appropriate in general only when the shock, as well as being permanent, is 'monetary' rather than 'real'. If there is a rise in the price of imports, this will register as a fall in the real exchange rate, but appreciating in response (as a constant-real-exchange-rate rule would demand) will aggravate any resulting payments problems and also further depress output (which may or may not be depressed in any case by the rise in import prices according to the elasticity of demand for the imports affected). Conversely, a permanent fall in capacity in the export industry, without any change in the terms of trade, may require a fall in real expenditure, as well perhaps as a real depreciation, and the constant-REER rule would not lead to this response.

A closely related point is made by Collier and Joshi (1989) when they point out that, for the SOE, a given set of changes may easily move the ratio of NT to exportable prices in one direction and of NT to importable prices in the other. An SOE that exports tin and imports oil may find that an oil-price rise and related world recession (which reduces the price of tin) lowers its price ratio of NT to importables but raises its price ratio of NT to exportables. Then the REER, as calculated by multiplying the nominal EER by the consumer-price index and dividing it by a (foreign-currency) import-price index, will probably show a fall (depreciation), whereas, if division is by the export-price index, it will show a rise (appreciation). Since the consumer-price index will be affected by the price of importables rather than that of exportables, finding the REER by dividing by a combined export-import price index will probably also show an appreciation, at least if the fall in export prices and the rise in import prices are of similar proportions. But, in response, neither an appreciation of the nominal EER (which would tend if anything to increase consumption of oil and to reduce production of tin) nor a depreciation (whose switching effects, though in the right direction, would probably be small and slow and be overtaken by NT price rises before they had produced much change) would probably be appropriate. The closer we go to an SOE, the less useful indexing the exchange rate by the usual measure of the REER will be.

In general, where there is a permanent 'real' shock, the appropriate response includes some change in real expenditure. An exchange-rate depreciation may sometimes be a valuable addition in the case of a negative income-shock, mitigating the ill-effects on output of the reduction in real expenditure, but if so a reduction in the rate of growth of money wages would fulfil a similar role and would have the advantage of tending to lower, rather than raise, the rate of growth of prices.

Even where the constant-real-exchange-rate rule might be appropriate, it is still worth remembering that, if the real exchange rate originally fixed had been at an inappropriate level, striving to maintain it would be the wrong response and might aggravate the difficulties. Moreover, a once appropriate real rate might be rendered inappropriate by real changes (Lipschitz, 1984; Adams and Gros, 1986).

To summarize: when there is an adverse movement in the external balance, the choice is (a) to do nothing, (b) devaluation, (c) reduction in the money wage, or (d) fiscal-monetary restraint (which may be combined with devaluation or with money-wage manipulation). If the change appears to be temporary and is one against which the fiscal discipline (see Chapter 13) has provided, or for which acceptable foreign accommodation can be obtained, the best response is to do nothing. Otherwise, the less the responsiveness of trade flows to relative prices (that is, the less the switching effects of devaluation), the less eligible is exchange-rate depreciation, which tends to be inflationary, in comparison with fiscal restraint, which does not. In fact, wage restraint, which may be combined with the fiscal restraint, may be used to exercise any switching effect that devaluation might have, and thus, like devaluation, to mitigate the depressing effect of the fiscal restraint on output, but without devaluation's tendency to raise prices.

If, however, the source of the shock that leads to the adverse external movement is an expansion in monetary expenditure which seems irreversible, and holding the exchange rate has little power to halt the resultant domestic inflation, while there is no other available measure for doing so, then devaluation to keep the real rate constant, and thus to preserve real output and the external balance, may be the best expedient available. These conditions arguably applied in Brazil when it used a crawling peg to maintain a constant RER in the face of high and variable domestic inflation in the late 1960s and 1970s.

Where fiscal and wage disciplines are good, there is a case for considering a rule of crawling *appreciation* to reinforce price stability in the face of some inflation from the rest of the world. The aim, as mooted earlier, would be to keep the foreign component of prices constant. The rule for such a crawl might be to act as if keeping a constant real rate *on the supposition that the domestic component of prices was constant*: to put it more simply, appreciating against the reference currency or basket as fast as the purchasing-power of that currency or basket was falling (as measured perhaps by the reciprocals of the export-price indexes of the foreign countries concerned). Botswana in 1980, and Papua New Guinea in 1976, 1977, and 1979, have appreciated, apparently to neutralize imported inflation, roughly in the way that such a rule would dictate. As with crawling depreciation to keep a constant RER, there are circumstances in which following this rule would not be ideal, even if the other disciplines required were present.

Peg to single currency or basket

Since the end of Bretton Woods, a number of countries have changed their pegs from a single currency to a basket. Collier and Joshi (1989) (in a table compiled from IMF data) show the number with a single-currency peg falling from 86 to 53 between 1973 and 1987, while the number using a basket rose from none to 37. These totals include those with both fixed and adjustable (jumping) pegs, but those with crawling pegs and 'limited-flexibility' arrangements, numbering eight at both dates, are excluded. The numbers with managed or independent (market) floating rose from three to 34. The single-currency pegs abandoned were mainly those with the dollar and pound, rather than with the franc. Clearly basket-pegging, like floating, has grown in favour.

Pegging may be designed to render trade and investment conditions more predictable, and the choice of peg should presumably take place with that in mind, coupled with a desire to fix or monitor either competitiveness or the foreign component of the price level.

If it is the price level that is overwhelmingly important in exchange-rate policy (probably implying an approach to the SOE type of economy) and (import) trade and investment relations are heavily with a country possessing a fairly stable price level, there may be sense in using that country's currency alone as the peg (whether it is designed as fixed, jumping, or crawling). Unless both these conditions are fulfilled, the case is stronger for a basket.

If it is competitiveness that is important, the relevant standard will almost inevitably not be a single currency, and a basket seems a natural choice. This is likely to be so even with a peg that is allowed to jump or crawl, since the aim in these cases is both to have a standard for administrative purposes and to move the peg no more than necessary. The dollar proved a very unsatisfactory peg in the 1980s, appreciating against other currencies over much of the first half of the decade and depreciating in the third quarter. This caused effective appreciations in currencies pegged to it early in the decade, such as the Dominican Republic, Guatemala and Chile (Collier and Joshi,

1989) and by 1985 Singapore, requiring then large jumps or other adjustments. The changes of the partner country's currency against third countries may not be at all appropriate for the home country's trade with those third countries.

A currency union is a special case of a single-currency fixed peg. Another country's currency is used (as in Panama) or a currency controlled by another country or group (as in the CFA). This is most relevant if the home country, beside the other requirements for a fixed peg, doubts its own capacity for exercising independent fiscal and monetary discipline or for the technical business of managing a monetary system. The experience of the CFA countries, by comparison with their African neighbours, is generally regarded as not wholly bad.

Choice of basket

The choice of the basket to which the currency will be pegged might be designed to keep either the price level or the degree of competitiveness as far as possible constant.

If the main objective is to keep the price level constant, it would seem best to peg to currencies subject to very little inflation most of the time, such as the German mark; around 1990 the SDR may not be a bad choice. A minority of those with a composite peg use the SDR as the basket. (The SDR is in fact somewhat more literally a basket of currencies than tailor-made 'baskets' of currencies used for pegging are likely to be, in that the ratio of the *number* of dollars to the number of yen within the SDR remains constant even if the dollar devalues against the yen, so that the *weight* that the dollar carries in the basket in that case falls. If we could be confident that a currency's effective depreciation accompanied a relatively high rate of inflation, this would impart a slight anti-inflationary tendency.)

If the main objective is to maintain a constant level of competitiveness, which means (more or less) a constant real exchange rate, the basket should be based on currencies whose countries are important in the home country's trade. The currencies that are relevant to the home country's competitiveness would seem to be those **of countries in which imports are bought or exports sold**. These are *not* necessarily the currencies in which the world prices of the goods are conventionally *denominated*. The fact that the rubber price is *quoted* in Malaysian ringgit does not set up any presumption that a rubber exporter should include that currency in its basket.

Sticking to a constant nominal rate against a basket based on the currencies of the main countries with which one's own is in competition will not of course guarantee a stable real effective rate. The real rate, however, is a compound of the effective nominal rate and the relationship between home and foreign price indices. Choosing the basket so that the rate against it is as close as possible to a relevant or correct effective nominal rate provides that at least one of these elements is fixed when the rate against the basket is fixed. To put it another way, choosing the basket to fix the most relevant effective rate ensures that the overall competitiveness will not change *simply because the effective exchange rate of one of the major partners has changed* (Lipschitz, 1979). It thus also tends to reduce the frequency with which the peg has to be moved.

Should the weighting system within the basket be based on proportions of partner countries in *imports* or in *exports* or in *total trade*? If stable competitiveness is generally desired, the basket should perhaps be composed of the currencies of countries important to the home country in markets for goods whose prices are related fairly closely and promptly to costs and whose demand is sensitive to their price. It may be that for many developing countries (and perhaps all those whose exports are heavily dominated by primary commodities) these are mainly the markets for imports. In that case the basket might be based on the importance of various countries in imports.

The choice was important for Botswana in the early 1980s. South Africa was overwhelmingly important in its imports but much less so in its total trade, and price-competitiveness was not a short-term consideration in most of its export markets, which were for primary commodities. In order to maintain its competitiveness against imports, Botswana found itself having to make repeated small devaluations against its basket, which weighted the South African rand much less than the importance of South Africa *as a supplier of imports* would justify. As the rand depreciated against most major currencies, Botswana found that sticking to the parity on its basket would have left it appreciating against the rand, with no import suppliers of comparable weight against whom it was depreciating. So Botswana had to keep on depreciating against its (very roughly) total-trade-weighted basket in order to maintain its competitiveness against South African imports and against imports in general. Presumably a more closely import-weighted basket, as was apparently eventually adopted, would have reduced the need to change the peg (Mmolawa, 1988).

The exchange rate in liberalization

Where it is desirable for a country to liberalize its external trade, it will be necessary for the official exchange rate to be depreciated to the point at which it is consistent with sustainable external balance under the degree of liberalization desired. As explained already, the combination of such a depreciation with the removal of tariffs and quotas on imports may actually reduce domestic prices for importables rather than increasing them.

Summary: choosing the exchange-rate regime

The scheme below, Table 14.2, is there to stimulate thought: it is not under any pretence of being a manual for choosing the regime. The 'hazards' are simply that: disadvantages that *may* be realized in certain circumstances. The 'indicators' are not all put forward as either necessary or sufficient conditions for the choice of a particular regime; they are circumstances whose presence might make the regime worth consideration or whose absence might raise doubts about it. Thus very high inflation is certainly not a *requirement* for choosing a managed float for an LOE, and may not even be a *sufficient condition*. The opposite extreme of firm independent discipline may also serve. Nor is having a dominant partner and an SOE-type economy necessarily a good *enough* reason for having a single-currency fixed peg, even if that is likely to help domestic disciplines; but the absence of these conditions weakens the case for it.

The choice of regime clearly overlaps with the choice of policy, since some choices of regime determine how the exchange rate is used.

Summary: choice of exchange-rate policy

The chapter started by saying that the choice of regime and policy would be conditioned by four factors: liberality of foreign relations, whether there was a world market in the country's currency, type of economic structure (on the SOE-LOE spectrum), and strength of other policy disciplines.

Regime	*Hazards*	*Advantages*	*Indicators*
Fixed peg	Loss of competitiveness; resort to controls	Low exchange risk	SOE; domestic disciplines needing support
Single-currency peg		Ease of administration	Dominant partner
Currency union		Ease of administration; monetary discipline	Dominant partner; political weakness
Jumping peg	Speculative losses, big shifts, or as for fixed peg, if rate out of line	Midway between benefits of fixed peg and floats	Moderate (or better) wage and fiscal discipline; low inflation
Single-currency peg	Increased chance rate out of line	Ease of administration	Dominant partner
Crawling peg depreciation for constant REER	Loss of fiscal and wage discipline	Limit to exchange risk; no shocks in adjusting	[LOE]; fairly high inflation with no remedy
Crawling peg appreciation for constant import prices	As for fixed peg	Neutralizing imported inflation; limit to exchange risk	[SOE]; good wage and fiscal discipline
Managed float	Loss of fiscal and wage discipline	No limit on use of rate as macro instrument	LOE; unbridled inflation; *alternatively* firm indepen't disciplines
Market float	As for managed; fluctuations in rate disturbing production	[External-balance objective can be ignored]	As for managed; search for equilibrium rate in liberalization; world market in currency

Table 14.2 Choice among exchange-rate regimes

We suppose first that it is desirable to have a fairly liberal regime and assume that this will be surrendered only as a last resort (a hope of course, rather than a historical generalization).

We also consider first the case where there is no market in the country's currency. This leaves two variables: economic structure and strength of other disciplines.

As an ideal we start with the 'small-open fiscal' assignment expounded near the end of Chapter 12. If you begin from a satisfactory position in internal and external balance:

(a) Use money-wages to stabilize the domestic component of prices;
(b) Use the exchange rate to stabilize the foreign component of prices;
(c) Use the fiscal balance and other fiscal devices (with monetary measures where appropriate) to keep expenditure, taken as including net overseas interest payments, at the trend of the sum of capacity output and net autonomous capital and transfer inflows.

(A reservation to (a) and (b) is that there may be 'real' changes, transient or lasting, such as harvest failures and world oil-price falls, that properly dictate a temporary or a lasting step rise or fall in one of the two price components relatively to the other.)

Following this rule strictly would leave the exchange rate assigned entirely to the price level, indeed to one component of it. The ideal would not fully be achieved by a fixed peg, though that might seem a reasonable approximation. To stabilize the foreign component of prices completely, we should probably need a rate allowed to crawl upwards against imported inflation. For a pure SOE, with other disciplines intact, that might be all there was to be said.

For an LOE, or an SOE with the possibility of moving toward the local production and export of tradable manufactures, another consideration might enter. This is the longer-term aspiration for the division of output between tradable and nontradable goods. A lower real exchange rate, coupled with whatever other changes are necesssary to restore internal and external balance, may bias development of production towards tradables and of consumption towards nontradables, and (because of the typically higher rate of technical improvement in the kind of goods that are tradable and the stimulating effect of overseas trade) this may make for faster growth. Underlying then the short-term use of the exchange rate for price stability (or other targets), there might reasonably be a slight downward pressure on the real exchange rate for this purpose. Since there are probably no pure SOEs, certainly none determined to remain SOEs for ever, this possibility may be potentially relevant to all. To be effective, this use of the exchange rate might need to be combined with wage policies that allowed the domestic component of prices to rise more slowly than the foreign component.

If fiscal policies are adequate to look after the external balance and to stabilize nominal expenditure, but wage policies fail, there is a dilemma for exchange-rate management. Should it continue to be used to stabilize prices, even reducing the level of the foreign component to compensate for the rise in that of the domestic component, at the cost of reducing competitiveness and hence output and employment? Or should it concentrate on output and competitiveness and allow the rate to crawl downward? In a pure SOE, competitiveness strictly speaking will not be in question. A rise in the REER will still tend if anything to divert spending from nontradables to tradables, so requiring output to be depressed. Yet, if there is very little substitution in use between tradables and nontradables, this may not be important in the short term. Thus, the closer to an SOE the economy concerned is, the less important is likely to be the short-term output effect of a REER rise, and the stronger the case will be for continuing to use the exchange rate for price stability. In practice, especially in an LOE, the compromise adopted may reasonably take account of how effective tradable-price suppression through the exchange rate is likely to be in helping to restore wage discipline.

If both wage discipline and fiscal (or fiscal-monetary) discipline are absent, the overriding concern must be for external balance. In an LOE, the exchange rate will probably have to be used as far as possible to this end, if rigorous exchange and trade controls are to be avoided. In an SOE-like economy, with few possibilities of using the exchange rate for substitution in production or consumption, such controls may well have to be applied in any case.

In any economy, but especially in the LOE, serious attempts to stabilize prices through the exchange rate will then probably appear too costly in terms of output and the external balance to be tolerable, and the substitute for fiscal discipline has to be the 'inflation tax', the fact that *unexpected* inflation, such as increasing rates of exchange-rate depreciation may introduce, acts like a tax in reducing real disposable income and spending. Since this means that continually increasing rates of inflation may be needed to maintain external and internal balance, and since the inflation-tax effect weakens as such inflation comes to be expected and formal or informal indexing takes over, it is likely that either internal balance must at some stage be abandoned or controls must be introduced, damping the growth of real capacity through misallocation. One instrument will not be enough to maintain two targets.

Bearing of type of economy and other policies on suitable targets for exchange-rate policy

Other policies:
Wage discipline or flexibility (WDF),
Fiscal-monetary discipline (FMD)

Type of economy	*Both strong* ⟷	*WDF weak, FMD strong* ⟷	*Both weak*
SOE	Price stability	Price stability	No answer, [controls used for external balance]
LOE	Price stability, [long-term division T to NT]	Choice of internal balance or price stability	External [or internal] balance, ['inflation-tax' &/or controls supporting]

Note: 'Internal balance' means full use of labour.

Table 14.3 Choice of exchange-rate policy

Variants of this position have been reached by numerous Sub-Saharan and Latin American countries in the 1970s and 1980s (and some before), destructive controls probably dominating in the former (which often tend to the SOE) and unharnessed inflation in the latter. Chapters 17 and 18 discuss possible paths out of these dead-ends.

With reservations similar to those uttered over Table 14.2, Table 14.3 summarizes these choices. A crawling peg indexed to stabilize the real exchange rate becomes more appropriate as we move downward and to the right in the table. A fixed peg or an upwardly crawling peg is more appropriate as we move upward and to the left. A roughly stable managed float is most appropriate in the lower left corner, and indeed it is reasonably well-disciplined LOEs in Asia that are prominent among the managed floaters; a fast-devaluing managed float may belong in the lower right corner.

Departures from the initial case

If non-fiscally-generated monetary fluctuations are significant, other monetary discipline is required to supplement the fiscal. However, most of those trying today to make sense of experience would probably still emphasize the prevailing importance of fiscal policy.

If, in addition, there is a world market in the country's currency, monetary policy can be thought of as an additional instrument, independent of fiscal policy, that can be used to influence a market-floated exchange rate or to support a pegged or managed rate. In the initial case (by implication) a market-floated exchange rate could only be influenced by fiscal or wage policy, or else by the authorities' buying and selling of foreign currency. Such intervention would be limited by the amount of foreign exchange available to the authorities. Intervention in domestic money markets can now be substituted as a means of influencing the exchange rate through the interest rate.

We can in this case think of three macroeconomic instruments: fiscal, wage, and monetary, policy, with monetary policy directed proximately to the exchange rate. The question of *what is to be done with the exchange rate* may still be answered in much the same way as in the initial model and as summarized in Table 14.3 above: stabilizing the foreign element in prices, with a long-term thought for the division of output growth between tradables and nontradables, so long as other disciplines are intact; a possible shift to other objectives as wage and fiscal disiplines weaken.

Exchange-rate arrangements
(as of 31 March 1990)

Currency pegged to:

US dollar	*French franc*	*Other currency*	*SDR*	*Other composite*
Afghanistan	Benin	Bhutan (Ind.rupee)	Burundi	Algeria
Angola	Burkina Faso	Kiribati (Aust.$)	Iran	Austria
Antigua	Cameroon	Lesotho (SA rand)	Libya	Bangladesh
Bahamas	Cen.Af.Rep.	Swaziland (SA rand)	Myanmar	Botswana
Barbados	Comoros	Tonga (Aust.$)	Rwanda	Cape Verde
Belize	Congo		Seychelles	Cyprus
Djibouti	Côte d'Iv.		Zambia	Fiji
Dominica	Equat'l Guinea			Finland
Ethiopia	Gabon			Hungary
Grenada	Mali			Iceland
Guyana	Niger			Israel
Haiti	Senegal			Jordan
Iraq	Togo			Kenya
Jamaica				Kuwait
Liberia				Malawi
Nicaragua				Malaysia
Oman				Malta
Panama				Mauritius
Peru				Mozambique
St. Kitts				Nepal
St. Lucia				Norway
St. Vincent				Papua New Guinea
Sierra Leone				Poland
Sudan				Romania
Suriname				São Tomé
Syria				Solomon Islands
Trinidad				Somalia
Yemen A.R.				Sweden
Yemen P.D.R.				Tanzania
				Thailand
				Uganda
				Vanuatu
				W.Samoa
				Zimbabwe

Flexibility limited in terms of a single currency or group of currencies		***More flexible***		
Single currency[1]	*Cooperative arrangements*[2]	*Adjusted according to a set of indicators*[3]	*Other managed floating*	*Independently floating*
Bahrain	Belgium	Chile	China	Argentina
Qatar	Denmark	Colombia	Costa Rica	Australia
Saudi Arabia	France	Madagascar	Dominican Republic	Bolivia
UAE	Germany	Portugal	Ecuador	Brazil
	Ireland		Egypt	Canada
	Italy		El Salvador	Gambia
	Luxembourg		Greece	Ghana
	Netherlands		Guinea	Guatemala
	Spain		Guinea-Bissau	Japan
			Honduras	Lebanon
			India	Maldives
			Indonesia	New Zealand
			Korea	Nigeria
			Laos	Paraguay
			Mauritania	Philippines
			Mexico	S.Africa
			Morocco	UK[4]
			Pakistan	US
			Singapore	Uruguay
			Sri Lanka	Venezuela
			Tunisia	Zaire
			Turkey	
			Viet Nam	
			Yugoslavia	

Notes:
1 Limited flexibility against the US dollar
2 Exchange Rate Mechanism of the European Monetary System
3 Crawling pegs
4 Moved to column 2 later in 1990

Source: IMF, *International Financial Statistics*, August 1990. (Note that some country names are abbreviated for the sake of fitting them in. Notes are adapted from those in the source.)

Table 14.4 Exchange-rate arrangements

15 Wage policies

The need for wage policies

Views of how wages are determined have been a critical ground of difference among the various schools of macroeconomic policy. Are they determined under conditions that simulate well-behaved markets in which the wage will, of its own accord, approximate to the market-clearing equilibrium price for labour, or is the market for labour often one of monopoly or oligopoly on one side and monopsony or oligopsony on the other? If the latter, what is implied is that there may at the time of negotiation be a **range** within which any wage rate may be fixed (see Chapter 5); the actual rate that emerges will have its position within the range determined by a bargaining process in which skills of negotiation and the power of the parties are important. In many developing countries a large proportion of the wage-workers are in the public sector, so that the government, directly or indirectly, is the employer. A large section of wage rates is then fixed by the government when it determines the pay for its own employees. It would not be surprising if these influenced any wages outside the public sector that were fixed under conditions of imperfect competition.

Thus in a formal sense the government normally has some power to determine a considerable part of the spectrum of money-wage rates and to influence the rest. It is also true that such powers are likely to be exercised in an intensely political environment, and there may well be limits to the degree of discretion that a government has.

However, the wages of its own employees are clearly something over which it must have a policy of some sort, even if the policy is to simulate the market. Insofar as wages outside the public sector can be regulated or influenced, the importance of the wage rate for the stabilization objectives suggests that there too a policy may be called for.

What can be called the New Keynesian approach has treated the fixing of the money-wage rate as potentially one of the instruments of stabilization policy. For any given (nominal) fiscal, monetary and exchange-rate setting in which the starting point is not one of excess demand for labour, **raising** the price of labour will tend to reduce real aggregate demand (and therefore real income and employment), will tend however to raise prices, and will probably worsen the external balance on current account; **reducing** the wage rate will tend to raise real income and employment, to reduce prices, and probably to improve the external current account. (The 'probably' inserted over the effect on the external current account is the same 'probably' as has to be inserted about the effect of exchange-rate movements on the external current account, and for the same reasons.)

The market-clearing Monetarist is inclined to think that a range of possible real wages, which would allow one of various rates for each class of labour to be adopted at equilibrium, does not exist: the equilibrium real wage for any activity at any time is at a particular level, and trying to influence it will probably be unsuccessful, and, if successful, simply cause misallocation by leaving either an excess supply of, or an excess demand for, labour. Yet, even if that Monetarist approach were broadly correct, it would still be important for the government, at least in regard to its own employees, to fix rates which could be regarded as equilibrium ones under the degree of inflation that it was expecting. A monopsony buyer of a class of labour (such as the government may be) has in effect to decide what it will offer. Even if it initially fixes the rate for every class of its employees at the lowest at which it can recruit the required number (which could be regarded as simulating profit-maximizing behaviour if there is a certain number that it must employ), it then has to decide how to vary each rate as circumstances, such as the price level, change.

At any time the government is faced with a particular pattern of existing money-wage rates, both for its own employees and for others. Any variation downward in money rates for any class of worker will cause resentment or worse, and any resulting fall in real rates can be criticized on welfare grounds for disappointing expectations. A fall in real rates as prices rise will also be resented, and there will be pressure to restore previous real rates by raising money wages. How should a government react? One response is indexation.

Wage indexation

Changes in circumstances, such as rises in the price level, or rises or falls in the particular local market or in the real *per capita* income of the society, lead either one party or the other to want to alter money wages. Negotiation is costly in several ways: it may, for example, lead to strikes. Wage indexation in its broadest sense is an attempt to remove the need for frequent negotiation by changing the money wage from time to time according to a formula. Since the most important reason for renegotiation is usually inflation of the general level of prices, the most common form of indexation of wages is in relation to the general price level. In its simplest form the wage level is adjusted in proportion to changes in a consumer-price index, so that the real purchasing power of the wage is held constant, or more accurately so that it is repeatedly restored to some base level with each round of adjustment.

But indexation is possible without keeping such strict proportionality between wage and price changes. The arrangements made may be such that a certain proportion only of any price-index change is reflected in the wage, or the wage may be indexed, in part or entirely, against some variable other than the general price index. Indexation is usually retrospective, that is, related to *past* price changes, but it may also be prospective, that is effected with reference to projected *future* events.

Indexation of wages and other particular prices is most often introduced in a situation of chronic inflation, and it is no accident that the pioneers in the subject should be in South America. What full retrospective indexation achieves under inflation is that the real wage is frequently and without argument restored to what it was when the index was last applied. In a continuing cycle of inflation what appears to be happening is that the various other groups of income earners and price setters are mostly doing something similar. As wages rise, other prices are raised so that the employers of labour may have their own real incomes restored. If money and credit are allowed to expand passively so as to accommodate this process, there is nothing to bring it to an end. Experience in Brazil and Chile (McNelis, 1987) suggests strongly that, when the period between wage adjustments is reduced, the inflation speeds up, and that it also speeds up if the completeness of the adjustment is increased.

In favour of general indexation of wages (and other payments such as housing rents), however, is the fairness argument that it ensures that the weaker among the payees, with worse information or lower bargaining power, are not disadvantaged purely on that account. It serves to protect them. Yet perhaps the protection that is reasonable in the circumstances can be achieved without invariable and repeated restoration to whatever the starting real wage happened to be. Such restoration under inflation will be in any case only transient, and the worker may be better off under a lower real target rate which, because of lower inflation, is more consistently maintained.

What seems to be implied, if the inflation continues, is that the total of the spending that would occur out of all the disposable real incomes if they were all restored to their peaks at the same time would be greater than the total of goods and services available for purchase by individuals and private-sector companies. Equality between aggregate suply and aggregate demand at any time is possible only because inflation begins to erode the real value of each income immediately after it is restored to its peak. The inflation will not stop unless some or all income-earners are prevailed upon, or obliged, to settle for less than the real incomes that they receive at their respective peaks. In principle this may be achieved either by fiscal and monetary restraint alone, which usually involves reduced employment and bankruptcies, or else by some kind of 'social contract' which may involve (at least temporary) control of wages and prices. The monetary restraint without the wage-price control or moderation is likely to be painful. Attempting to have the wage-price controls without the monetary restraint may well be ineffective because the controls are not observed. Brazil's experience in 1986 (see Chapter 18) suggests that, against a past of high inflation, it is difficult, both politically and technically, to get the price and wage controls right: not to keep them rigid either too briefly or too long, and to know how and how far to relax them without losing the public confidence which is necessary to maintain restraint in income demands.

A change in the system of wage indexing so that it relates to projected future, rather than to past, inflation tends naturally to increase the speed of inflation when it is already rising and to reduce it when it is falling.

Indexing wages 100-per-cent to a price index has the disadvantage that it does not allow any downward adjustment in the real wage as 'real' conditions change. To have an equilibrium set of wages which will clear at the 'right' level, so as to make it possible to maintain the highest available steady path of real output, may seem a difficult ideal to realize, but some attempt must be made to approach it. Any set of wages that is to approximate to it will need to fall in real terms whenever there is a 'permanent' fall in real average national labour product in purchasing-power terms, through a 'permanent' fall in real export earnings (that is, in the income terms of trade), for example, or in productive capacity as a result of climate change. In the opposite contingencies it will need to rise.

It is always difficult politically for a government to manipulate wages in what appears to be an arbitrary fashion. Yet real wages as a whole do need to adjust from time to time, unless other claims can be reduced instead. If money-wage rates can not be adjusted in the appropriate way and there is a given external-balance constraint, the outcome must be either price-inflation or a deficiency in real output and employment.

Modified wage indexation

To resolve the dilemma, it might be possible to get by with an indexing formula that takes account of what might be called the economy's capacity to pay. A first element of the indexing might be such as normally to maintain real wages as they have been at a certain starting date. However, the formula might be modified by introducing a second element which would adjust the real wage in line with estimated 'permanent' movements up or down in real national income per worker such as might arise as a result of changes in external trade or interest-rate conditions or domestic *per capita* food output. Since there is no reliable way of determining whether a change that occurs in one year is temporary or permanent, a 'permanent' change for this purpose could be estimated as a movement in a moving average of the previous say three or five or eight years' figures.

The workforce might be prepared to accept such a deal without too much complaint, since it would provide for real movements up as well as down and would be some protection against sharp downward changes in the real wage. If so, the arrangement might combine the advantages of indexation (avoiding the need for negotiation, and protecting groups in a weak position from sudden and drastic changes in real income) with those of flexibility (reducing real claims, in order to maintain employment and to prevent real output from falling below capacity, in response to a shock that has reduced that capacity).

As with the fiscal rule proposed in Chapter 13, the policy would have to rely on the existence of foreign reserves (or alternatively on the international accommodation that might be hoped for if a reasonable discipline is patently being observed but there happens to be an exceptionally bad period) to provide the resources for allowing real expenditure to be maintained, or very slowly reduced, while a gradual downward adjustment of real wages is being made.

It is important to point out that such arrangements need not, and should not, prevent changes in the relative earnings of particular groups of wage-earners. Improvements for any body of employees, on account of a productivity deal or a shortage of the particular type of labour, might be agreed to by a tribunal or by negotiation. The indexation would mean that the wage, once agreed, would change with the price index and with whatever other national indicators were included. It would be a matter of choice and judgement how far the state considered that it needed to restrict such specially arbitrated or negotiated changes for groups of workers or to limit the conditions under which they could be awarded. While absolute rigidity of relative wages would almost certainly be harmful, the result of a free-for-all might reflect monopolistic bargaining power rather than simply the needs of allocative efficiency. Also, where there were inflationary traditions and expectations, a spiral might easily be restarted with such *ad hoc* deals. All groups of income-earners need in such conditions some assurance that changes in relativities will be the exception without the need for fighting politically to keep their own relative positions.

Those industrialized nations, most notably Japan, Sweden and Austria, but also to a considerable extent Norway and Finland, that have found acceptable ways of varying wage settlements to take account of the factors that affect the community's ability to pay, have been able to maintain high employment through the 1970s and 1980s. In Japan, according to Dore (1985), ordinary people show considerable knowledge of the national economic indicators that must be taken into account in the annual wage settlements.

A further problem that might arise, however, is that the original real wages on which the indexed figures are based turn out to be too high to allow 'full-capacity' working unless they are repeatedly eroded by inflation in each adjustment period. There may have been a 'mistake' in the starting position. In that case, if no *other* income-earners agree to modify their claims, there may have to be a once-for-all modification of the indexing proportion in one round, or possibly in several rounds until the result seems roughly right. There is, however, an intrinsic difficulty of knowing when you have reached the right point, and again a real-wage rate that looks wrong on the ground of a one-year experience should not perhaps have its apparent deficiency taken very seriously until later observations confirm it.

If politics (and the welfare losses from sudden and unexpected changes in personal income) could be ignored, the government might be able to use the wage rate at its discretion, without indexation, as one of say three instrument variables for maintaining the stabilization targets. In practice, however, indexation that also takes into account real-income shocks may prove much more acceptable, because of its transparent rationality and the safeguards built into it. Indexation of this sort may also have the advantage of making the unpleasant decisions early and in small doses rather than leaving them until they are overdue and involve serious changes in living standards. Where there is no rule, it is almost inevitable that the government will tend to postpone unpopular decisions in the hope that the need for them will go away.

Real-wage moderation according to a formula that takes into account external shocks may be thought of in the context of a fiscal stabilization rule such as that outlined in Chapter 13. That rule aims to stabilize the course of real government, or national domestic, expenditure. 'Real' expenditure in this context may be thought of either in terms of its cost in foreign-exchange equivalent or in terms of what goods and services it delivers. A given amount of real expenditure by the foreign-exchange measure may mean a larger amount of real government services delivered if the real wage rate is lower. If real government expenditure in the foreign-exchange sense must fall, then any fall in real wage rates that occurs at the same time will tend to maintain the services delivered (unless of course it makes real wages so low that jobs can not be filled). Modifying real-wage rates by the same indicators of 'permanent' changes which signal that real expenditure in foreign-exchange terms should fall means that the sacrifice is partly borne by the workers who continue to provide the services and not wholly by the recipients of the services and those workers who lose jobs or fail to gain them.

A modified wage-indexation formula

A formula that meets the requirements of adjusting the real wage as real national income changes might be based on three indicators: the consumer-price index, an index of average productivity of labour, and a net-barter-terms-of-trade index.

To adjust the wage in accordance with *permanent* movements in real national income strictly requires some distinction to be drawn between temporary and permanent changes. Since there is no satisfactory way of doing this, a compromise would be to express the productivity and terms-of-trade indexes in 'smoothed' form by using moving averages. This means that a year-on-year or quarter-on-quarter change in these indicators is not met by an immediate full proportional response, but, if the change persists, eventually the shift to a new level will be reflected fully in the real wage.

Suppose that the principle to be followed is that the real purchasing-power of each wage rate should change in proportion to the real purchasing-power of national income per worker. Indexing fully by the consumer-price index alone would keep the purchasing power of the wage constant. Multiplying further by the ratio in which an index of real purchasing power of national income per worker has changed would make the further adjustment required.

The second of these moves is best seen as consisting of two steps. First, find the ratio in which national disposable income (net national product *plus* net inflows of foreign transfers) at producers' prices per worker has changed and deflate this by an appropriate price index for reducing the income per worker to its purchasing power in terms of domestic goods and services. (Usually there will be a GDP-deflator index that will serve reasonably well for this purpose.) Since the income-per-worker index that we have worked out is based on national product rather than domestic product, it will take into account the effect on income of changes in world interest rates. Let d be the ratio of change in this index, that is, the ratio of its value in period (t - 1) to its value in period (t - 2).

But we want the index to show changes in purchasing power over the goods that are actually bought, not over domestic product. So the proportion of national product that is sold abroad will need to be readjusted to take account of any changes in the purchasing power of exports over imports. This is the second step. Call that proportion 1/x. Strictly it will be the ratio to national disposable income of the contribution to domestic product of exports (of goods and services) *plus* (gross) inflows of property income and transfers. (The contribution of exports to domestic product will not be the same as gross export proceeds; it will be those gross proceeds *minus* the imports embodied in them: the domestic value-added in exports.)

This part, 1/x, of d would need to be adjusted so as to reflect changes in purchasing power over imports rather than over domestic goods. So it must be adapted in the ratio (call it b) of change in the net barter terms of trade, which is the ratio of export price index to import price index.

The ratio by which the real wage would be multiplied to reflect the change in real national, disposable income would now not be simply d but

$$[(b + x - 1)/x] \quad \text{multiplied by} \quad d$$

If d were 1.20, indicating that real average productivity per worker had grown by 20 per cent, but b were 0.60, indicating that the terms of trade had fallen by 40 per cent, and 1/x were 0.25, meaning that a quarter of disposable income came in the form of foreign purchasing-power, the ratio to be used would work out at 1.08. Why this is so is that a quarter of the 1.20 that expresses the ratio of this year's product to last year's, that is 0.30, would have to be reduced by 40 per cent of its value, that is by 0.12 of last year's product, so that the 1.20 would be reduced to 1.08.

To keep the real wage changing in proportion to the purchasing power of national disposable income per worker, where p is the ratio of change of the consumer-price index, we should then multiply last period's wage by

$$p.(b + x - 1).d/x$$

But there is a further adjustment that should be made. If, with an indexing formula, we are to allow for some changes in relative wages, these must probably be thought of as being realized through rises of certain wage rates in more than the ratio provided by the index. This means that, to keep the *average* real wage per worker rising in proportion to the purchasing-power of real national disposable income per worker, the index should reflect only a proportion of the rise in the national figure. Call that proportion y. Since y is less than one, the formula, if it treats rises and falls symmetrically as implied in the formula below, will have the effect that, when the aggregate is falling, the real wage will fall less than in proportion, which is the opposite to the way that this adjustment is meant to work. However, if the long-term prospect is for rises rather than falls, this may be thought of as simply another element in the smoothing of the effect of changes in the indicators.

The indexing formula may now be written as:

$$w_t = w_{t-1} . p_{t-1} . [1 + y\{(b_{t-1} + x - 1)d_{t-1}/x - 1\}]$$

where subscripts t, (t-1), etc. refer either to individual periods, or to moving averages of periods ending in, t, (t-1), etc.

- w is any wage rate
- π is the consumer-price index
- β is the net-barter-terms-of-trade index
- δ is an index of average productivity of labour
- $p_{t-1} = \pi_{t-1}/\pi_{t-2}$
- $b_{t-1} = \beta_{t-1}/\beta_{t-2}$
- $d_{t-1} = \delta_{t-1}/\delta_{t-2}$
- 1/x is the proportion to national disposable income at factor cost of X', where X' is the contribution of exports to domestic product *plus* gross receipts of property income and gross transfers from abroad
- y is a policy-chosen number less than one

The adjustment by y might be further refined.

Where the exchange rate is over-valued, the value of 1/x as estimated from the national accounts may understate the importance of foreign earnings in total purchasing power.

The formula is put forward on the supposition that the price index, like the productivity and terms-of-trade indexes, is based on a moving average of annual figures.

This has the possible advantage that a 'rogue' consumer-price rise, occurring in one year because of factors peculiar to that year such as a bad harvest, has its effect muted, with less hazard that it may be passed on after the special conditions have changed. However, the period adopted for the moving average for consumer prices would have to be fairly short to meet its purpose of providing protection and satisfying employees that renegotiation is unnecessary.

The period best used for the various moving averages would be related to the character of the series concerned, in particular whether it is thought of as having an underlying 'natural' trend or not, and if so whether the period-to-period fluctuations are large in relation to the movement of the trend. β and δ, but not π, may be thought of as having trends related to 'real' factors. With β the fluctuations are likely to be much larger in relation to trend movements than with δ. Hence, the moving-average period adopted would probably need to be longer with β (perhaps five or six years) than with δ (perhaps three or four), and shortest of all with π (perhaps one or two years where prices are fairly stable, but in situations of high inflation arguably shorter still).

The measures of year-to-year changes in 'physical' productivity will probably not be very reliable, and, instead of the moving average of the index (reduced in effect by y), some standard figure might be applied each year to allow for a certain fraction of what the longish-term growth is thought to be, replacing both the d and the y factor.

Wage-indexation and the domestic component of prices

The development of the indexation rule in this chapter has been discussed as if its main aim was to keep the average of real wages close to an 'equilibrium' level that would maintain a pre-existing 'internal balance', that is full use of available labour. It is directed to doing this, whether or not the level of prices is stable.

In Chapters 12 and 14 the ideal purpose of wage policy was seen as keeping the domestic component of prices constant. In principle keeping the domestic component of prices constant is most directly achieved by pegging the nominal wage and varying it (if at all) only with real national income per worker, ignoring the consumer-price element in the indexation formula given above. This, however, is unlikely to be tolerable for long unless domestic-price changes that arise *for reasons other than changes in controlled wages* are small and randomly distributed about zero, as might be the case if all other disciplines were working ideally. The choice or dilemma is somewhat comparable to the one explored in Chapter 14 over the exchange rate: whether to peg it in nominal terms (or even to appreciate it against world inflation) on the one hand or to respond to domestic inflation by keeping a constant real rate on the other. Whether we are considering exchange rates or wage rates, the dilemma disappears only when other instruments are being managed in an ideal fashion.

Keeping money-wages changing so that in each period the average real wage rate changes in the same proportion as the real purchasing power of national disposable income in the previous period will of course not necessarily achieve or restore a stable domestic component of prices. If consumer-prices start to rise and other instruments are geared to maintaining capacity real output, the indexation formula is likely to keep the domestic component of prices rising and so help to continue the rise in consumer-prices.

However, *if prices start from a position of reasonable stability* and *the foreign component of prices is kept stable by the exchange rate*, keeping average real wage rates changing in proportion to real national disposable income per worker will tend to keep the nominal *labour-cost* per unit of output constant. With a constant rate of markup of selling prices of goods over their labour costs, this would make *total domestic costs* per unit of output constant.

But how realistic is it to assume that the rate of markup will be constant? Are those (other than wage-earners) who have the capacity to set their own prices likely to vary their markups in a way that could be inflationary even if their nominal wage costs are constant? In our account of persistent inflation, we have supposed that these price-setters, like wage-earners, feed the inflationary process by repeatedly trying to restore their real incomes to some previous level from which wage and other price rises have since dislodged them. If that is so, there is no need for them to engage in this activity of restoration once other prices are stable and nominal wage costs per unit output are held constant.

Let us suppose now not only that prices start from a position of reasonable stability and that the exchange rate is used to stabilize the foreign price-component, but also that (through fiscal and if necessary monetary policy) *purchasing-power in money terms is not allowed to rise out of proportion to real national disposable income*. Then there is a reasonable hope that price-setters will fix their prices so that, under general price stability, they will roughly maintain their real incomes. When real national income falls, some of them may strive to maintain the absolute amounts of their real incomes and so to increase their relative shares, but in such conditions those producers who are price-takers (for example in agriculture) will suffer falls in their absolute incomes and probably also in their shares of income. Hence, under initial price-stability when national income per worker is falling, a fall in real wages may be enough to allow those non-wage-earners who have price-setting power to maintain their real incomes without raising prices. There is reasonable ground for hope that, from a starting-point of stable prices, with fiscal and monetary discipline and with the exchange rate used to the same non-inflationary end, an indexing formula of the kind indicated will keep the domestic component of prices fairly stable.

This account simplifies a much more complex reality. Oligopolistic power to set prices is always limited. Competition does have some effect on prices, and by fostering it governments may encourage the downward adjustment of real non-wage-earner claims when income is falling.

When prices are rising, the indexing formula will tend to continue the rise, though it is not always obvious that, in the absence of *formal* indexation, the average rate of rise in money wages would be any less. **Stopping the inflation without depressing output and employment may require a break in the indexation** or a period in which the consumer-price component is reflected less than fully, as well as the appropriate fiscal and monetary discipline. To gain acceptance for such a break may be no more difficult politically, and much less costly in terms of output and welfare, than bringing the share of real wages down by monetary contraction alone.

16 Interest-rate policies

The roles of interest rates

In present-day 'open-economy' macroeconomics, the interest rate may have several roles. As a price of money or of loanable funds, it will serve to **allocate credit** and to **moderate the level of investment.** It may **influence the level of saving** out of income or the amount of saved resources that goes into formal-sector intermediaries. Its movements will also **attract or repel short-term capital** from abroad, and will thus serve for shoring up or reducing the net external balance or for raising or lowering the exchange rate. Because of its influence on investment and consumption, it may **affect the general level of activity and the general level of prices**, and it can be regarded as an **instrument for setting the level of money-supply or liquidity.**

Conflict between external and domestic roles

In those developing countries for which there are undeveloped financial markets and little overseas holdings of their currency, the short-term stabilization effects on the external account, on internal balance, and on the price level, may seem largely irrelevant. In such cases, we can concentrate on the domestic long-term role of interest rates in allocation. However, there are always likely to be some locally-owned assets in financial form which the owners will keep at home if real-interest prospects are good but which they will otherwise do their utmost to convert into currencies in which they can expect a better return, in spite of legal and administrative barriers. Hence the external effects of interest rates can not be completely ignored.

There are also comparatively large and semi-industrialized economies such as Brazil and Argentina with active financial markets that have had at least semi-liberal foreign-exchange policies at certain times in the last twenty years. If residents lose faith in the local currency, there may be currency-flight, which may later be reversed as confidence is restored. If the authorities are to halt the currency flight, let alone reverse it, without administrative controls, it may be necessary for them to allow interest rates to rise very high in real terms. Such high interest rates prove very restrictive internally. Dornbusch (1982) records that in early 1981 *real* rates of interest were 35 per cent in Chile and 135 per cent in Argentina, apparently as confidence in the two countries' stabilization schemes disappeared. This incident followed one of strong capital inflows a year or so earlier. Several writers (Fernandez, 1985; Corbo, 1985; Hanson and de Melo, 1985) agree that the financial liberalization in Argentina, Chile and Uruguay complicated those countries' attempts at stabilization over 1978-82.

In the light of that experience, even writers of a fairly liberal cast accept that there may need to be capital controls on foreign exchange in such situations to prevent the interest rate, with its important domestic functions, from becoming the plaything of external capital movements. It may be that, if we were starting from a period of stability of prices, growth, and external-payments, we could leave fiscal and wage policies to stabilize the growth path of real income and the external current account over the medium term, and could then allow short-term interest rates to fluctuate so as to neutralize any disturbing movements of the short-term capital balance or the exchange rate, without the need for quantitative exchange controls. In a period of instability and uncertainty, however, attempts to use the interest rate in this way may lead to excessive fluctuations in the rate which are altogether too disturbing to the domestic economy.

In all developing countries interest rates have a vital long-term role in influencing domestic saving or intermediation and also investment. In countries with developed financial markets, they have an additional importance in moderating liquidity creation by the private sector. If the external role of the interest rate under exchange freedom jeopardizes these domestic functions, there is a strong case for saying that the needs of the latter should take precedence over the external function, with exchange controls on foreign capital movements introduced if that should prove necessary. Exchange controls are a tricky area, in which developing countries have already been far too much involved, with plenty of resulting waste and exploitation, and a decision to introduce or maintain them, even on a limited range of transactions, should not be taken lightly; but recent painful experiences suggest that they may sometimes be the lesser evil.

Short-term domestic uses

The question of domestic monetary policy for stabilization, which must be considered separately from fiscal policy wherever financial markets and private-bank credit are important, is still sunk in controversy and confusion. This book makes no serious attempt to cover it. One school that could be regarded as left-Keynesian, following Kaldor (e.g. 1986), treats the private supply of money (in a financial system that is not rigidly controlled) as responding to demand for it, so that attempts to reduce liquidity, and hence the nominal rate of spending, by increasing interest rates will not be successful. Raising interest rates may as well raise the demand for money as reduce it. Measures such as decreasing the rate of growth of nominal wages, or decreasing inflationary expectations, will be necessary. Raising interest rates will not be effective unless incidentally it has these effects, or, not so happily, it decreases business confidence and the desire to invest. The difficulty for this view is that the measures associated with raising interest rates (often increased government sales of bonds or bills) do generally seem to have the effect of bringing down inflation, though often at the cost of reducing output. This school would answer that any favourable effects might better be achieved by other means.

The opposite view is that the private-sector supply of liquidity may be controlled actively by the government through market purchases and sales of financial instruments or through requirements of bank liquidity. The difficulty with this view is the lack of any satisfactory indicator of whether monetary policy is loose or tight enough. Despite the apparent desirability of having a rule for controlling the money supply, authorities have been largely thrown back on to something very like 'fine-tuning': raising interest rates when there are signs that inflation is rising or the external account faltering. The 'International Monetarist' alternative of an exchange-rate rule to determine whether liquidity is at the right level may not yet have been completely discredited, but it supposes a floating rate with minimal deliberate intervention in the exchange markets themselves, and it has in itself no satisfactory way of dealing with changes in real conditions, such as a commodity boom in an oil or coffee exporter, which would put upward pressure on the exchange rate and by the standard rule would dictate monetary expansion.

Perhaps the best advice that can be given for countries in which private-sector creation of liquidity is important is that all available measures of liquidity should be *monitored*, with some presumption for restraint if any shows a marked apparent departure from trend in real value; and that the external account should similarly be monitored for changes that appear to be of monetary origin. At the same time the entities that are likely to affect the demand for money, such as the exchange rate and wage rates, should be moderated in ways suggested in previous chapters. This is not entirely satisfactory, in that it leaves too much to discretion and 'judgement', which without a firm set of indicators is too likely to be overruled by political convenience; but in the existing state of understanding it may have to serve.

Long-term domestic uses

Since the early 1970s experience has accumulated to support the arguments of McKinnon and Shaw to the effect that keeping interest rates below equilibrium levels is more likely to obstruct productive investment than to encourage it. This is because the interest rates offered by banks and other financial intermediaries seem to have a direct effect on the volumes of funds deposited with them. The reason may be either that allowing real interest rates to rise toward a 'market-clearing' level encourages saving, or that allowing them to rise in modern-sector financial institutions attracts funds that would otherwise be allocated by more informal channels or simply hoarded. If such a change does not actually increase saving, it may make the saved resources more productive than they would otherwise be by directing them through banks and similar intermediaries.

It is taken for granted that the 'equilibrium' interest rate will be positive in real terms. But in fact LDC governments have often set rigid or maximum interest rates, for bank deposits for example, and have found themselves with negative real rates. It is probably true to say that the tide is turning, however, and more and more governments have recognized the damaging effects of such policies.

Ideally the short-term uses of interest rates to help stabilize prices are not in conflict with the longer-term uses for allocation and the savings-investment balance. Commonly interest rates become low or negative in real terms during times of abnormally high inflation. Raising nominal short-term rates with a view to reducing inflation thus tends to restore the incentives for saving and intermediation. However the reality is not always as good as this suggests because capital markets are not perfect, and in particular because of the servicing patterns of most loans. A large rise in nominal interest rates, even though to a level which, deflated by current inflation, is low or negative, may cause liquidity problems, especially to small businesses and house-buyers, who often cannot raise additional loans at the new rates to defray the much higher current real payments that they now have to make. Raising interest rates in a time of inflation thus often has its effect through killing a number of businesses which, apart from having failed to predict the macroeconomic situation and policy management or mismanagement, are perfectly sound and useful. This defect leads to the question of indexation of interest rates.

Indexation of interest rates

The main point of indexation of interest rates is to provide for steady real rates in order to create a stable environment for investment, intermediation, and possibly saving: suitably encouraging to saving and intermediation, and able to act as an efficient allocator of funds for investment. A second important purpose is to reduce the 'front-end load' that results under inflation from the usual systems of servicing of long-term loans and also to blunt the sudden increase in burden that may create liquidity problems as nominal rates rise. Moreover, it seems quite likely that the uncertainty attaching under an unstable price level to the real value and cost of loans, from both lender and borrower points of view, may actually discourage lending and borrowing. Complete indexation to a price-level index will remove the uncertainty about the real value of a unit of debt-servicing.

The front-end-load problem can be explained as follows. Unindexed long-term loans, whether on fixed or on sliding interest-rate terms, are likely in the absence of 'financial repression' to have their nominal interest rates large enough to take account of inflation, expected or actual. A typical arrangement in some countries is to have a regular and equal nominal amount of servicing to be paid each year, composed of the interest due together with increasing nominal amounts of principal as the amount of interest due each year falls. But where the inflation rate is persistently high, the *initial* servicing payments will be very high in real terms because the nominal interest rate is high. If the nominal interest rate is 54 per cent, for example, to take account of a real interest rate of 10 per cent and an inflation rate of 40 per cent, the borrower will have to pay in the first year an amount equal to somewhat more than 54 per cent of the nominal value of the loan. If this is paid at the end of the first year and inflation has actually occurred at the rate of 40 per cent, the *real* value of the payment will be more than 38.6 per cent of that of the original loan. Later the payments due may dwindle to virtually nothing. In real terms the servicing is enormously biased towards the early period.

Some borrowers, often those planning to build or to buy a house, find the high real annual or monthly payment in the early stages an obstacle, because it represents too large a proportion of their incomes. Instead an indexed loan, with a constant real rate of interest, and the outstanding amount of principal increased in nominal terms each year to take account of inflation, may be used to spread the real value of servicing payments evenly over the years and so break down some of the hurdles in the way of borrowers.

There is a strong case for government to index any lending rates over which it has direct control. It is quite likely that rates on loans not directly controlled will come into line.

Various governments have indexed lending and borrowing. A notable case is that of Colombia which in the early 1970s, on the advice of the one-time New Deal economist Lauchlin

Currie, set up housing-finance intermediaries which were both to borrow and to lend at significantly positive indexed rates. The policy was spurred on by Currie's view that housing construction represented a large potential source of growth for many LDCs because of (a) its capacity to use their abundant resource of low-skilled labour, and (b) its high income-elasticity of demand which meant that the increased income generated by construction would lead to further demand for housing. In other words, releasing the latent demand for housing would increase the capacity for growth by directing expenditure to goods that used abundant local resources rather than scarce foreign exchange. The housing market was held to need only appropriate financial arrangements for its high latent demand to be released and to contribute substantially and continuously to growth. The brief full-scale experiment with indexed housing finance, which was wound down with a change of government in 1974, was associated with a big increase in lending for house-building, and seems to have led to a construction boom that added considerably to wage-employment and to national output and investment (Sandilands, 1980, pp. 57-81). It seems likely that capital which would otherwise have found its way abroad was attracted by the substantial real interest rates that were offered, and possibly also that those who could not have afforded to borrow on unindexed terms at lower real rates were paradoxically able to do so at higher real rates because of removal of the 'front-end-load' effect.

The arithmetic of indexing loans

Suppose that a loan of 100 pesos in year-0 prices has a real interest rate of 5 per cent and terms under which 10 per cent of the original real value of the principal will be repaid each year. After the first year, inflation has been 20 per cent, and the original 100 pesos has risen to 120 pesos in current year-1 prices. The borrower then pays 5 per cent of 120, that is 6 pesos, as interest, and another 10 per cent, 12 pesos, towards repayment. The unredeemed principal in year-1 prices has now fallen to 108 pesos. Over the second year, there is 40 per cent inflation, and the 108 pesos has become 151.2 pesos in year-2 prices. The borrower now pays 7.6 pesos interest and 15.1 pesos towards repayment, reducing the unredeemed principal to 136.1 pesos in year-2 prices.

If the whole transaction had been expressed in year-0 prices, the borrower would have paid 15 pesos after the first year, 14.5 after the second, and so on.

It would be quite possible to arrange a schedule of payments which, so long as the real interest rate remained constant, could be constant in real terms from year to year and result in complete repayment by an agreed date. It would also be possible to have a sliding real rate, with a fixed term date but with the annual rate of payment changing as the real rate changed. But an indexed real rate is likely to change less widely than an unindexed nominal rate, and the resulting pattern of real servicing payments over time is likely, other things equal, to be smoother.

*****

Resumé: wage rates, interest rates and exchange rates in stabilization

Exchange rates, wage rates, and interest rates: all are prices. All have potential allocative roles. All also have potential uses in macroeconomic management, and the two functions overlap. All respond to some extent to market forces, but there are plausible doubts about the wisdom of leaving any of them unreservedly to the market: the exchange rate because of speculation and the possibility of disturbing movement in response to transient factors; the wage rate because of monopoly or oligopoly in labour (and product) markets; the interest rate because speculation and hedging may lead to large international capital movements. So all three are often, on plausible grounds, controlled, monitored, or targeted.

The first task of policy over these rates, in the approach suggested here, is **for the spectrum of wage rates, the exchange rate, and the spectrum of interest rates, to be set at levels such that the corresponding real rates will, in normal conditions, roughly clear their respective markets,** implying neither 'permanent' excess demand nor 'permanent' excess supply of labour, foreign exchange, or loanable funds. The various particular wage rates and interest rates should also be such as roughly to clear their particular markets. Market forces will naturally be relied on to indicate the appropriate levels, even though the rates are not wholly abandoned to the dictates of the markets. Such rates will tend to give the best available quantity and allocation of employed labour, foreign exchange and investment. The rough general fulfilment of this condition can be regarded as dealing with the long-term allocative question including the size and character of the wage-labour force.

Overlying this requirement is a need **for the real rates to be stabilized against temporarily disturbing factors and to be moved in response to relevant permanent changes.** Indexing of wage and interest rates, and where relevant indexing of the exchange rate, may be seen in one or other of these lights. So may exchange controls on short-term capital movements if they are considered necessary to avoid the disruption arising from unduly fluctuating interest rates. These measures may be seen as present to avoid disturbances to internal balance ('full employment') through undue slipperiness or stickiness of the prices concerned.

A further objective is **for the nominal rates to be stable for the sake of price stability.** The rules suggested for exchange and wage rates imply in each case that to have stable nominal rates *as well as the appropriate real rates for internal balance* is the 'first-best' choice. Each of the two instruments has the possibility of meeting both requirements provided the other is being managed with the same objective in view and provided that fiscal (and where relevant monetary) policy is also under control. Where one of the two instruments is failing to be used in such a way as potentially to serve both purposes, the management of the other will at best have to choose between them, sacrificing either internal balance or price stability. If the choice has to be made, the guidelines given here presume that generally internal balance should be pursued.

This implies that external balance is primarily the responsibility of fiscal (and where relevant monetary) policy. Changes in wage rates and exchange rates, unless they have been artificially kept well out of line with their respective free-market equilibria, provide at best temporary palliatives for external imbalances, and their use for this purpose interferes with their other functions. The same applies to changes in interest rates except insofar as they affect domestic nominal expenditure. Wage rates may be manipulated to a limited extent to help reduce nominal government expenditure and so influence the external balance by that route. Active manipulation of exchange rates with primarily external targets in mind should be a last resort.

17 Adjusting from gross imbalance

The previous four chapters have been written on the assumption that the starting-point of policy is one of stability. In reality most economies most of the time find themselves in some other place than where they would like to be. When the divergence is small, a gentle pull on the appropriate instruments, or trusting the automatic pilot of the existing rules to weather the storm, may be enough. But many developing countries, especially during the 1980s, have shown strong and chronic tendencies to external-payments problems or inflation or both. Often they have added to this a highly illiberal system of foreign trade and payments that discourages the earning of foreign exchange and misallocates what is earned, and often a considerable amount of domestic regulation as well, with the resulting efficiency losses. Though these two phenomena, misallocation and macreoconomic imbalance, are separable, their causation is often connected, and increasingly over the 1980s the view has become prevalent that escape from the two of them should be coupled and that indeed it may be hard to eliminate one without also dealing with the other.

This chapter can do little more than raise some questions for thought about an immensely difficult practical problem.

Let us say that there is a **dual aim**: first, to restore a 'balance' between aggregate supply and demand at stable prices ('aggregate adjustment'); and second, to make a radical improvement in allocation ('structural adjustment'), both for its own sake and to make it easier to achieve the other objective.

The main **obstacles** to adjustment are the political and welfare ones: that activities would be eliminated or curtailed, and that people employed or otherwise earning from these activities would have their sources of income removed. The activities concerned include those of a purely parasitic nature, such as gaining privileged access to imports at an overvalued exchange rate and reselling them at market prices: an example of so-called 'rent-seeking' behaviour. Yet they are also likely to include services that are useful in themselves or would be so under different circumstances; and the people affected may be conscientious and law-abiding, and some of them are often among the poorest and most vulnerable.

Three main **questions about the process** of adjustment may be posed. Should it happen quickly or slowly? Should liberalization precede, accompany, or follow, stabilization? And how can the process be designed and phased to maximize the gain or minimize the loss in output and to spread the costs equitably or acceptably, minimizing the harm to the weakest and finding a way to deflect the opposition likely to stem from those whose interest is to block the reforms?

The following are **considerations in answering these questions.** Which choice would keep the most favourable path of total output? As a way to answer this: which steps need to precede or accompany others to make those others effective? Which will do least to render any group of people destitute or greatly disrupt their lives? And which will do most to neutralize effective opposition?

What pattern would do most to raise output? A simple answer is to make the allocative improvements as early and quickly as possible. This would bring forward entry into the promised land. However, the allocative improvements associated with liberalization are likely to bring initial losses because existing capacity is forced out of operation by foreign competition or changes in costs and prices. The total loss in output may be greater when changes are made together and at once, because there is less opportunity then for threatened enterprises to find ways of surviving by adjusting to changed conditions, and it is more difficult to reallocate displaced workers promptly. Even without these drawbacks and on the (unrealistic) assumption that the losses could be shared equally across the population, there must be doubts whether a higher average output, over the decade say, would be worth the greater instability that comes with a sharp initial dip.

Which changes are necessary to make others effective? A common hunch is that balancing the budget (whatever precisely 'balancing' is taken to mean) should come first: or at least steps that convey a credible determination to balance it. Without this, the other stabilizing reforms are unlikely to be effective: inflationary expectations will not be removed; liberalization of foreign transactions will not be sustainable for external-payments reasons; with an uncontrolled budget deficit, an attempt to avoid undue domestic-credit creation at stable prices is likely to disturb liberalized domestic financial markets (Smith and Spooner, 1990).

On the side of structural adjustment, a recent paper suggests that three reforms should come first because of their importance for others. These are to decontrol essential imports of inputs, to move the exchange rate to a level at which it is likely to be market-clearing under the degree of trade liberalization eventually designed, and to make foreign exchange available for critical development of infrastructure (Smith and Spooner, 1990, with some extrapolation). (It is implied that import trade in general, and external capital movements, may still be controlled at this stage.) This gives an early start to those improvements that will probably be slow in bearing fruit (export expansion and infrastructure). At the same time it makes the most of the opportunities for quick increases in output that can result if hitherto restricted materials and components for industry are made more freely available (even if their import prices also rise considerably). It hands immediate increases in income to export-producers, without necessarily penalizing in full measure and at once those interests that will lose from liberalization on the import side.

The same writers suggest that the next set of liberalizing steps needs to be in domestic financial and labour markets. This will need to precede the next stage again, the liberalization of domestic agriculture, if the latter is to be effective in expanding output and improving allocation. The hazard is that freeing agriculture will raise food prices unduly, and to avoid this producers need to have as much opportunity as possible to expand output and increase the efficiency of trade and transport of food. Smith and

Spooner would next remove price controls in industry, and only after that complete the liberalization of trade on the import side. The final step in liberalization would be the freeing of international capital flows; reasons have already been given here in Chapter 16 for suggesting that this should take place, if at all, only after all stabilization disciplines are in working order.

Which sequence would do least to render any group of people destitute or grossly disturbed? The answer seems to be a programme that proceeds only gradually in pursuing any necessary change that involves displacing workers and closing enterprises. The more slowly these things happen, the easier it is for those displaced to adapt, and the more feasible for government to foster alternative sources of income for them, temporary or permanent. If the government workforce or the extent of construction activity has to be cut down, doing this gradually may minimize dismissals or the number obliged to move out of the industry, and instead rely more on reduced recruitment.

Which would do most to deflect opposition? It is difficult to give any answer in general terms rather than with respect to a particular balance of political forces. Again gradualness in liberalization seems the safest course, once more to give time for adaptation. Suddenness is attractive to theorists and those of a radical cast of mind, but it is seldom welcome to those in the firing line. There are plenty of cases of radical reforms which governments have launched, only to retreat in the face of powerful opposition.

There are, however, possible arguments for haste and for liberalizing while stabilization is being attempted. One is that the liberalization will bring a dividend in increased output that can be used to compensate losers from the stabilization. This may be valid in certain cases, but it supposes both a rather extreme degree of misallocation from which the changes are to be made and the entrepreneurial and managerial attributes that enable new opportunities to be seized quickly. It may be (see Chapter 18) that these conditions were met in Ghana in the mid-1980s.

A second argument is that a comprehensively radical programme may be treated as a showcase by donors and receive serious international help in mitigating the damage. Again Ghana may be an example; but there is no assurance that a dozen other Ghanas would be treated so generously.

A third argument is that the endpoint of the adjustments needs to be known so that current investments take it into account, but that, if the endpoint is known in advance, those who stand to lose will mobilize against it without waiting for all the changes to be realized. There is, therefore, no political gain from delay. Against this is the point already made that those adversely affected may be less hard hit if the changes are gradual and they have time to adapt. From this exchange we might draw one further point, however: on balance, there is probably gain in **announcing the main proposed reforms at the start of the process,** *both* so that those adversely affected will have warning and time to adapt *and* so that the allocative effects that are hoped for can begin to be reflected in new investments before the reforms are all in place (a point again made by Smith and Spooner). (The European Community announced its 1992 single-market project a number of years in advance but with a date attached, and so stimulated much activity designed for taking advantage of the changes when they occurred.)

To avoid extreme welfare losses, and to deflect some political opposition, there needs to be attention to **compensation or alternative means of support** for those displaced or grossly disadvantaged. Some of the enthusiasts for liberalization have assumed too readily that all will be well in the end. Few worse things can happen to a family than to lose its livelihood. Where policy has this result, those affected have a right to expect at least some transitional relief.

Relevant differences in circumstances

The choice of solution probably depends on whether the most prominent problem is inflation, external imbalance, or stagnation through gross misallocation.

Where the main problem is inflation, as with Israel in 1985, adjustment may have comparatively few real costs and few people need be greatly disadvantaged. What is needed above all may be a kind of 'social contract', with enough immediate state enforcement to convince people to abandon inflationary expectations. It is probably asking for trouble to introduce disturbing measures of liberalization simultaneously.

Where the main problem is external imbalance, aggregate sacrifices will probably have to be made: expenditure will need to be reduced unless output can be sufficiently raised. Here some, perhaps rather selective, early liberalization on the lines suggested above may help to increase output and so mitigate the need for falls in expenditure.

Where there is stagnation due to gross misallocation, the misallocation has obviously to be faced, but it may be advisable to take the less disturbing bits first, while making no secret of the longer-term plan. Where there has also to be adjustment of aggregate expenditure to output, it is probably also necessary that this be done promptly, for reasons give above, but, insofar as the contraction involves, for example, displacement of government employees or falls in construction or removal of food subsidies, means should be sought of phasing those parts of the adjustment over a longer period.

Possible sequences

Here it may be useful to divide suggestions according to the nature of the problem. Two cases outlined at the end of Chapter 14 may be taken as typical: (a) fiscal indiscipline, a passive wage policy, and high inflation; (b) fiscal indiscipline, comprehensive controls, and misallocation. Either malaise may or may not be complicated by serious external deficit. The two may overlap: inflation may be serious in the latter case and misallocation in the former. But often one of the two elements will be dominant. In case (a), it may seem necessary to freeze prices *temporarily* in order to halt inflationary expectations. In case (b), prices have to be freed. The following are suggested sequences for consideration.

For both cases

A plan should be set out with clear timing and in a form that the general public, potential investors, and international institutions and foreign governments, are likely to find comprehensible and credible. As far as possible, any interest groups that have the potential for wrecking the proposals (labour unions perhaps) should be brought in to the formulation of the plan and given whatever guarantees are consistent with its objectives; and those interests who will gain from it (perhaps farmers) should be mobilized in support. Bids should be made for international help.

Where disruption to employment or food prices is likely to occur, there should be arrangements made to facilitate the redeployment of labour to expanding activities and for providing strictly targeted and limited food or cash or both to support those that would otherwise be destitute.

As a first step in reform, an 'unbalanced' budget will have to be 'balanced'. The government should examine all the available measures for doing this and adopt promptly those that (failing other bad side-effects) will not have serious welfare or political repercussions. Possible moves include reducing outlays on defence equipment (most of it usually bought overseas), improving the efficiency of tax enforcement, tightening tax legislation at existing rates, increasing tax rates, reducing non-food subsidies, raising public-utility prices, reducing government payrolls through natural wastage and non-replacement, reducing government wages, reducing food subsidies (with possible targeted programmes replacing them), reducing government capital construction, laying off government employees. In welfare, and probably political, terms, the measures higher up this list are generally preferable to those lower down. Any higher up that are available might be adopted at once; others, if they are necessary, phased in over time. Reducing food subsidies seems a prime example of a reform that should be made gradually and also in harness with measures to increase food supplies in the markets and with special programmes to increase the food entitlements of the very poor. There is no necessary reason why reducing food subsidies should not be associated with *reduced* malnutrition.

Case (a): mostly high inflation

The device of temporarily freezing the exchange rate, wage rates, possibly interest rates, and many other prices, as a means of convincing the public that inflation is ending, was popular in the mid-1980s and sometimes seemed to work. The frozen prices have to be mutually consistent under reasonably free markets, as far as it is possible to calculate. The duration of the freeze should be clearly laid down, and also what rules will be applied afterwards: with government-influenced wages, with the exchange rate, and with public-utility prices. Foreign accommodation may be particularly valuable in making possible temporary additional importing in order to prevent shortages from occurring during the period of the freeze, and also to prevent prices from rising just after it is over and before any new investment or improved allocation has time to bear fruit.

Where further liberalization is deemed desirable, much of it may be left to a subsequent stage, though the arrangements for freezing and unfreezing prices foreshadowed above mean that the questions of an appropriate exchange rate, and of appropriate public-utility prices, and of how far food prices should be left to the market, have to be addressed with the initial measures.

Case (b): mostly misallocation

As suggested above, the least offensive measures of liberalization, which also seem likely to be the best facilitators for other reforms, should be undertaken first (official devaluation which is allowed to raise the rewards of exporters, increasing imported supplies of industrial inputs and of inputs for infrastructure), with plenty of notice given of the more disturbing items to come later. The sequence of subsequent liberalizing changes outlined above from the schema of Smith and Spooner (drawing on Edwards, 1987) seems a reasonable one on political and distribution, as well as on output, grounds (reforming domestic labour and financial markets, freeing agricultural prices and movements, freeing industrial prices, completing foreign-trade liberalization, freeing foreign-capital movements). Attention should be given to the possibility that reducing the official exchange rate while liberalizing trade may actually reduce consumer prices by increasing the amount of import purchases that can be made; and the changes should be co-ordinated so that there is the greatest chance that this will happen. Some people will lose from liberalization, but if it does not increase the price of essentials in relation to typical incomes, much of the popular steam may be taken out of the issue.

*****

Sketches of some actual programmes of adjustment will be found in the chapter that follows.

Part 6

Case-Studies and Conclusions

18 Some recent experiments and experiences

The four brief studies that follow are about experiments of various kinds. Some apparently succeeded. Some failed. Obviously we must try to draw lessons from them, but the lessons are not always easy to extract. A policy that fails in one situation appears to succeed in another that is superficially similar. We must try to surmise what the critical difference is: whether it lies in the details of the measures attempted, or in the immediate situations to which they were applied, or in the fundamental nature of the economies concerned, or in the degree to which governments could and did effectively carry through the policies projected.

Each economy was faced with a problem that was either present or threatened. In several cases a large part of the trouble was an unacceptably high rate of inflation. In one case the problem was mainly prospective: the instability in income, employment and public programmes that seemed likely to result from fluctuating export earnings if advance action were not taken.

Ghana: out of the abyss

Ghana's experiment in the 1980s is interesting for a number of reasons. During the late 1970s and early 1980s Ghana had come to be considered the supreme example in Black Africa of economic mismanagement. Twenty years earlier it had been probably the richest of the Black African countries at or on the verge of independence, and the most advanced educationally. It did not suffer a civil or an international war. Its misfortunes could not, like those of some other African countries, be attributed to a sustained adverse shift in its terms of trade, or to natural disasters, or to trouble among its neighbours, even if these sources of difficulty were not altogether absent. Its immediate neighbour, the Côte d'Ivoire, with similar physical environment and main export crop, throve while Ghana declined. By general consent bad management had greatly outweighed bad luck in creating the predicament in which Ghana found itself in 1983.

The other extremely interesting feature of Ghana's case is that the measures taken in the mid-1980s seem to have succeeded remarkably quickly in reducing inflation to an acceptable level while simultaneously restoring, after many years, a comfortably fast rate of growth. The measures followed lines favoured by the IMF and the World Bank, and they were introduced by a revolutionary government, which, when it first came to power, had a left-wing populist complexion.

Ghana's 'short-term' problem of stabilization was tackled in a programme also directed to its 'long-term' problem of efficient allocation and growth. In fact the prevailing view in the international organizations has recently been that stabilization of the price level and restoration of a sustainable external balance are likely to depend on, or at least to be greatly furthered by, 'supply-side' measures, that is measures to improve the efficiency of resource allocation. The supply-side measures in this context can be summarized as principally **liberalization** and improvement in certain key elements of **infrastructure**.

An account of the predicament that Ghana faced before the first Economic Recovery Program (ERP I) of 1983-6 must dwell first on the gradually worsening growth of income. GDP per head had in fact remained fairly static from 1963 to 1974 (falling from 1965 to 1968 but recovering from 1968 to 1971), but thereafter had fallen, so that in 1980 it was only 80 per cent, and in 1983 only 63 per cent, of its 1970 level (Huq, 1989, p. 288). Gross domestic capital formation had fallen in real terms, so that in 1982 and 1983 it was less than half of its level of 1977 and less than a third of its level of 1964, and in the same two years *net* domestic capital formation is estimated as so near to zero that the difference is well within the margin of error (Huq, 1989, p. 295).

The growth of export earnings declined much further than the growth of total output. Recorded exports, which over 1970-2 bore an average proportion to GDP at current prices of 21.8 per cent, represented an average of only 4.7 per cent over 1981-3, when GDP was actually lower in real absolute terms (Huq, 1989, p. 289). Though Ghana's net barter terms of trade declined markedly after 1979, they had in fact risen at an average rate of 6.9 per cent a year between 1970 and 1979, and much of the fall in export earnings from the early 1970s to the early 1980s was due to a fall in export *volume*, which declined by about half from 1970 to the average of 1979-81 (World Bank, 1984, pp. 8, 9). The resulting fall in the capacity to import is indicated by the fact that imports at 1970 prices in 1982 and 1983 averaged only 44 per cent of their average level of 1970-2 and only 36 per cent of their average level of 1960-2 (Huq, 1989, p. 290).

Tax revenue had at the same time declined from 13.3 per cent of GDP in fiscal 1975-6 to 6.3 per cent in fiscal 1981-2 (World Bank, 1984, p. 21). Large budgetary deficits were being recorded from the mid-1970s: that for 1980-1 amounted to 14.6 per cent of GDP and 65 per cent of total government expenditure (World Bank, 1984, p. 21).

Inflation on the previous year, as judged by the GDP deflator, was 50 per cent, 77 per cent, 28 per cent, and 123 per cent, respectively, in the four years from 1980 to 1983 (Huq, 1989, p. 296). During the last of these years drought and fires, and the sudden expulsion of a million Ghanaian workers from Nigeria, had admittedly contributed to shortages.

Though it is hard to put all these figures together with complete consistency, the story is clear enough. Ghana, despite its apparent advantages, had become markedly poorer and less productive. Its capacity to import per head had declined much more sharply again. Inflation, though certainly high enough to be a cause of great concern, is perhaps best regarded as a side-effect of the malaise in the 'real' economy and an aggravation of the suffering which that malaise rendered inevitable.

The reasons for the decline cannot be fully explored here. Ghana from Nkrumah's time had been a pioneer within Africa of a pattern of policy involving heavy government intervention in industry, laxity in dealing with state-supported and aid-supported projects, the use of state enterprises for political patronage, over-protection of manufacturing, currency-overvaluation, and generally price relationships implying discouragement of agriculture and of exports. There had been some remission in these approaches under the National Liberation Council and Busia governments (1965-71), but the succeeding military and civilian regimes returned to a not dissimilar pattern until the Rawlings government announced its Economic Recovery Program in 1983. The Ghanaian cedi was fixed at 2.75 to the dollar in September 1978 and remained officially at that level until surcharges began to be applied in April 1983. The unofficial rate is estimated to have been already 10 cedis to the dollar in September 1978, 40-45 in October 1981, and 70-80 in March 1983 (Huq, 1989, p. 196). The *real effective exchange rate* against the industrial nations implied by this official rate is estimated to have appreciated *ninefold* between 1973 and 1981 and more than *fourfold* between 1978 and 1981 (World Bank, 1984, p. 11).

Distortions in the price system had discouraged production of social value and provided large returns to administrative privileges, encouraging corruption and the parallel economy. Infrastructure had deteriorated and the public services declined as the real value of tax revenue fell. There had been large dividends in the system for those who had access to political influence, and governments had lacked the capacity or the will to make radical changes.

The Economic Recovery Program was planned in two stages: the former (ERP I, 1984-6) emphasizing stabilization, and the latter (ERP II, 1987-9) structural adjustment and development, though in fact the stabilization measures of the former phase were associated with a prompt resumption of growth.

Policies in ERP I included financial discipline, rationalizing the exchange rate, reviving agriculture especially cocoa, dealing systematically with foreign debt, and beginning to restore the infrastructure. Foreign assistance at roughly twice the rate of the previous four years was secured (Republic of Ghana, 1987, pp. 3, 4). The exchange rate of 2.75 cedis to the dollar was gradually changed between early 1983 and early 1987 through various systems of multiple rates to a predominantly market-based single rate determined by auction; early in 1989 this was about 230-235 cedis to the dollar. One stage in the process had been to have a fixed rate applicable to certain classes of receipts and payments while the rate for other transactions was determined by weekly auctions. The government account moved into surplus in 1986, apparently as a result in part of measures to enhance the tax system. Considerable reduction in overseas indebtedness inherited from earlier years was also achieved. Reserves at the same time were raised: by about 150 per cent from end-1983 to mid-1987, after which they fell sharply (Huq, 1989, pp. 277-81; Republic of Ghana, 1987, p. 8).

Growth at an average rate of 6.3 per cent a year was recorded for the three years from 1984 to 1986 (Republic of Ghana, 1987, p. 4), though from an exceptionally low base in the drought and bushfire year of 1983. Manufacturing output grew at 14 per cent a year over the period, and capacity utilization moved from 10-15 per cent at the end of 1981 'towards and beyond 50 per cent' for most industries by end-1986 or mid-1987. Export volume grew at 13 per cent a year over the same period (Republic of Ghana, 1987, pp. 7, 8), with an increase of over a third in (recorded) cocoa exports over the two years from 1983-4 to 1985-6. Inflation came down as low as 15 per cent in 1986 (Huq, 1989, pp. 278-80).

ERP II aimed to increase public investment to 25 per cent, and domestic savings to about 15 per cent, of GDP, and to increase social expenditure (Republic of Ghana, 1987, p. 10). A continual process has been the reduction of government employment and the redrafting of workers to sectors where more labour is needed such as some rural activities. Latterly, attempts have been made toward substantial increases in the real wages of such government servants as remain.

Much more could be said, but enough has no doubt already been recorded to make the reader think that it is all too good to be true. So much seems to be at odds with the experience of various other African countries that were in difficulties during the 1980s and which either (like Zambia) for long rejected the IMF/World Bank-type prescription or else (like Malawi) accepted it but with dubious benefit. Why was a reduction of the official dollar exchange rate of the cedi to about 1-2 per cent of its previous level over about five years associated with a marked *reduction* in the rate of inflation, when devaluation in Malawi in the 1980s seemed to be fairly closely followed by corresponding *rises* in the domestic price level? Why was fiscal and monetary restraint followed by a sustained spurt in growth?

There are two elusive questions: why was the government able to carry through policies which elsewhere were apparently too unpopular to be sustainable; and why did these measures bear fruit so quickly?

It seems that the leading members of the Rawlings government, when they came to power, were genuine outsiders with no stake in the existing system of controls. They were also prepared to be quite authoritarian and executed some of their predecessors for corruption. Probably they, rather than established high-ranking officers, controlled the armed forces. Thus those who might otherwise have obstructed devaluation and liberalization were neutralized. They could also the more easily reduce employment in government service in that they were not heavily involved in the system of political patronage.

Why did it work? The answer is probably: precisely because mismanagement, rather than lack of resources, had been so largely responsible for the mess. There was so much potential that had simply been wasted. Once the price system was allowed to reflect relative scarcity and to allocate resources, activities that were of negative net value were abandoned, while the skills and capacity were already there to expand many activities of positive worth. In 1983 the World Bank's *World Development Report* examined the relationship between growth rates and price distortions in thirty-one developing countries over 1970-80. Ghana was highest on distortions and second-lowest on growth (for a period before the ERP), while Malawi was lowest on distortions and at about a third of the way from the top on growth. Ghana's troubles, this suggests, were man-made and home-made. Given the will to act, they were easy to remove. Malawi's were largely natural or external. Malawi could 'adjust' through more or less painful restraints, but there were no miracles waiting to be performed.

The official exchange rate in Ghana in 1983 probably had little direct bearing on the domestic price level. Huq (1989, pp. 311-12) gives survey results suggesting that 'official' sources of goods purchased were very unimportant for many people by the early 1980s. The prices that most people paid for goods embodying foreign exchange would almost certainly reflect mainly the scarcity value, rather than the official price, of the foreign currency. Raising the official price did not make goods bought with foreign exchange more scarce. Hence it probably contributed little or nothing to domestic price inflation. When the markets were released, foreign exchange began to go where it was needed, free of the 'political tax' that much of it had borne under the system of controls. In Malawi again all this was probably much less true; the exchange rate, though not market-determined, probably acted much more as an allocating device in the early 1980s than it did in Ghana.

The final puzzle is why fiscal restraint did not, even initially, inhibit the restoration of growth. The answer may be partly that the government was able and determined to redeploy many of those 'shaken out' of the public sector, and perhaps more importantly that there were simultaneously strong inducements to expand productive output with resources already present. Some of the recorded growth may have come about because transactions in the parallel markets and 'smuggling' of cocoa to neighbouring countries for export ceased and were replaced by legal activities that were recorded. Nevertheless the increased openness itself would have social advantages, reducing certain real costs at the same time as it increased the tax base.

The government matched one of the recommendations of Chapter 17 above in taking active measures to redeploy workers who had been displaced by the reforms. As admitted in that chapter, however, much of Ghana's experience seems to go against the argument offered there for gradualism in liberalization. Ghana seems to be the star example of what can be achieved by liberalization in record time. But the success may reflect special factors, such as the extent of previous mismanagement, the human resources, and the firmness with which the authorities were able to act. Ghana also seems to have been lucky in having two very good foodcrop years at just the right time in the adjustment programme (Taylor, 1988). Not all of this can necessarily be replicated. Yet thoughts about Ghana's uniqueness should not lead policy-makers elsewhere to ignore the positive lessons of its experiment.

The Southern Cone exchange-rate experiments: all the eggs in one basket

Over the years 1978 to 1982, Argentina, Chile and Uruguay adopted policies of a distinctive kind, and much the same from one to the other, in order to reduce their very high rates of inflation. All three had recently liberalized their external-trade, finance, and foreign-exchange, arrangements, and the corrective devices were conceived in a liberal framework. The policies concerned can be regarded as reflecting, if not entirely following, one version of the Monetarist approach: that described earlier in this work as 'International Monetarism'. They differed from what is usually regarded as the Keynesian approach of 'fine-tuning' in that they aimed to influence expectations by sticking to a simple pre-announced rule or set of actions. They differed also from typical Keynesian approaches of the present day in actively using only one macroeconomic instrument for stabilization, rather than several independent instruments simultaneously, and from Structuralist approaches in generally avoiding administrative controls. The strategy departed also from the standard Friedman version of Monetarism, in which the exchange rate is to be allowed to find its own level.

All three countries aimed to use the exchange rate to stabilize the domestic price level. In the recent past the exchange rate had by contrast accommodated domestic inflation through repeated devaluations. This is one way, systematized to some extent by Brazil, of living with persistent high inflation: devaluation may be used to keep the real exchange rate roughly constant and so preserve the international competitiveness of the country's tradable goods. Fashionable thought at the time, however, suggested that giving way to inflation in this way was unnecessary. The 'rational-expectations' hypothesis seemed to imply that, if the authorities could induce the markets to believe that they would adhere to certain exchange rates without wavering, everyone who mattered would realize that the inflation rate would adjust to a level consistent in the long term with those exchange rates and would immediately begin to aim at wage rates, interest rates, and profit margins, that would be appropriate to that rate of inflation. In this way competitiveness, and hence real output and the external balance, would not be damaged by the exchange-rate policy, except possibly very transiently, and inflation would be brought down to any rate that the authorities chose.

The policy involved *initially* raising the real exchange rate. The proponents of the device apparently believed that there would be a natural tendency (operating through expectations that would be based on a faith in the government's declared intention) for the previous, acceptable level of the real exchange rate to be rapidly restored after every disturbance. This restoration of the real exchange rate would come about through a reduction in the rate of inflation of the prices of factor services and nontradable goods. Hence the process of restoring the real exchange rate after each change would reduce the rate of inflation.

Accordingly, Uruguay (in October 1978) and Argentina (in December 1978) each published what was called a *tablita* setting out a sequence of monthly exchange-rate devaluations that would proceed in decreasing proportions until they ceased altogether. Argentina's annual inflation rate in 1977 had been 176 per cent (Fernandez, 1985); Uruguay's had been at a peak of 97 per cent in 1973 but had been falling generally since and stood at 44 per cent in 1978 and 67 per cent in 1979. Chile, which started with a lower inflation rate than the others (a rate implying annual inflation of about 34 per cent, according to Corbo, 1985), declared in June 1979 that it would freeze its exchange rate immediately. It seems to have been assumed that there would in all three countries be fiscal and monetary restraint to the degree necessary to sustain the declared exchange rates. However, the doctrine supposed that it would be unnecessary to follow any particular wage policy; accordingly existing indexation arrangements seem to have been untouched, notably in Chile, where they applied not only to wages but also to rents and school fees (Corbo, 1985). Changes of the previous few years also meant that there were no significant controls on international capital movements, reduced controls on external trade, and no controls on domestic interest rates.

At first the policies seemed to show some success. Inflation fell: in Argentina to 1980 (when it bottomed at 101 per cent), in Chile to 1982 (at 10 per cent), in Uruguay to 1982 (at 19 per cent). Unemployment also fell, but generally more briefly: in Argentina to 1979, in Uruguay to 1980, in Chile to 1981. The reason for these falls in unemployment may have been an initial increase of confidence inspired by the policies. But in all three cases these improvements in inflation and unemployment rates were then reversed. Chile's unemployment rate rose from 11.1 per cent in 1981 to 22.1 per cent in 1982 (Corbo, 1985). Argentina's inflation rate had gone back up to 165 per cent in 1982 and 344 per cent in 1983. By early 1981 (Dornbusch, 1982), real interest rates were enormous: 35 per cent to commercial borrowers in Chile, 135 per cent in Argentina, both *in real terms*. The exchange-rate promises were eventually abandoned: in Argentina after the first quarter of 1981, in Chile after June 1982, in Uruguay after November 1982.

What went wrong? There are two sets of observations which help to illustrate how the policies failed. One effect, catalogued clearly for Argentina (Fernandez, 1985), is that capital first moved in, probably attracted by the prospect of greater price stability, and then, when faith in the maintenance of the exchange-rate policy waned, began to move out in large volume, making it necessary for domestic interest rates to rise to the levels mentioned, apparently to compensate for the much higher future inflation which the market by then expected. The other set of observations, which probably shows *why* the markets did not expect the exchange-rate policy to persist, consists of indices of competitiveness, which are another way of expressing real effective exchange rates, falling when the real exchange rate appreciates. Two competitiveness indices for Uruguay, both set at 100 for the second quarter of 1978, reached troughs respectively of 45 in the first quarter and 54 in the third quarter of 1982, implying that relative costs for purposes of international competition had roughly doubled over the period of a little under four years (Hanson and de Melo, 1985). Corbo (1985) shows that various competitiveness indices for Chile fell greatly between early 1976 and early 1982: by proportions ranging between 60 and 72 per cent, and mostly over 1979-82, suggesting that relative costs had risen about threefold over those six years.

Clearly the real exchange rate had not returned quickly to its original level after the disturbances caused by the exchange-rate policy. The fact that it remained out of line disrupted output and employment, and hence threw doubt on the continuance of the policy. Once doubt had crept in, capital movements became perverse, and the survival of the policy became ever less credible.

Various reasons have been suggested why the policies failed. Ferenandez (1985) argues in relation to Argentina that the experiment was an attempt to manage expectations, and there was no reason in the country's past record to suggest that the government would find that easy. Indexation, and in particular retrospective indexation, of wages, rents, and school fees, in Chile (Corbo, 1985) were no doubt a contributing factor to the inertia of inflation there. Bruno (1985) has argued that it was mistaken to surrender control over capital flows under conditions of such instability. Fiscal discipline was not observed. It is also mentioned (Fernandez, 1985) that Argentina had not only given up control over bank credit but positively encouraged monetary ill-discipline by guaranteeing bank deposits. Each of these criticisms implies that at least one other instrument beside the exchange rate needs to be managed to achieve the required adjustment.

Dornbusch (1982, p. 704), making a similar presumption, gives an explanation of a more root-and-branch type. He supposes that monetary restraint combined with disinflationary exchange-rate targeting *will* lead to real appreciation, that the damaging effect on output will be aggravated by rises in real interest rates, that such rises in real interest rates are likely to follow if monetary restraint is not matched by fiscal restraint, and to be enhanced by any rise in the demand for money that follows from expectations of falling inflation, and that indexing wages to past inflation promotes real appreciation and further reduces the real value of money balances. He concludes (pp. 707-8) that disinflation by exchange-rate targeting is not likely to succeed unless backed by other policies, such as over wages, real interest rates and the fiscal balance. Any monetary targeting must be adjusted, moreover, to allow for the fact that success in reducing expectations of inflation is likely to increase the demand for real money balances. Furthermore an announcement may not be enough to convince the markets that the exchange rate will hold: the government must lock itself into the targeted exchange rate by buying its own currency forward.

Shortly after these unsuccessful experiments in the Southern Cone of South America, Ecuador tried a similar device with apparent success. In early 1983, the central bank tied itself to a fixed exchange rate by doing something like the last of Dornbusch's recommendations: it agreed to settle the dollar debts of residents in exchange for the domestic currency, the sucre, thus laying itself open to considerable loss if the exchange rate of the sucre should fall below the rate projected. Within a few months the inflation rate fell from 80 to 20 per cent (according to *IFS* from an annual rate of 75 per cent between the first two quarters of 1983 to an annual rate of 19 per cent between the fourth of 1983 and the first of 1984), apparently without adverse effects on employment and without de-indexation of wages (McNelis, 1987). The lower inflation rate seems to have been maintained more or less thereafter: 28 per cent to 1985, 23 per cent to 1986; though depreciation against SDR and dollar in fact continued.

It may be that the 'locking in' to the exchange rate by such a manifest act of faith in the currency really did the trick with expectations, so that Ecuador matched the apparently successful initial phase of the other countries' stabilization policies without suffering from the subsequent loss of credibility. But perhaps there is a danger of making too much of Ecuador's fast inflation of early 1983, which was of very brief duration.

Tests of the rest of Dornbusch's recipe may be sought in the next set of experiments, which followed a few years later.

Structuralist ventures: pulling out all the stops

At various times in 1985 and 1986, Brazil, Argentina, Israel and Bolivia entered upon programmes to cut inflation, the first three at least of which might well have been a direct response to Dornbusch's critique just mentioned. In all cases the exchange rate was to be rigidly fixed from a certain day, but there was to be a bevy of other measures, and, except in Bolivia, the general approach would pass as Structuralist rather than Monetarist, in either the North Atlantic or the Latin American sense of the latter term. As in the 1978-82 experiments, to change expectations was regarded as crucial. The difference is that more than one instrument was used to that end: the measures were *comprehensive, synchronized*, and designed to bring down inflation *drastically and immediately* (Blejer and Cheasty, 1988, p. 870). Brazil, Argentina and Israel sought a combination of fixes that were intended to disinflate with minimal disruption to the real economy. It could reasonably be supposed that the less disturbance the policies involved the more credible their continuation was likely to be.

The prongs of the approach could be described (from Blejer and Cheasty, 1988, adapted) as:

(a) fixing and freezing, at least temporarily, a number of absolute and relative prices, in order to avoid output losses (that might otherwise arise through squeezing competitiveness and returns), and hence also to help reduce inflationary expectations;

(b) making fiscal changes, some permanent and some temporary, in order to reduce (perhaps temporarily to over-reduce) real demand pressures, and again, in so doing, to increase the credibility of the policy;

(c) breaking retrospective indexation of wages and financial contracts, for at least the initial period, so that past inflation should not be fed into costs and prices after the realignment, and so that the fall in inflation should not put a real overload on those paying wages and interest.

The risk in freezing relative prices is that, if the freeze continues for long, they may fall out of line with market-clearing prices, so possibly distorting allocation, and in the short term depressing output of certain goods or unduly stimulating their consumption or import. On the other hand, if the freeze is too brief, it may not have the intended effects. A further source of miscalculation is that a rapid fall in the inflation rate will alter the real impact of a number of fiscal measures and may also alter the demand for money in relation to income.

Israel's rate of inflation, high for a number of years, had greatly increased since 1983; there was very comprehensive indexation of wages, interest, and a number of other prices. The stabilization programme of July 1985 had been shortly preceded by three brief attempts to curb inflation, which had had some trade-union support, had operated mainly through reducing subsidies on goods and cutting real wages, and had left the inflation rate reduced from its 1984 peak but rising rapidly once again (Kreis, 1989).

Argentina and Brazil each introduced a new currency to add to the psychological effect: the austral and the cruzado respectively. All four froze the exchange rate chosen for the new programme: in Argentina it appears officially constant against the dollar over the ends of four quarters from June 1985; in Brazil over the ends of three from March 1986; in Israel of six from September 1985; in Bolivia of four from March 1986. (Israel subsequently depreciated by only 17 per cent from end-September 1985 to end-February 1989. Bolivia, which introduced a new currency at the start of 1987, went on to a floating rate shortly after, and is now regarded by the IMF as independently floating, but devalued by only 23 per cent against the dollar from end-March 1985 to end-1988, though rather more against the SDR.) In Argentina and Israel the new fixed exchange rate implied, with the other measures adopted, an immediate real depreciation against the dollar (Blejer and Liviatan, 1987).

Argentina, Israel and Brazil froze wages; in the first two this led fairly quickly to a fall of about 20-25 per cent in real wages, which then gradually rose again, but Brazil started with a planned rise of 8 per cent in real wages over the average of the previous six months.

All four aimed to reduce their budget deficits as proportions of GDP. Israel and Argentina at first succeeded in reducing the proportion by more than half; Israel's deficit continued to fall and was reduced close to zero by mid-1986, but Argentina's rose. Brazil seems to have been unable, even in 1986, the first year of its 'Cruzado Plan', to reduce its real budget deficit, which was financed passively by the central bank (Blejer and Liviatan, 1987; Bresser Pereira, 1987; Baer, 1987).

Israel's budget balancing in the first year was greatly assisted by special help from the US. As percentages of GNP, the budget deficit before foreign grants received fell from 29.2 to 20.6 between 1984-5 and 1985-6. This was due almost entirely to revenue measures, though there were also reductions of expenditure, especially in subsidies on goods and services. But simultaneously, grants received (almost entirely from the US) rose from 13.9 to 19.3 per cent of GNP; so that the remaining deficit after grants was reduced from 15.3 to 1.3 per cent. In the next fiscal year, however, grants fell back somewhat to 15.7 per cent of GNP, and, partly because some of the revenue measures taken the previous year were temporary, revenue fell; but this time expenditure was reduced by 4 per cent of GNP, more than half the reduction being on imports of military equipment. The effect projected for 1986-7 was that the deficit after grants would be only 0.6 per cent of GNP (Kreis, 1989). Hence the deficit before grants was halved over the two years, and the deficit after grants virtually eliminated.

Sudden changes in the rates of growth of consumer prices were associated with corresponding changes in the rate of growth of the money stock. In Israel, precisely as expected *a priori*, the velocity of money rose when the inflation rate was rising and fell when it was falling, but in Bolivia surprisingly something like the reverse was true. Brazil showed a sudden sharp fall in velocity, as might be expected, at the start of its plan (*IFS*; Baer, 1987).

At first, all four countries seemed to be successful in reducing the rate of inflation drastically and quickly. But, while low rates continued in Bolivia and Israel, Brazil and Argentina within a couple of years found themselves back on the familiar round of hyperinflation. Israel's consumer-price inflation was 300, 48, 20 and 16 per cent respectively in the years 1985, 1986, 1987 and 1988; and Bolivia's was 11,748, 276 and 15 per cent in 1985, 1986, and 1987. In Brazil, however, interest rates of over 600 per cent in January 1987, less than a year after the plan had been introduced, seemed to betray a breakdown in credibility. Prices of a number of items in Brazil were raised sharply near the end of 1986, and these helped to trigger changes in wages which had been set to occur once an agreed 20 per cent threshold in living-cost rises had been passed. Tantalizingly Brazil through much of 1986 experienced inflation below 20 per cent and a growth rate of real income that was almost without precedent. Argentina found it necessary, as so often during previous attempts at stabilization, to give in to wage demands, and began increasing wages in January 1986, only a few months after the start of its plan, and again in May. It devalued from its new 'frozen' exchange rate over February and March 1986 (Epstein, 1987; *IFS*).

Why did Bolivia and Israel succeed while Brazil and Argentina failed despite their cruzados and australes? Perhaps most important was the lack or loss of fiscal control in Brazil and Argentina. Closely related were the deficiencies in the way their wage policies performed. Argentina's, designed apparently to reduce real wages, broke down under union pressure within a few months; Brazil's plan had originally been designed to set real wages at their average rate of the previous six months, but the authorities had given in before the start of the plan and set them 8 per cent higher. On the face of it, setting wages 8 per cent higher than appeared to be consistent with existing employment at existing prices was inviting either employment to fall or prices to rise. For whatever reasons a social contract seems to have held in Israel but to have been weak or non-existent in Argentina and fudged in Brazil. No doubt the difference in performance on wages explains some part of the differences in budget performance, and there are other differences as well. In Brazil a number of other factors, some of them direct results of the anti-inflation measures, served to reduce government revenue or increase outlays (Baer, 1987, p. 1026). Both Brazil and Argentina were under newly democratized regimes; there were interests that had to be propitiated. The degree of effective control that a government has must be critical in any radical experiment. The best-laid plans for painless adjustment will always leave some people as losers, and they may refuse to co-operate. Argentina's Peronistas, with their trade-union connections, were in opposition to the governing party. Brazil's main democratic and populist party was technically in power, but under an unpopular President who had no firm political base.

Israel, by contrast, seeing itself as in a perpetual state of siege, could probably rely on a greater degree of social solidarity.

Apart from being lucky in having extra American aid to call on, Israel does seem to have phased its budget adjustments with some care, concentrating on measures to increase revenue in the first round, and leaving most of the reductions in expenditure (other than subsidies) to the second, and even then making the bulk of the cuts in overseas purchases that had no direct effect on either employment or services. Unemployment rose in Israel from 1984-5 (July to June) to 1985-6, but by scarcely more than it had risen over the previous year, and in 1986-7 it was back virtually to the level of two years earlier (Kreis, 1989, p. 365).

Bolivia's experiment was different in concept from the others. Its plan appears to have been one of severe austerity, entailing strong monetary restraint and day-to-day balancing of fiscal expenditure to revenue, big tax rises and public-utility-price rises, with widespread loss of jobs, rather than resting to a great extent on price control; wages were frozen, but prices of goods were not. Bolivia also releived itself of considerable burdens by refusing to service its debt to the banks and having this stand tacitly accepted abroad (by the US and the IMF) until it could begin buying back the debt at enormous discounts in 1988 (see Chapter 11 and Sachs, 1989). (Peru under Garcia, which defaulted less wholeheartedly at about the same time, but did *not* pursue other policies approved by the IMF, did not receive the same indulgence.) In spite of the austerity, the experiment apears to have been sufficiently popular in retrospect for its architect, Gonzalo Sanchez de Lozada, to receive most votes (though not an absolute majority) in the presidential election of 1989, and the other main candidates did not campaign against it.

Mistakes that can be identified in retrospect may have contributed to failure in Brazil and Argentina. Baer (1987) believes that Brazil continued too long with frozen prices though they were giving rise to over-consumption and excessive imports. Waiting until after the November 1986 election to correct them led to a sharp rise in the general price level and thence to triggered wage rises. But by that stage there may have been no way of escape. Freezing prices in a market economy, hard on the heels of fast inflation, is a knife-edge business, and indeed it may well be that the lack of fiscal discipline and the deliberate real-wage rise at the start of the Plan ruled out continued success in stabilizing prices.

By contrast with Israel's liberal financial support from the US and Bolivia's daring but tolerated default, Argentina and Brazil were still labouring under enormous international debts, whose burden had been aggravated after 1982, as elsewhere, by the drying up of further lending.

The experiments of 1985-6, like those of 1978-82, depended on managing expectations. Once failed, attempts of this sort are all the harder to repeat. So the various ingredients for success should perhaps be ensured before the attempt is made. These seem to be: either a firm bargain with labour unions over a wage discipline or else authoritarian powers; a clear plan to control the budgetary balance, probably making dismissals a last resort; machinery for modifying international capital flows if necessary in order to stabilize rates of interest as credibility waxes and wanes; contingency plans for use if things begin to go wrong; and preferably rich foreign friends committed in support.

Papua New Guinea's fiscal disciplines: making the rough places plain

Papua New Guinea's is the experiment on which the model of fiscal discipline given in Chapter 13 is based. Its strategy from 1974 depended on simultaneous management of public expenditure, the exchange rate, and wage rates, within a liberal framework of trade and payments. The distinctive feature of this form of management was its dependence on stable rules related to longer-term projections. Anything resembling fine-tuning applied only to the exchange rate. The main instruments and targets were considered together, but it was a premiss of the strategy (as expressed at the end of this section in a quotation from its principal architect) that, if public-expenditure and wage disciplines were observed, the exchange rate could be assigned to influencing the domestic price level.

Papua New Guinea became officially self-governing in December 1973 and independent in September 1975. It probably comes as close as any country to the SOE model. Its export earnings had been derived mainly from a number of agricultural products, principally coffee, copra and cocoa; but in 1972 it began to be a major exporter of copper and other metals, which quickly came to predominate in its export receipts. In the early months of self-government the Cabinet began to renegotiate the revenue arrangements over what was then the country's single large mine. The new agreement, completed in November 1974, provided for revenue flows to the government that would be highly responsive to the mine's year-by-year profitability and that would hence be likely to fluctuate much more even than its gross sales revenue. The arrangements were retrospective and captured a significant share of the earnings from the period of high metal prices that was ending.

In order to prevent the fluctuations in revenue from unduly disturbing fiscal expenditure, the government at the same time put through legislation imposing a certain discipline on itself and its successors. A Mineral Revenue Stabilisation Fund was created, into which all the government earnings from mineral projects, whether as taxes and royalties or as dividends, were to be paid. Payments out of this Fund into the ordinary revenue of the state were to be made according to a formula which would relate the amount to the *expected* revenue from minerals, as estimated according to a real-terms formula from prices for a certain number of past years, with some latitude given to both the Fund's Manager and the Minister for Finance to vary the amount paid out within certain proportions.

Such legislation was no guarantee that the spirit of the provision would be perpetually observed. A future government might succeed in obtaining alteration of the law, and a Minister for Finance who chose to do so could in any case probably find ways of getting around the limitation. Nevertheless the provision was at the very least a forceful reminder to governments that stability in expenditure was unlikely to be achieved unless they were prepared to accumulate reserves in times of high revenue receipts rather than increasing spending whenever those receipts rose. It provided also a convenient rule for observing such restraint. The fact that the period to which the law applied began with a time of high prices and profits in copper meant that the Fund started with large reserves, which could be run down in the process of helping to stabilize expenditure over the years of very low prices that followed. In the late 1970s (Daniel and Sims, 1986, p. 27) payments from the Fund into the 'budget' were indeed far more stable than its receipts of revenue. The country was fortunate in having further large mines that were to come on stream during the 1980s, so that, in spite of the prolonged relative depression of copper prices, new sources of mineral revenue were emerging.

Also in late 1974, a Budget Priorities Committee was formed, composed of civil servants (mainly heads of co-ordinating agencies). Its function was broadly to translate objectives set by the political leaders into guidelines for spending and then into packages of proposals which could thereafter go back, through a further filter of a National Planning Committee which included the main 'co-ordinating' Ministers and government party leaders, to the Cabinet. Its proposals were to be contained within limits set by the Minister of Finance on macroeconomic grounds.

Stability in the environment in which public-expenditure decisions were taken was enhanced by an agreement with Australia, the country's major aid donor, in early 1976, guaranteeing aid in untied cash grants, with minimum amounts specified for five years in advance (Garnaut, 1981, p. 178), and by arrangements for public-servant and urban wages that, after big real rises in 1974-5, provided broadly for indexation up to a certain inflation limit, but with an understanding from 1977 that no more claims, other than on performance grounds in particular cases, would be made for three years. Both aid and wage agreements were renewed on rather similar terms when these periods had expired.

Before the budget prepared in 1977, a further fiscal discipline was introduced. A National Public Expenditure Plan was prepared for 1978-81, under which it was agreed that the real value of budgeted government expenditure on goods and services should rise each year by 3 per cent. It can be said that this rule influenced the size of the next four budgets, and it is estimated that the growth in government expenditure on goods and services as defined did in fact increase by an average of 3 per cent a year between 1978 and 1981, though not at a steady rate from year to year (Daniel and Sims, 1986, pp. 14, 51 ff., 80; IMF figures in *IFS* on different definitions give a slightly, but not markedly, different picture). This again was an attempt to adopt a simple policy rule which would take the size of government expenditure out of day-to-day politics and would allow it to be considered in a wider perspective. One part of the purpose of the expenditure policy was to reduce the country's dependence on foreign grants which continued to cover a substantial part of government expenditure. The proportion has indeed been decreasing: from 43 per cent in 1975 to 22 per cent in 1987 (*IFS*). A second purpose seems to have been the provision of firm limits within which allocation decisions over expenditure could be made. Without such known limits politicians and officials may try to avoid difficult choices, and the effect of their doing so may easily lead to outlays that are excessive from the viewpoint of stability.

The discipline was tested over 1980-2, first by a substantial real rise in revenue in what was thought to be the start of another mineral boom, and then by a much larger decline between 1980 and 1982. Though *ex post* real expenditure on the IMF definition appears to have risen in 1979 by more than 3 per cent, 1980, largely governed by the 1979 budget, shows a very modest real rise, within a 3 per cent limit, and 1981, when expenditure might have been expected to be affected by the optimism of 1980 and by the parliamentary manoeuvres that led to a change of government in that year, saw a similarly modest rise. (Daniel and Sims explain the caution on the part of both government and opposition that brought about this result as having much to do with the rules and procedures earlier established.) The budget prepared in 1981, having to take account of the world slump in commodity prices and rise in interest rates, reduced expenditure significantly, as well as introducing a number of measures to increase revenue. This fiscal restraint was associated with a fall in wage-employment of about 12 per cent between mid-1981 and mid-1982. The idea of pre-planned limits to changes in expenditure, however, was maintained. There were to be real falls, it was decided, for two years, and thereafter rises of 1 per cent a year (Daniel and Sims, 1986; Garnaut and Baxter, 1983).

Provided that the positions of reserves, foreign debt, and the price level, have remained fairly satisfactory, one way of testing the success of the expenditure disciplines is to observe the relative variability of expenditure and revenue. When revenue (including foreign-aid grants) and expenditure are reduced to 1980 prices by the consumer-price index, and year-on-year percentage changes calculated, it is found that the average magnitude of the percentage change of revenue is 8.9, with a peak fall of 17.8 per cent between 1980 and 1981 and a peak rise of 17.9 per cent between 1982 and 1983, while the corresponding average for expenditure is 3.5, with a peak fall of 7.5 per cent to 1982 and a peak rise of 7.7 per cent to 1979. In the face of a sharp fall in Australian aid between 1975 and 1976, expenditure was cut then by 6.2 per cent, even though revenue and grants combined were actually rising. This initial austerity allowed reserves to rise and set a conservative starting point for expenditure.

Beside the budget, a further contributor to the stability of domestic expenditure lay in the stabilization funds for the three main export crops. In the coffee, cocoa and copra booms of the late 1970s, these were allowed to build up very large reserves; the funds for coffee and cocoa levied half of any excess of actual over 'expected' (long-term-average) producer prices. (There were no significant taxes on crop production or export.) In 1980 falls in price required payments out of the funds for all the three commodities (Daniel and Sims, pp. 28, 50).

But was this success bought at the expense of unacceptable or dangerous positions of reserves, inflation, or foreign debt? *Reserves*, after rising markedly from 1975 to 1977, stayed extremely stable in nominal US-dollar terms over the next ten years, the lowest end-year value (1981) being 79 per cent of the highest (1979); in real terms there must have been a slight downward trend from 1977, but the very stability of the reserves in proportion to their size, even in the downward shock of 1980-2, suggests that they have remained more than adequate. *Consumer-price inflation* reached its highest rate, for any one year from 1975 to 1987, in 1980 at 12.1 per cent, and the average compound rate over the twelve years from 1975 to 1987 was 6.5 per cent. Until the end of 1982, government long-term *foreign debt* was exceeded in value by international reserves. Net government borrowing (a budgetary deficit) is recorded for every calendar year from 1975 to 1987, and total overseas debt has become quite high: total long-term debt service in 1985 being 27.3 per cent of exports of goods and services or 17.3 per cent of GNP; but only about half this debt is public or publicly guaranteed: in 1985 debt service on *public* debt amounted to 6.0 per cent of GNP (*World Development Report, 1987*). Papua New Guinea had not, through the 1970s and 1980s, been obliged to make any conditional borrowing arrangement with the IMF (Daniel and Sims, 1986, p. 81). The first credit facility from the IMF was in fact granted in early 1990, largely under the CCFF, when the IMF pronounced approvingly on policy reforms then under way.

Altogether there seems to have been considerable success with the stabilization strategy, by the standard of economies facing similar conditions over the 1970s and 1980s. Through a decidedly shaky thirteen or so years for copper and for primary commodities generally, instability in government expenditure was surprisingly low, and only the rise of foreign debt might cause concern.

The exchange rate of the Papua New Guinea kina, initially tied to the Australian dollar, was first appreciated against it several times in 1976 and 1977, in order to reduce imported inflation, and then fixed against a basket of currencies. It was appreciated by 5 per cent against this basket at the end of 1979 in the face of enhanced world inflation. It generally rose against the SDR from 1976 to 1981, altogether by 19 per cent, and then fell each year, altogether by 36 per cent, to 1987. The fall was, however, associated with generally declining inflation. This picture is probably related to falling world inflation and to effective depreciation of the Australian dollar, which had a high weight in the country's exchange-rate basket.

Essential background to Papua New Guinea's measure of success with stabilization was the 'hard-currency strategy', the determination to control inflation and to build confidence in the economy by maintaining the fiscal and wage conditions in which there could be fairly free transactions in foreign exchange together with an exchange rate subject to discretionary shifts. In the words of the policy's progenitor:

> The theory of the 'hard currency strategy' had two main elements. First, foreign prices and the kina exchange rate were together the main determinants of the price level in Papua New Guinea. Second, Papua New Guinea could choose fairly freely the foreign exchange value it wished the kina to have so long as the average real level of public expenditure over a number of years was within the limits set by the average real level of internal revenue, plus grants from foreign governments, plus surplus savings of the PNG private sector, plus sustainable levels of foreign borrowings (the latter being kept low in line with the general objective of reducing reliance on foreign aid in course of time). The art of the 'hard currency strategy' was to establish mutually consistent and sustainable trends in *real* government expenditure, *real* wages, and *real* aid levels, and to co-ordinate changes in *money* levels of these variables with changes in the exchange rate and price level. It was essential that the exchange rate, and the kina-denominated levels of government expenditure, wages, and foreign aid, move in a consistent manner. Low inflation was considered to be important in itself...and it would facilitate the careful allocation of resources in line with government priorities. (Garnaut, 1981, p. 171)

Fiscal restraint in 1976, fortified by a serious public-education campaign, was probably the necessary springboard for maintaining control and creating an image and tradition of reliability. Relaxation then might have spoiled the picture, sapping international confidence, which itself probably provided a useful buffer, and leading sooner or later to much more serious problems of adjustment. The systematized prudence in public expenditure of which the budget of 1976 was the first practical test does seem to have had an important stabilizing effect, and there is little in the experience of other primary-export-dominated economies in the last two decades to suggest that much of value was lost by Papua New Guinea's quest for stability.

19 Concluding lessons

Certain tentative lessons may be drawn from experience with stabilization policy in developing countries, much of it equally applicable in any country. The following aphorisms and prescriptions are set down for consideration. Where they are not self-evident, an attempt has been made to defend them in earlier chapters. A number are controversial, however. The reader should not take them as gospel. Many of these questions are by no means closed.

1. It is much more difficult to correct a large imbalance than a small one, and therefore policy should be directed to correcting imbalances as early as possible and better still to forestalling them.

2. It is more difficult politically to make satisfactory adjustments by discretionary action than in pursuit of an established rule. This is one of several reasons why rules should be developed wherever they can be made applicable.

3. Fiscal control is a key element in any system for maintaining or restoring macroeconomic stability.

4. Rules for fiscal control are best directed to maintaining, as a primary objective, an external account that is sustainable when good years are taken with bad.

5. This does not imply that what is needed is a mechanical year-by-year equation of expenditure with revenue according to particular arbitrary definitions. The definition of the appropriate 'balance' to be sought between government domestic revenue and expenditure depends on beliefs about the habitual level of the domestic private surplus or deficit (of saving over investment) and government net capital and transfer receipts from abroad. It may also (see rule 9 below) be appropriate to relate expenditure to 'permanent' or expected receipts.

6. Wherever wages are fixed under politicized conditions or in imperfect markets, government should seek to influence their general level systematically for purposes of allocation and stabilization, and (if other instruments are directed primarily to maintaining external balance and the external component of the price level) particularly for purposes of approaching 'internal balance'. The goal of internal balance implies that an underlying objective of wage policy should be to approach a general level and structure of money-wages that would be market-clearing under a stable general price level.

7. In the short term, adjustments to money-wages may ideally be directed to keeping the domestic component of the price level constant, though, where other instruments are working less than ideally or shocks impinge, it may be necessary to modify this pursuit.

8. Wage-rate indexation for inflation is potentially valuable in avoiding disputes and protecting the vulnerable, but it should be modified systematically to take account of the need to adjust, upwards or downwards, to 'real' shocks arising from changes in domestic supply, or in world supply of the country's imports or demand for its exports, or in foreign debt or interest-rates.

9. However, rules applying to the control of fiscal expenditure and wage-rates will generally be more conducive to stability in real disposable income and

living standards, and more politically acceptable, if they are adjusted to appropriately smoothed, rather than simply to year-on-year or quarter-on-quarter, changes of revenue or of indicators such as the terms of trade.

10. The use of a single macroeconomic instrument, such as domestic credit or the exchange rate, without attention to other instruments, is unlikely to maintain the required degree of stability in real disposable income and prices under a sustainable external balance, and is especially unlikely to be effective, without severe costs, in eliminating established high inflation.

11. Ideally, the exchange rate should be thought of primarily as useful for purposes of efficient allocation, and secondarily as a means of contributing to price stability in the face of inflation of external origin. Its active short-term manipulation for maintaining external or internal balance or for correcting inflation of domestic origin is to be considered only in support of other measures or if other measures are not available.

12. Accordingly, the aim should be to have an exchange rate that 'on average' is roughly market-clearing. If the special conditions favouring a fixed peg to a single currency are not thought to prevail, the rate should normally be pegged or tacitly held or targeted with reference to a basket of currencies representing the country's import or total-trade partners, with possible provision for upward crawling against world inflation if the domestic component of prices can be kept reasonably stable, or for downward crawling if control of the domestic component of prices is weak or has been abandoned. The crawling may be done under a publicly explicit rule (as a crawling *peg*) or less formally on criteria known only to the authorities (under 'managed floating'), or under less direct influence (in a 'market float').

13. Interest rates have an important function in allocation of resources. Their levels should be allowed to respond to domestic supply and demand, but limitations on international capital movements may have to be imposed if, usually under instability arising from some other cause, external factors would otherwise be unduly disturbing to this function.

14. Indexation for price-level changes of the debt-servicing on all domestic long-term loans whose terms are subject to government control or influence has important potential for reconciling the demands of stability with those of efficient allocation and growth.

15. Domestic measures for stabilizing the incomes of producers of agricultural exports, through marketing institutions, or through taxes and subsidies that vary with commodity prices, have a useful role in stabilization if they can be sheltered from abuse.

16. To make the practice foreshadowed in rule 9 consistently workable, international economic arrangements should provide developing countries with a reliable form of insurance against external and domestic-supply shocks.

17. Earnings insurance is a more promising form of international support for primary-exporting countries than commodity-price-stabilization agreements. Its use as a means of encouraging responsible domestic stabilization policies, beyond what is now possible under IMF arrangements, needs to be explored.

18. Since excessive debt has come to render the capital flows into many developing countries consistently negative, there is a strong case for international action and institutions that will revalue debt in order to reduce its burden to the debtors and its insecurity to the creditors, and that will, by selective guarantees, both support and moderate new lending.

19. The elimination of habitually high inflation, or the reversal of chronic decline that has arisen through misallocation, will first of all require fiscal discipline. For this or other reasons, it is also likely to need a strong and honest government, the use of a number of macroeconomic instruments, public education, care for the needs of the losers, the co-operation of workers' organizations, proper phasing of any liberalization measures (so that those that are least disturbing, or likely to bring favourable supply responses most quickly, or that are prerequisites for the effectiveness of other measures, come first), and international support.

Further reading

Works listed here are identified by author and publication year. The bibliography gives details.

Chapters 1 to 5

The reader without previous training in economics should work through the macroeconomic section and the introductory microeconomic section of a standard basic-economics text, such as Begg *et al.* (1988 or other edition), parts 4 (especially chapters 19-25) for macro, and 1 for micro, or Wonnacott and Wonnacott (1990 or other edition), parts 2, 3, (4, 5,) for macro, and 1, (6, 7,) for micro. An alternative approach to macroeconomics, geared to the primary-export-dominated economy, is given by Harvey (1985). Historical background and a simple introduction to the Keynesian revolution are provided by Stewart (1986). Keynesian and Monetarist views on inflation are integrated, briefly and simply, in Trevithick (1980). A more extended comparison of Keynesian and Monetarist views, together with those of British structuralists, appears in Cuthbertson (1979). For a historical survey of the quantity theory, see Friedman (1989), and for an account of Monetarism and its variants and controversial positions, see Cagan (1989): both in the *New Palgrave*. Those who want to know more about the international monetary system, from the post-War settlement until after the end of Bretton Woods, can read Tew (1982 or other edition).

Chapter 6

The various approaches to the balance of payments may be explored further in Williamson (1983), chapters 8, 9. Other standard international economics and finance textbooks, such as Kane (1988), parts 1-3, might also be consulted. Alexander (1952) is the original work on the absorption-injection approach. Polak (1957) shows the thinking that set the monetary approach in motion. Frenkel and Johnson (eds) (1976) present a number of articles on the approach; and Kreinin and Officer (1978) give an advanced discussion of it.

Chapters 7 and 8

An example of a small-open-economy model in Monetarist form, carried to its extreme and applied to a particular country's experience, occurs in King (1979). A sophisticated discussion of the effects of money-supply changes, under market-clearing rational-expectations assumptions, in a small-open-economy model, is given by Montiel (1987), showing deductively that such changes, even if anticipated, may have real effects on output and employment. Nowak (1984) discusses the implications of the existence of an unofficial market for foreign currency under administrative controls, a question also discussed by Krueger (1982). A special issue of *World Development*, **17** (12), December 1989, is devoted to parallel markets in developing countries. On structuralism, Arndt (1985) gives the historical setting; Seers (1962) attempted to formalize the assumptions at a time when they were considered more respectable than they are today; Jameson (1986) examines the logic; Bresser Pereira (1987) interestingly relates the various strands of structuralist thought to the Brazilian 'heterodox' experiment in stabilization of 1986. On the question of whether money supply determines nominal income or *vice versa*, there is a rather condensed survey by Desai (1989) in the *New Palgrave*.

Chapter 9

On commodity-price-stabilization agreements, Gilbert (1987) gives a then up-to-date survey of practice which anyone at all interested in the subject should read. MacBean (1987), in the same issue of *World Development*, discusses the issues in more general terms. Anderson and Gilbert (1988) explore the collapse of the tin buffer stock. Johnson (1977) presents a contentious case against commodity agreements, with a somewhat-too-abbreviated argument about the conditions in which a buffer stock used to stabilize prices may destabilize earnings. Nguyen (1979, 1980) undertakes two formal analyses that tend to diminish the importance of this destabilizing effect on earnings. On the use of market devices for stabilizing producer prices, the enthusiast can read Gemmill (1985), Gilbert (1985), and Powell and Gilbert (1988).

Chapter 10

An excellent and informative summary of the two main international earnings-compensation schemes, with a discussion of their extension or improvement, is given by Hewitt (1987). Dell (1985) criticizes what he considers the emasculation of the Compensatory Financing Facility after 1983, and Love and Disney (1976), writing near the beginning of the life of Stabex, call attention to its defects. Kumar (1989) assesses the stabilizing effect of the CFF over 79 countries. Helleiner (1986) is useful background to the extent of instability of external origin and its various causes, and of domestic responses to it, over a number of developing countries in the crises of the 1970s and 1980s. Bacha (1987) proposes a two-way conditionality, which may be an interesting supplement to the suggestions in this chapter.

Chapter 11

There is an abundance of material on the world debt crisis of the 1980s. The present writer's prejudices come out in his recommending first Griffith-Jones (1988), especially her opening and closing chapters, a short article by Griffin (1988), and Sachs (1989). A strongly anti-IMF, anti-liberal set of papers is presented in Körner *et al.* (1986). There is solid material in Frenkel, Dooley and Wickham (eds) (1989), among which Corden (1988) on an international debt facility is reproduced with minor changes, and an article by Greene gives a survey of Sub-Saharan African external debt.

Chapter 12

Anyone interested in the history of the targets-and-instruments analysis can consult Tinbergen (1952), Swan (1955), Meade (1951), and Mundell (1962). King (1979) presents a model discussed here. Meade (1978 and 1983), though referring particularly to Britain, may also be of interest, especially for those countries with extensive domestic capital markets and currencies traded internationally.

Chapter 13

Mansfield (1980) and Tanzi (1982) introduce some of the concepts used in this chapter. Garnaut (1981) and Garnaut and Baxter (1983) provide the source of the main thought behind it but may be hard to obtain.

Chapter 14

Consult the issue of the *Oxford Review of Economic Policy* on exchange rates, **5** (3), Autumn 1989, especially the article by Collier and Joshi (1989) on exchange rates in developing countries. Wickham (1985), Adams and Gros (1986), and Lipschitz (1979, 1984) are also worth reading.

Chapter 15

Gros (1986) and McNelis (1987) are worth reading on the implications of wage indexation, as is Sandilands (1980) (see below).

Chapter 16

Oxford Review of Economic Policy, **5**, (4), Winter 1989, is devoted to finance and economic development; articles by Collier and Mayer and by McKinnon aim to give a current review of the arguments and evidence on financial repression and liberalization and their effects. Sandilands

(1980) outlines the indexation experience of Columbia, Brazil and Chile up to the mid-1970s.

Chapters 17 and 18

On the sequencing of stabilization and structural adjustment (especially liberalization), Smith and Spooner (1990) produce a stimulating summary directed to agricultural markets but raising the main issues, and drawing on Edwards (1987). On the Ghana experiment, see Huq (1988), especially 'Overview' and 'Postscript'. For background on previous policy in Ghana, see the rest of the same book and also Killick (1978). On the Southern Cone experiments of 1978-82, see the special issue of *World Development*, **13** (8), August 1985, and Dornbusch (1982). On the experiments of 1985-6, see the special issue of *World Development*, **15** (8), August 1987, Blejer and Liviatan (1987), Blejer and Cheasty (1988), and Kreis (1989). On the Papua New Guinea experiment of 1974 and after, see Garnaut (1981), Garnaut and Baxter (1983), and Daniel and Sims (1986).

Bibliography

ACFOA (Australian Council for Overseas Aid) (1987), *Life After Debt*, Development Dossier No 23, Canberra.

Adams, C. and Gros, D. (1986), 'The consequences of real exchange rate rules for inflation', *IMF Staff Papers*, **33** (3), September, pp. 439-76.

Alexander, S. (1952), 'The effects of a devaluation on a trade balance', *IMF Staff Papers*, **2** (2), April, pp. 263-78; reprinted in Caves and Johnson (1968).

Allen, W.R. (1989), 'Specie-flow mechanism', in Eatwell, J., Milgate, M., Newman, P. (eds), *The New Palgrave: Money*, London: Macmillan, pp. 316-19.

Anderson, R.W. and Gilbert, C.L. (1988), 'Commodity markets and commodity agreements: lessons from tin', *Economic Journal*, **98** (389), March, pp. 1-15.

Arndt, H.W. (1985), 'The origins of structuralism', *World Development*, **13** (2), February, pp. 151-9.

Bacha, E.L. (1987), 'IMF conditionality: conceptual problems and policy alternatives', *World Development*, **15** (12), December, pp. 1457-68.

Baer, W. (1987), 'The resurgence of inflation in Brazil, 1974-86', *World Development*, **15** (8), August, pp. 439-76.

Begg, D., Dornbusch, R., Fischer, S. (1988), *Economics: British Edition*, 2nd ed. London: McGraw-Hill.

Blejer M.I. and Liviatan, N. (1987), 'Fighting hyper-

inflation: stabilization strategies in Argentina and Israel, 1985-6', *IMF Staff Papers*, **34** (3), September, pp. 409-30.
Bresser Pereira, L. (1987), 'Inertial inflation and the Cruzado Plan', *World Development*, **15** (8), August, pp. 1035-44.
Bruno, M. (1985), 'The reforms and macroeconomic adjustments: introduction', *World Development*, **13** (8), August, pp. 867-9.
Cagan, P. (1989), 'Monetarism', in Eatwell, J., Milgate, M., Newman, P. (eds), *The New Palgrave: Money*, London: Macmillan, pp. 195-205.
Caves, R.E. and Johnson, H.G. (1968), *Readings in International Economics*, Homewood, Illinois: Irwin.
Chenery H.P. *et al.* (1974), *Redistribution with Growth*, Oxford: Oxford University Press.
Collier, P. and Joshi, V. (1989), 'Exchange-rate policy in developing countries', *Oxford Review of Economic Policy*, **5** (3), Autumn, pp. 94-113.
Collier, P. and Mayer, C. (1989), 'The assessment: financial liberalization, financial systems, and economic growth', *Oxford Review of Economic Policy*, **5** (4), Winter, pp. 1-12.
Corbo, V. (1985), 'Reforms and macroeconomic adjustments in Chile during 1974-84', *World Development*, **13** (8), August, pp. 893-916.
Corden, W.M. (1989), 'An international debt facility?', in Frenkel *et al.* (eds) (1989), pp. 151-71; a slightly modified version of an article of the same title in *IMF Staff Papers*, **35** (3), September 1988, pp. 401-21.
Cornia, G.A. *et al.* (1987), *Adjustment with a Human Face*, Oxford: Oxford University Press.
Currie, L. (1971), 'The exchange constraint on development---a partial solution to the problem', *Economic Journal*, **81** (324), December.
Currie, L. (1974), 'The "leading sector" model of growth in developing countries', *Journal of Economic Studies*, **NS 1** (1), May, pp. 1-16.
Cuthbertson, K. (1979), *Macroeconomic Policy: The New Cambridge, Keynesian and Monetarist Controversies*, London: Macmillan.
Daniel, P. and Sims, R. (1986), *Swings, Shocks and Leaks: The Making of Economic Policy in Papua New Guinea, 1980-82*, Brighton, Sussex: Institute of Development Studies Discussion Paper, February.
del Drago, G. (1978), *International Comparisons of Levels of Development*, Milton Keynes: Open University Statistical Series, Unit 15.

Dell, S. (1985),'The fifth credit tranche', *World Development*, **13** (2), February, pp. 245-9.
Desai, M. (1989), 'Endogenous and exogenous money', in Eatwell, J., Milgate, M., Newman, P. (eds), *The New Palgrave: Money*, London: Macmillan, pp. 146-50.
Dore, R.P. (1985), *An Incomes Policy Built to Last*, London: Tawney Society Pamphlet.
Dornbusch, R. (1982), 'Stabilization policies in developing countries: what have we learned?', *World Development*, **10** (9), September, pp. 701-8.
Edwards, S. (1987), 'Sequencing and economic liberalisation in developing countries', *Finance and Development*, **24** (1).
Emmanuel, A. (1972), *Unequal Exchange*, New York: Monthly Review Press,
Epstein, E.C. (1987),'Recent stabilization programs in Argentina, 1973-86', *World Development*, **15** (8), August, pp. 991-1005.
Feldstein, M. (1987), 'Latin America's debt', *Economist*, 27 June, pp. 21-5.
Fernandez, R.B. (1985), 'The expectations management approach to stabilization in Argentina during 1976-82' *World Development*, **13** (8), August, pp. 871-92.
Frank, A.G. (1965), *Capitalism and Underdevelopment in Latin America*, Harmondsworth: Penguin.
Frenkel, J.A. and Johnson, H.G. (eds) (1976), *The Monetary Approach to the Balance of Payments*, London: Allen and Unwin.
Frenkel, J.A., Dooley, M.P., Wickham, P. (eds) (1989), *Analytical Issues in Debt*, Washington, DC: IMF.
Friedman, M. (1989), 'Quantity theory of money', in Eatwell, J., Milgate, M., Newman, P. (eds), *The New Palgrave: Money*, London: Macmillan, pp. 1-40.
Garnaut, R. (1981), 'The framework of economic policy-making', in Ballard J.A. (ed.), *Policy Formation in a New State*, Brisbane: University of Queensland Press.
Garnaut, R. and Baxter, M. (1983), *Exchange Rate and Macro-Economic Policy in Independent Papua New Guinea*, Port Moresby: Papua New Guinea Government Printer and Department of Finance.
Gemmill, G. (1985), 'Forward contracts or international buffer stocks? A study of their relative efficiency in stabilizing commodity export earnings', *Economic Journal*, **95** (378), June, pp. 400-17.
Gilbert, C.L. (1985), 'Futures trading and the welfare economics of commodity price stabilization', *Economic Journal*, **95** (379), September, pp. 637-61.
Gilbert, C.L. (1987), 'International commodity agreements:

design and performance', *World Development*, **15** (5), May, pp. 591-616.
Goreux, L.M. (1980), *Compensatory Financing Facility*, Washington, DC: IMF Pamphlet Series no 34; cited Hewitt, 1987.
Griffin, K. (1988), 'Towards a cooperative settlement of the debt problem', *Finance and Development*, **25**, (2), June, pp. 12-14.
Griffith-Jones, S. (ed.) (1988), *Managing World Debt*, Hemel Hempstead: Harvester Wheatsheaf.
Hanson, J. and de Melo, J. (1985), 'External shocks, financial reforms, and stabilization attempts in Uruguay during 1974-83', *World Development*, **13** (8), August, pp. 917-47.
Harris, J.R. and Todaro, M.P., (1968),'Urban unemployment in East Africa: an economic analysis of policy alternatives', *East African Economic Review*, December, pp. 17-36.
Harris, J.R. and M P Todaro, M.P. (1970), 'Migration, unemployment and development: a two-sector analysis', *American Economic Review*, March, pp. 126-42.
Harvey, C. (1985), *Macroeconomics in Africa*, Revised Pan-African ed., Macmillan, London.
Helleiner, G.K. (1986), 'Balance-of-payments experience and growth prospects of developing countries: a synthesis', *World Development*, **14** (8), August, pp. 877-908.
Herrmann, R. (1983), *The Compensatory Financing Facility of the IMF: Analysis of Effects and Comparisons with Alternative Systems*, Kiel: Kieler Wissenschaftsverlag Vauk; cited Hewitt (1987).
Hewitt, A.P. (1987), 'Stabex and commodity export compensation schemes: prospects for globalization', *World Development*, **15** (5), May, pp. 617-31.
Huq, M.M., (1989), *The Economy of Ghana*, London: Macmillan.
IFS (International Financial Statistics), monthly, Washington, DC: IMF.
Jameson, K.P. (1986),'Latin American structuralism: a methodological perspective', *World Development*, **14** (2), February, pp. 223-32.
Johnson, H.G. (1962), *Money, Trade and Economic Growth*, London: Allen and Unwin.
Johnson, H.G. (1977), 'Commodities: less developed countries' demands and developed countries' response', in Bhagwati, J. (ed.), *The New International Economic Order*, Cambridge, Massachusetts: MIT Press, pp. 240-51.
Kaldor, N. (1986), *The Scourge of Monetarism*, 2nd ed., Oxford: Oxford University Press.

Kamas, L. (1986), 'Dutch disease economics and the Colombian export boom', *World Development*, **14** (9), September, pp. 1177-98.
Kane, D.R. (1988), *Principles of International Finance*, London: Croom Helm.
Karmel, P.H. and Polasek, M. (1978), *Applied Statistics for Economists*, 4th ed., London and Melbourne: Pitman.
Keesing's Contemporary Archives.
Killick, T. (1978), *Development Economics in Action*, London: Heinemann.
King, J.R. (1979), *Stabilization in an African Setting: Kenya 1963-1973*, London: Heinemann.
Körner, P. *et al.* (1986), *The IMF and the Debt Crisis*, London: Zed Books.
Kravis, I. *et al.* (1978), 'Real GDP *per capita* for more than one hundred countries', *Economic Journal*, **88** (350), June, pp. 215-42.
Kreinin, M.E. and Officer, L.H. (1978), *The Monetary Approach to the Balance of Payments: a Survey*, Princeton, NJ: Princeton Studies in International Finance No 43, Princeton University.
Kreis, E.S. (1989), 'The inflationary process in Israel, fiscal policy, and the economic stabilization plan of July 1985', in Blejer, M.I. and Chu, K.-y. (eds), *Fiscal Policy, Stabilization, and Growth in Developing Countries*, Washington, DC: IMF, pp. 309-45.
Krueger, A.O. (1982), 'Analysing disequilibrium exchange rate systems in developing countries', *World Development*, **10** (12), December, pp. 1059-68.
Kumar, M.S. (1989), 'The stabilizing role of the Compensatory Financing Facility: empirical evidence and welfare implications', *IMF Staff Papers*, **36** (4), December, pp. 771-809.
Lewis, W.A. (1954), 'Economic development with unlimited supplies of labour', *Manchester School*, May.
Lipschitz, L. (1979), 'Exchange rate policy for a small developing country, and the selection of an appropriate standard', *IMF Staff Papers*, **26** (3), September, pp. 423-49.
Lipschitz, L. (1984), 'Domestic credit and exchange rates in developing countries: some experiments with Korean data', *IMF Staff Papers*, **31**, (4), December, pp. 595-635.
Little, I.M.D. (1982), *Economic Development*, New York: Basic Books.
Little, I.M.D., Scitovsky, T., Scott, M.FG. (1970), *Industry and Trade in some Developing Countries*, Oxford: Oxford University Press.
Love, J. and Disney, R. (1976), 'The Lomé Convention---a

study of its likely benefits with special reference to Ethiopia', *Journal of Economic Studies*, **NS, 3** (2), November, pp. 95-116.
Macbean, A.I. (1987), 'International commodity agreements...', *World Development*, **15** (5), May, pp. 617 ff.
McKinnon, R.I. (1989), 'Financial liberalization and economic development: a reassessment of interest-rate policies in Asia and Latin America', *Oxford Review of Economic Policy*, **5** (4), Winter, pp. 29-54.
McNelis, P.D. (1987), 'Indexing, exchange rate policy and inflationary feedback effects in Latin America', *World Development*, **15** (8), August, pp. 1107-17.
Mansfield, C.Y. (1980), 'A norm for a stabilizing budget policy in less developed export economies', *Journal of Development Studies*, **16** (4), July, pp. 401-11.
Meade, J.E. (1951), *The Balance of Payments*, Oxford: Oxford University Press.
Meade, J.E. (1978), 'The meaning of "internal balance"', *Economic Journal*, **88** (351), September, pp. 423-35.
Meade, J.E. (1983), 'A new Keynesian approach to full employment', *Lloyd's Bank Review*, 150, October, pp. 1- 18.
Mmolawa, A. (1988), dissertation for MSc in Finance, Strathclyde University, Glasgow.
Montiel, P.L. (1987), 'Output and anticipated inflation in the dependent economy model', *IMF Staff Papers*, **34** (2), June, pp. 228-59.
Morgan, D.R. (1979), 'Fiscal policy in oil-exporting countries, 1972-1978', *IMF Staff Papers*, **26** (1), March, pp. 55-86.
Morton, K. and Tulloch, P. (1977), *Trade and the Developing Countries*, London: Croom Helm.
Mundell, R.A. (1962), 'The appropriate use of monetary and fiscal policy under fixed exchange rates', *IMF Staff Papers*, March.
Nguyen, D.T. (1979), 'The implications of price stabilization for the short-term instability and long-term level of less developed countries' export earnings', *Quarterly Journal of Economics*, **93**, (1), February, pp. 149-54.
Nguyen, D.T. (1980), 'Partial price stabilization and export-earning instability', *Oxford Economic Papers*, 32, July, pp. 340-52.
Nowak, M. (1984), 'Quantitative controls and unofficial markets in foreign exchange', *IMF Staff Papers*, **31** (2), June, pp. 404-31.
Polak, J.J. (1957-8),'Monetary analysis of income formation...', *IMF Staff Papers*, pp. 1-50.
Powell, A. and Gilbert, C.L. (1988), 'The use of commodity

contracts for the management of developing country commodity risks', in Currie, D. and Vines, D. (eds), *North South Macroeconomic Relations*, Cambridge: Cambridge University Press.
Radetzki, M. (1976), 'The potential for monopolistic commodity pricing by developing countries', in Helleiner, G.K. (ed.), *A World Divided*, Cambridge: Cambridge University Press.
Rangel, I. (1963), *A Inflacao Brasileiro*, Tempo Brasileiro; cited Bresser Pereira (1987).
Republic of Ghana, (1987), *National Programme for Economic Development (Revised)*, 1 July, Accra.
Sachs, J.D. (1989), 'New approaches to the Latin American debt crisis', *Essays in International Finance*, No. 174, July, Princeton NJ: International Finance Section, Department of Economics, Princeton University.
Sandilands, R.J. (1980), *Monetary Correction and Housing Finance in Colombia, Brazil and Chile*, Aldershot: Gower.
Seers, D. (1962), 'A theory of inflation and growth in underdeveloped countries based on the experience of Latin America', *Oxford Economic Papers*, **14** (2), pp. 173-95.
Smith, L.D. and Spooner, N.J. (1990), 'The sequencing of structural adjustment policy instruments in the agricultural sector', CDS Occasional Paper No. 6, Glasgow: Centre for Development Studies, University of Glasgow.
Stewart, M. (1986), *Keynes and After*, 3rd ed., Harmondsworth: Penguin.
Swan, T.W. (1955), 'Longer-term problems of the balance of payments', reprinted in Arndt, H.W. and Corden, W.M. (eds) (1965), *The Australian Economy: Selected Readings*, Melbourne: Cheshire.
Tanzi, V. (1982), 'Fiscal disequilibrium in developing countries', *World Development*, **10** (12), December, pp. 1069-82.
Taylor, L. (1988), *Varieties of Stabilization Experience*, Oxford: Oxford University Press and WIDER.
Tew, B. (1982), *The Evolution of the International Monetary System, 1945-81*, 2nd ed., London: Hutchinson.
Tinbergen, J. (1952), *On the Theory of Economic Policy*, Amsterdam: North Holland.
Trevithick, J.A. (1980), *Inflation*, 2nd ed., Harmondsworth: Penguin.
Wickham, P. (1985), 'The choice of exchange-rate regime in developing countries: a survey of the literature', *IMF Staff Papers*, **35** (2), June, pp. 248-88.
Williamson, J. (1965), *The Crawling Peg*, Princeton, NJ: Princeton Essays in International Finance, No. 50,

December, Princeton University.
Williamson, J. (1983), *The Open Economy and the World Economy*, New York: Basic Books.
Wonnacott, R. and Wonnacott, P. (1990), *Economics*, 4th ed., New York: Wiley.
World Bank (1984), *Ghana: Policies and Programs for Adjustment*, Washington, DC: IBRD/World Bank.
World Bank, *World Development Report*, annual, Washington, DC: IBRD/World Bank.

Index

absorption-injection
  approach to external
  balance 82-5, 89-91
adjustment from imbalance
  see imbalance, adjustment
  from
administrative controls
  102-5, 107
appreciation of exchange
  rate 35
  effects of 41-2
Argentina 8, 49, 116, 208,
  236, 261-71
assets, definition 24
asset market *see* bond market
assignment of instruments to
  targets 170-72, 178-81
Association of Tin Producing
  Countries 130
Australia 33, 117

balance of payments *see*
  external balance
Bangladesh 99
bank credit, lack of,
  implications 100, 107
Bolivia 8, 266-71
bond market, lack of,
  implications 100, 107
Botswana 118, 151, 210, 213
bottlenecks in inflation
  115, 120
Brady, Nicholas 162
Brazil 105, 106, 116, 130,
  141,142, 208, 225, 236,
  266-71
Bresser Pereira, Luis 115-6
Bretton Woods system 37, 38
budgetary policies and rules
  see fiscal policies and
  rules
budgetary neutrality 185
Buffer Stock Financing
  Facility (IMF) 129
buffer-stock schemes 130-39

Canada 33, 117

capital flows,
international,
short-term, modifying 43-4
long-term 47-8
cartels, producer 129-30
Chile 8, 49, 106, 208, 211, 225, 236, 261-5
China 8, 126, 130
Classical models 28-9, 68, 88 *see also* New Classical models
closed and open economy *see* open and closed economy
cocoa agreements 131
Colombia 106, 114, 239-41
coffee agreements 131, 132
Common Fund for Commodities (UN) 129
Communauté Financière Africaine (CFA) 203, 212
Compensatory (and Contingency) Financing Facility (IMF) 144, 146-8
competitiveness effects of exchange-rate movements 48-50, 97-9
comprehensive shock insurance 152-3
consumption, in social accounts 19-20
controls, administrative *see* administrative controls
convertibility 34
Côte d'Ivoire 114, 142, 145, 164, 256
covered-interest parity 44
Cruzado Plan (Brazil) 266-71
Cuba 126
currency union 212, 215
Currie, Lauchlin 239-41

debt, foreign 106, 156-65
crisis 125-6, 156-8
default 164-5
guarantees 159-60
rescheduling 157
debt-management agency 160-62
Denmark 117
depreciation of exchange rate 18, 35
effects of 38-41
under exchange controls 103-5
devaluation of exchange rate *see* depreciation of exchange rate
diminishing marginal utility of income 4-6
disappointed expectations 5-6, 8
disposable income
national 18, 23
personal 18
distribution of income
effect of inflation on 8
domestic credit, definition 86-8
Dominican Republic 211
Dornbusch, Rudiger 264-5
'Dutch disease' 99

earnings-compensation schemes 143-55
Economic Commission for Latin America (UN) 108
Ecuador 265
elasticity approach to external balance 76-81, 84-5
European Community 144-6, 148-9, 248
exchange controls *see* administrative controls
exchange market
unofficial 103-5
international, absence of, implications 106
exchange rate
basket peg 211, 212-4
changes, effects of 39-42
choice of poicy targets 218, 242-3

choice of regimes and policies 197-221 *esp.* 215, 242-3
classification of regimes 198-200
crawling peg 200-201, 204-5
determination in free market 46-8
effective, meaning of 35
fixed and flexible 35
fixed peg 201-4
forward 44
in liberalization 200-201, 214
jumping peg 200
moving, mechanism of 44-6, 206-11
pegged and floating 35, 106, 200-203
real, meaning of 48-50, 98-9
under restrictions 42-3
Exchange Rate Mechanism of European Monetary System 37-8
expenditure (domestic, national),
definitions, relationships 15-23
fluctuations, stability 3, 4-7,10-12
export controls (quotas) 130, 132, 133, 138-9
export-earnings compensation schemes 143-55, 193, 196
Extended Structural Adjustment Facility (IMF) 163
external balance 3, 9-10, 13, 30-33
and international reserves 30
basic balance 31-2
capital account 32
current account 32
and domestic balance 33
management of 76-91
merchandise-trade balance 31
net balance 31-2
trade balance in goods and services 31

Fiji 126
Finland 227-8
fiscal policies and rules 184-96
food production
as constraint on output 112-13
food-supply insurance 151
foreign exchange supply as constraint on output 102, 112-13
forward purchases and sales 139
Friedman, Milton 68-71, 72
Friedman models 68-71, 88-9 95, 99, 101, 115, 116, 179-80, 195
full employment 10-13, 54-6, 243
futures markets 139

Germany 8, 33
Ghana 38, 106, 126, 142, 145, 202, 206, 247, 256-71
gold 34
gold standard 35-6
Goodhart's Law 28
gross and net social-accounting aggregates 18
Guatemala 211

Hansen, Alvin 57
Harris-Todaro model 11-12
hedging contracts 139-41
Hicks, John 57
hoarding and dehoarding of money 90
Hong Kong 95, 126
Hume, David 35

imbalance, adjustment from 244-51, 255-71
income, national
comparisons over time 20-21
definitions, relationships 15-23
indexation
of exchange rate 106, 208-9
of interest rates 239-43
of wage rates 224-34
India 126
Indonesia 8
industrial revolution and spread of industrialism 96
inertial inflation *see* inflationary inertia
inflation,
endemic 105-6, 107, 108-9, 115-16
oligopolistic elements in 115-16, 120
price-stability objective 3, 7-9, 10, 217-8, 232-4, 243
inflationary inertia 116, 120-21
instability, sources of 125-8
instruments in stabilization *see* targets and instruments in stabilization
insurance of export earnings *see* export-earnings compensation schemes
interest-rate
policies 235-43
roles, conflicts 234-5, 242-3
interest-rate repression 103, 238-9
Integrated Program for Commodities (UN) 129
internal balance *see* full employment
International Bauxite Association 130
International Cocoa Organization 131
International Coffee Agreements 131,132
International Monetarist models 69-71, 88-9, 179-80, 238, 261-2
International Monetary Fund (IMF) 34, 37, 141, 144, 146-9, 154-5, 157, 159, 162-4
International Tin Council and Agreements 130-32, 141
investment, in social accounts 33
IS-LM analysis 56-68
Israel 8, 116, 266-71
'inverted conditionality' 154-5
Ivory Coast *see* Côte d'Ivoire

Japan 33, 62, 227-8

Kaldor, Nicholas 115, 237
Kenya 118, 173-4
Keynes, J.M. 36, 37, 53-5, 72-4
Keynesian models 53-68, 74-5, 95, 99, 100, 115, 118-19, 179-80, 223, 237
King, J.R. model 173-4, 179-80
Korea 126
Kuwait 95

labour supply
implication of high elasticity 101-2, 107
see also Harris-Todaro model
large-open-economy models 97-9, 177-8
less-developed countries
features, variety 96-7

Lewis, Arthur 101-2
liabilities, as negative
  assets 24
liberalization, reducing
  exchange rate in 43, 103-5
liquidity 24-6
LM-IS analysis *see* IS-LM
  analysis
Lomé Convention 144-6

Malawi 118, 259-61
marketing-board
  stabilization schemes
  141-2
Mauritius 99
Meade, J.E. models 179-80
mineral-revenue
  stabilization funds
  150-51, 271-2
'modified wage indexation'
  226-32
'Monetarist' as against
  'Structuralist' 108-9, 111
Monetarist models 28-9, 63,
  68-75, 119, 179-80, 223
'monetary approach to the
  balance of payments' 85-91
'monetary repression' *see*
  interest-rate repression
money, 24-9
  demand 28-9
  Quantity Equation 28
  Quantity Theory 29
  supply change endogenous,
    hypothesis 115, 120, 237
  supply, definitions 27-8
Multilateral Investment
  Guarantee Agency 159

national accounts 15-23
Netherlands 117
New Cambridge model 117, 179
New Classical models 69-71,
  101
New Keynesian models *see*
  Keynesian models; Meade,
  J.E. models
New Zealand 117
Nigeria 38, 99, 106, 126,
  144, 202
Nixon, Richard 37
nontradables, switching
  demand to, as growth and
  stabilization strategy
  114, 121
Norway 227-8

open and closed economy
  identities 16-18
  models 99-100, 179-80
options purchases and sales
  139-41
Organization of Petroleum
  Exporting Countries (OPEC)
  129-30, 131

Pakistan 124
Papua New Guinea 118, 151,
  194, 210, 271-6
Pereira, Luis Bresser *see*
  Bresser Pereira, Luis
'permanent revenue' 184
Peru 270
Philippines 164
Phillips, A.W. 63-4
Phillips Curve 63-4, 105
Prebisch, Raul 110
price level, domestic
  indexes 21-2
  instability 3, 7-9, 10
  see also inflation
price-stabilization
  agreements 129-39
prices, purchasers' and
  producers', in social
  accounts 19
primary-commodity dominance
  in exports, implications
  97-100, 107
'primary-export-dominated
  economy', definition 185
product, domestic and
  national, definition,

relationships 15-23
purchasing-power parity 46-8

quotas, export *see* export controls
quotas, trade *see* administrative controls

real exchange rate *see* exchange rate, real
reserves, international 30-33, 34
restrictions on trade, exchange 42-3
see also administrative controls
risk-aversion 6-7
risk-sharing in loans 158

Sanchez de Lozada, Gonzalo 270
Saudi Arabia 99
saving, in social accounts 19-20
Seers, Dudley, Structuralist model 111-12
Senegal 145
Singapore 95, 114, 126, 211
Singer, Hans 110
skills as constraint on output 102
small-open-economy models 97-9, 173-7, 271
social accounts 15-23
South Africa 213
Special Drawing Rights 34, 35, 212
specie-flow mechanism 35-6
Sri Lanka 127
Stabex 144-6, 148-9,
Structural Adjustment Facility (IMF) 163
Structural Adjustment Loans (World Bank) 163
Structuralism 108-21
experiments 266-71
meanings of term 109-10
Sudan 145
sugar agreements 133
Sweden 62, 227-8
Sysmin 144
System of National Accounts (UN) 19, 23

Taiwan 33, 126
targets and instruments in stabilization 169-81
taxes
in social aggregates 20
net indirect, in social accounts 19
terms of trade, hypothesis of secular decline for primary commodities 110
tin agreements 130-32, 141
Todaro, Michael *see* Harris-Todaro model
trade controls *see* administrative controls
transfers, international, in social accounts 18, 20, 23

Uganda 202
unequal-exchange theory 110
Union of Socialist Soviet Republics 99
United Kingdom (UK) 33, 38, 49
United Nations Conference on Trade and Development 129
United States of America 33, 38, 54
Uruguay 49, 208, 236, 261-5

value-added, meaning 17
velocity of money 28

wage-determination models 62-4, 222
wage policy 61-4, 222-34, 242-3
wheat agreements 130-31
World Bank 141, 159, 162-4

Zaire 144
Zimbabwe 144
Zambia 126, 127, 144, 202, 259